INTERACTIVE
ACCOUNTING

This manual has been designed for use in conjunction with the Byzantium software to familiarise the student with the technical skills associated with introductory financial and management accounting. If a more theoretical approach is required, the student should refer to appropriate literature.

Consortium Members

G. J. Wilkinson-Riddle	De Montfort University
A. Patel	De Montfort University
D. Gallagher	Huddersfield University
A. M. Cook	Liverpool John Moores University
S. Grant	Liverpool John Moores University
M. Simpson	Middlesex University
L. M. Lindley	University of Plymouth
A. Tonge	University of Teesside

INTERACTIVE ACCOUNTING

The Byzantium Workbook

Edited by
Gregory Wilkinson-Riddle and Ashok Patel

Written by
A. M. Cook, S. Grant and L. M. Lindley

BLACKWELL
Publishers

Copyright © Byzantium consortium, 1997

First published 1997

2 4 6 8 10 9 7 5 3 1

Blackwell Publishers Ltd
108 Cowley Road
Oxford OX4 1JF
UK

Blackwell Publishers Inc.
350 Main Street
Malden, Massachusetts 02148
USA

British Library Cataloguing in Publication Data

A CIP catalogue record for this book is available from the British Library.

Library of Congress Cataloging-in-Publication Data
Interactive accounting : the Byzantium workbook / edited by Gregory
    Wilkinson-Riddle and Ashok Patel.
        p.   cm.
    Includes bibliographical references and index.
    ISBN 0-631-20750-3 (alk. paper)
    1. Byzantium (Computer file) 2. Accounting—Computer programs.
I. Riddle, Gregory Wilkinson. II. Patel, Ashok.
HF5679.I599   1997
657'.0285'5369—dc 21   97-16960
                                                                    CIP

Typeset in 10 on 12 pt Times
by Archetype IT Ltd, Stow-on-the-Wold, http://www.archetype-it.com
Printed in Great Britain by T.J. International, Padstow, Cornwall

This book is printed on acid-free paper.

GENERAL CONTENTS

FINANCIAL ACCOUNTING

Manual

CONTENTS

Supplementary chapters available on the web at
http://www.blackwellpublishers.co.uk/interacc

Introduction to Financial Statements

INTRODUCTION TO THE BALANCE SHEET

Introduction

Organisations, ranging from multi-national companies to small sports clubs, will produce financial statements at least once a year. These financial statements will be of interest to many user groups, e.g. owners, banks, the Inland Revenue.

General accounting principles, i.e. the underlying rules which govern accounting practice and which underpin financial statements, apply to ALL organisations. These concepts will be applied in the examples in each tutorial and explained in more detail in Tutorial 17.

All the examples in this manual will relate to sole traders, i.e. businesses owned by one person.

The two main financial statements, collectively known as "the Final Accounts", are:

- the Balance Sheet (introduced in this tutorial)
- the Profit & Loss Account (introduced in Tutorial 2)

The Balance Sheet

The Balance Sheet shows in monetary terms:

- business assets such as machinery, stock, debtors and cash
- business liabilities such as creditors and loans to the business
- capital, i.e. owner's investment in the business (also known as "equity")

Example

Jake starts a business, selling denim clothes, trading as "Cowboys Clothing Co." On 1st January, Jake opens a business bank account with £30,000 of his own money.

Cowboys Clothing Co.

Balance Sheet as at 1st January

	£
Assets	
Cash & Bank	30,000
	30,000
Representing Equity	
Owner's Capital	30,000
	30,000

Fig. 1

Notes

THE BALANCE SHEET

The Balance Sheet lists business assets, business liabilities and capital at a specific date, in this example as at 1st January.

Assets are resources which have a value to the business, e.g. machines, vehicles, stock, debtors, cash.

Liabilities are amounts owed by the business to people other than the owner or to businesses other than the owner's, e.g. loans, trade creditors.

The capital of a business represents the owner's stake in his own business. This is sometimes known as "equity".

THE BALANCE SHEET EQUATION

A Balance Sheet is constructed in two sections. The totals of the two sections of the Balance Sheet are always equal in value. This is known as "the Accounting Equation".

Every transaction of the business will affect TWO items on the Balance Sheet. In this example the two items are:

- the asset of cash at bank
- Jake's capital

Both aspects of each transaction must always be observed, as they underpin the accounting equation (DUAL ASPECT CONCEPT).

BUSINESS ENTITY

For accounting purposes, the owner and the business are treated as two separate entities (BUSINESS ENTITY CONCEPT). In the above example, Jake may have assets which have nothing to do with the clothing store, e.g. his private house. These assets will not appear on the Balance Sheet of Cowboys Clothing Co.

The Effect of Transactions on the Balance Sheet

The effect on the Balance Sheet of various transactions will be illustrated by the example of Cowboys Clothing Co. Three additional transactions will be illustrated and their effect on the business will be shown by drawing up a new Balance Sheet after each transaction.

The opening Balance Sheet of the business was as follows:

Cowboys Clothing Co.

Balance Sheet as at 1st January

	£
Assets	
Cash & Bank	30,000
	30,000
Representing Equity	
Owner's Capital	30,000
	30,000

Fig. 2

i. *On 2nd January, Jake buys a second-hand delivery van for £8,000, paying with a business cheque.*

Cowboys Clothing Co.

Balance Sheet as at 2nd January

	£
Assets	
Motor Vehicles	8,000
Cash & Bank	22,000
	30,000
Representing Equity	
Owner's Capital	30,000
	30,000

Fig. 3

Notes

The TWO items on the Balance Sheet affected by this transaction are:

- the asset of motor vehicles   (+ £8,000)
- the asset of cash & bank   (− £8,000)

Jake's capital is unchanged, as he personally has neither introduced nor withdrawn business resources.

The transaction is recorded at cost, i.e. the monetary value placed on the van is, in the first instance, its cost of acquisition (HISTORICAL COST CONCEPT).

ii.   On 5th January the business buys denim jeans from the manufacturer to sell to customers. The jeans cost £6,000. Cowboys Clothing Co. will pay the supplier next month.

Cowboys Clothing Co.		
Balance Sheet as at 5th January		
Assets		£
Motor Vehicles		8,000
Stock		6,000
Cash & Bank		22,000
		36,000
Less Liabilities		
Creditors		6,000
		30,000
Representing Equity		
Owner's Capital		30,000
		30,000

Fig. 4

Notes

The TWO items on the Balance Sheet affected by this transaction are:

- the asset of stock   (+ £6,000)
- the liability to creditors   (− £6,000)

The term used for goods held by a business for resale is "stock". Stock is normally valued at historical cost. Prudence dictates that profit should not be recognised until it has been realised, i.e. until the goods have been sold (PRUDENCE CONCEPT and REALISATION CONCEPT). Stock is therefore not normally valued at selling price, as this would anticipate an element of profit.

The term "liabilities" is used for amounts owed by the business to creditors. Liabilities are usually subtracted from assets on the Balance Sheet to indicate that these creditors have a claim on the assets of the business. Assets remaining after deducting liabilities represent the owner's claim on the assets.

THE ACCOUNTING EQUATION (IRON RULE OF ACCOUNTING)

NET ASSETS = CAPITAL

In the above example:

NET ASSETS (Assets – Liabilities) £30,000 = CAPITAL £30,000

iii. On 7th January, all of the stock is sold, for £9,500 in cash.

This transaction will involve accounting for:

a. The income from the sale.

b The cost of making the sale.

These will be considered separately:

a. The income from the sale

Cowboys Clothing Co.	
Balance Sheet as at 7th January	
	£
Assets	
Motor Vehicles	8,000
Stock	6,000
Cash & Bank	31,500
	45,500
Less Liabilities	
Creditors	6,000
	39,500
Representing	
Equity	39,500
Owner's Capital	
	39,500

Fig. 5

Notes

The TWO items on the Balance Sheet affected by the sale transaction are:

- the asset of cash & bank   (+ £9,500)
- capital   (+ £9,500)

Capital has increased, in accordance with the Balance Sheet equation, because the £9,500 income from sales has increased the net assets of Cowboys Clothing Co.

b.   *The cost of making the sale*

In the above Balance Sheet the total sales income was recognised. However, this income has not been earned without COST to the business, i.e. the business has parted with its stock. The value of the stock which the business no longer owns, i.e. the cost of sales, must be recognised.

	£
Cowboys Clothing Co.	
Balance Sheet as at 7th January	
Assets	
Motor Vehicles	8,000
Stock	—
Cash & Bank	31,500
	39,500
Less Liabilities	
Creditors	6,000
	33,500
Representing Equity	
Owner's Capital	33,500
	33,500

Fig. 6

Notes

The TWO items on the Balance Sheet affected by this transaction are:

- the asset of stock   (− £6,000)
- capital   (− £6,000)

Capital has decreased, because the £6,000 expense of cost of sales has decreased the net assets of Cowboys Clothing Co.

Capital before the goods were sold was £30,000. Capital after the sale is £33,500. The difference of £3,500 is due to PROFIT:

	£	£
Opening Capital		30,000
Add Sales income	9,500	
Less Cost of sales	6,000	
Profit		3,500
Closing Capital		33,500

If the business makes a profit, net assets and capital will increase. Conversely, if the business makes a loss, net assets and capital will decrease.

Profit is the return on the owner's investment of time and money in his own business. Profit is instead of a salary and interest which could have been earned if the owner's time and money had been used elsewhere. An entrepreneur accepts the risk that his business may make losses.

This transaction has increased net assets by £3,500; the asset of stock (£6,000) was exchanged for the asset of cash (£9,500). At this point profit is recognised, because it has been realised.

Sales will be the main source of income for most businesses. All business income increases profit and, therefore, increases capital. Other examples of business income are

- interest receivable
- rent receivable

Cost of sales is an expense of the business. All business expenses reduce profit and, therefore, reduce capital. Other examples of business expenses are:

- wages
- electricity
- postage
- interest payable

The Classification of Assets and Liabilities

For the benefit of the users of Final Accounts, Balance Sheet items are presented in a standardised format rather than appearing at random.

The following example illustrates the standard format of the Balance Sheet of a business.

Any Business

Balance Sheet as at 31st December

	£	£
Fixed Assets		
Machinery		120,000
Motor Vehicles		30,000
		150,000
Current Assets		
Stock	15,000	
Debtors	8,000	
Cash & Bank	500	
	23,500	
Creditors payable within 1 year		
Creditors	9,000	
Net current assets		14,500
		164,500
Representing		
Creditors payable after 1 year		
Loans		40,000
Equity		
Owner's Capital		124,500
		164,500

Fig. 7

Notes

Assets appear on the Balance Sheet in order of liquidity, i.e. starting with those items least likely to be converted into cash.

Assets are categorised as:

- *Fixed Assets*, which are acquired by the business with the primary intention of use rather than resale, e.g. land & buildings, machines, vehicles
- *Current Assets*, which will normally be converted to cash within one year, e.g. stock, debtors, cash

Liabilities are classified as:

- *Creditors payable within 1 year* – these are often called "current liabilities" – e.g. trade creditors, bank overdrafts
- *Creditors payable after 1 year* – these will include long term loans

The total of Current Assets and Current Liabilities is netted off on the Balance Sheet to show Net Current Assets, sometimes called "working capital".

The Net Current Assets figure may be used as a measure of liquidity, i.e. to assess the ability of the business to pay its short term debts.

Balance Sheet Formats

The Balance Sheet of "Any Business" shown, in Fig. 7 above, uses one of several alternative formats. Examples of other formats of the Balance Sheet which may be used are shown in Fig. 7a below.

Any Business

Balance Sheet as at 31st December

Fixed Assets	£	£
Machinery		120,000
Motor Vehicles		30,000
		150,000
Current Assets		
Stock	15,000	
Debtors	8,000	
Cash & Bank	500	
	23,000	
Creditors payable within 1 year		
Creditors	9,000	
Net current assets		14,500
Creditors payable after more than 1 year		164,500
Loans		40,000
		124,500
Representing Equity		
Owner's Capital		124,500
		124,500

Any Business
Balance Sheet as at 31st December

Fixed Assets	£	£
Machinery		120,000
Motor Vehicles		30,000
		150,000
Current Assets		
Stock	15,000	
Debtors	8,000	
Cash & Bank	500	23,500
		173,500
Trade Creditors		9,000
Loans		40,000
Owner's Capital		124,500
		173,500

Fig. 7a

Tutorial Questions

1.1   Classify the following items (i–vii) for Balance Sheet presentation purposes, i.e. as either:

- Fixed Assets
- Current Assets
- Creditors payable within 1 year
- Creditors payable after 1 year
- Equity

i.   Cash at bank.
ii.   Bank overdraft.
iii.   Office equipment.
iv.   Trade debtors.
v.   Trade creditors.
vi.   Owner's capital.
vii.   5 year loan to the business.

1.2   The following transactions relate to a new business.

i.   The owner starts a business by introducing cash of £15,000.
ii.   A vehicle costing £9,000 is bought and paid for immediately.
iii.   Goods for resale costing £2,500 are bought on credit.
iv.   All the goods are sold on credit for £3,500.
v.   Wages of £200 are paid.
vi.   £1,800 is paid to trade creditors.
vii.   £1,400 is received from trade debtors.

Required

a.   Identify the two items affected by each transaction. Indicate whether the transaction increases or decreases the items.
b.   Using the standard format, draw up the Balance Sheet of the business after accounting for all the transactions.

1.3   The following Balance Sheet relates to an established business.

Any Business		
Balance Sheet as at 31st December		
	£	£
Fixed Assets		
Machinery		120,000
Motor Vehicles		30,000
		150,000
Current Assets		
Stock	15,000	
Trade debtors	8,000	
Cash & Bank	500	
	23,500	
Creditors payable within 1 year		
Trade Creditors	9,000	
Net current assets		14,500
		164,500
Representing		
Creditors payable after 1 year		
Loans		40,000
Equity		
Owner's Capital		124,500
		164,500

The transactions for January of the following year are as follows:

i.   Additional long term loans of £20,000 are taken out.
ii.   Machinery costing £5,000 is bought and paid for immediately.
iii. A van costing £12,000 is bought on credit.
iv.   All the stock shown on the December Balance Sheet is sold on credit for £27,000.
v.   Wages of £2,000 are paid.
vi.   A bill is received from the garage for van repairs costing £600, to be paid for in February.
vii. Goods are purchased on credit for £13,000.
viii. Cash of £30,000 is received from trade debtors.
ix.   £18,000 is paid to trade creditors.

Required

a.   Identify the two items affected by each transaction. Indicate whether the transaction increases or decreases the items.

b.   Draw up the Balance Sheet of the business after accounting for January's transactions.

c.   Explain why the owner's equity has changed from £124,500 to that shown in your answer to b.

1.4   Consider the Balance Sheet of "Any Business" and answer the following questions. Use the original Balance Sheet as at 31st December as shown in question 1.3 above.

a.   Why is the owner's private house not shown on the Balance Sheet?

b.   Why is the stock shown at £15,000, when it is expected to be sold for more than £20,000?

c.   Do you consider that the business has liquidity problems, as its creditors exceed its cash?

d.   Is it true to say that the owner of the business is worth £124,500 at 31st December?

1.5   Apart from the owner, identify other parties who would be interested in the financial statements of a business.

INTRODUCTION TO THE PROFIT & LOSS ACCOUNT

Introduction

The two main financial statements of a sole trader are:

- the Balance Sheet
- the Profit & Loss Account

The Balance Sheet is a statement of an organisation's financial position at one point in time.

Profit earned during an accounting period will be reflected by an increase in the owner's capital.

The details of the profit earned during an accounting period are shown separately, in the Profit & Loss Account.

A business must produce a Profit & Loss Account at least once a year. This statement provides vital business information. Profit is one of the most important indicators of business success. A profitable business should prosper and everyone associated with it should benefit.

In Tutorial 1, profit was calculated with only one expense, cost of sales. Businesses have many other expenses, e.g. wages, telephone, rent, insurance, electricity, travel and loan interest. Any business expense reduces profit and therefore reduces capital.

Profit & Loss Account Layout

The Profit & Loss Account is divided into two sections. The first section calculates gross profit; the second section calculates net profit.

The layout of the Profit & Loss Account of a retailer is shown below.

Any Business		
Profit & Loss Account for the year ended 31st December		
Sales		X
Less Cost of Sales		X
Gross Profit		X
Less Overhead Expenses		
Wages	X	
Telephone	X	
Rent	X	
Insurance	X	
Electricity	X	
Travel	X	
Loan Interest	X	X
Net Profit		X

Fig. 8

Gross profit

Gross profit is the difference between sales and cost of sales. Many businesses set their selling prices to include a standard gross profit percentage (%). E.g.,

Cost price per unit	£80
Selling price per unit	£100
Gross profit per unit	£20

Gross profit margin $\dfrac{£20}{£100} \times 100 = 20\%$

The gross profit % provides useful management information.

If the standard gross profit margin is applied to all sales, this gross profit % should remain at a constant 20% irrespective of volume of sales. E.g., if 400 units are sold:

Sales income (400 @ £100)	£40,000
Gross profit (400 @ £20)	£8,000

Gross profit margin $\dfrac{£8,000}{£40,000} \times 100 = 20\%$

Any unexpected deviation from the standard gross profit % will provide an indicator of possible problems, e.g. theft of stock and/or cash.

Net profit

Net profit is the profit after overhead expenses have been deducted from gross profit. For a business to make a net profit, gross profit must be sufficient to cover all the overheads.

The Interlocking Nature of the Profit & Loss Account and the Balance Sheet

There are three reasons for a change in owner's capital:

TRADING TRANSACTIONS

Trading transactions, involving business income and business expenses, have an increasing or a decreasing effect on owner's capital. Details of trading transactions are shown on the Profit & Loss Account, where they are netted off to arrive at net profit.

DRAWINGS

Capital will also change if the owner of the business takes business assets for his own use. These transactions are called "drawings" and will reduce capital.

CAPITAL INTRODUCED

Capital will increase if the owner introduces his own personal assets into the business. The Balance Sheet will show that the owner's capital has changed, but it will not show the details of the change.

Example

Sheila is in business, trading as a florist. According to the last set of Final Accounts, the capital of the business was £1,000. The following details relate to the next accounting period.

i. *Goods which had cost £3,200 are sold for £4,000 cash*
    Cash +£4,000; Capital +£4,000
    Stock –£3,200; Capital –£3,200
ii. *Wages of £200 are paid*
    Cash –£200; Capital –£200
iii. *Electricity of £100 is paid*
    Cash –£100; Capital –£100

iv. *The owner withdraws £300 cash for personal use*
    Cash –£300; Capital –£300

The Profit & Loss Account is the analysis of how capital has changed due to the trading activities of the business. In the above example, the Profit & Loss Account will be drawn up as follows:

Profit & Loss Account for period ended		
	£	£
Sales (i)		4,000
Less Cost of Sales (i)		3,200
Gross Profit		800
Less Overhead Expenses		
Wages (ii)	200	
Light & heat (iii)	100	300
Net Profit		500

Fig. 9

The changes in equity can be summarised as follows:

Capital Movements	
	£
Net Profit for the period	500
Less Drawings during the period (iv)	300
Retained Profit for the period	200
Add Opening Capital and Capital Introduced during the period	1,000
Closing Capital	1,200

Fig. 10

NOTES

- A business will need to retain ("plough back") sufficient profits for survival and growth.
- The closing capital of £1,200 will be shown on the final Balance Sheet.

Accruals Accounting

The division of the life of a business into accounting periods creates the problem of deciding where this year's transactions cut-off and next year's transactions begin. E.g.

the Profit & Loss Account of a business for Year 3 should include income and expenses for Year 3 only; the Balance Sheet at the end of Year 3 should show assets, liabilities and capital as at that date only.

THE LIFE OF
ANY BUSINESS
(YEARS)

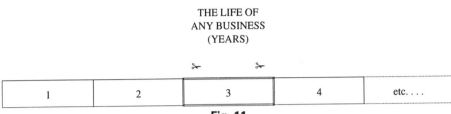

| 1 | 2 | 3 | 4 | etc. . . . |

Fig. 11

Profit is calculated by matching income earned during an accounting period with expenses incurred during that period. This is known as the ACCRUALS CONCEPT.

Income and expenses will be recognised during an accounting period even though the cash may be received or paid in a different period. E.g.:

• Sales made on credit in Year 3 will be included in the income for Year 3, even though the debtors may not pay until Year 4.
• The cost of electricity used up during Year 3 will be included as an expense on the Profit & Loss Account for that year even though the bill may not be paid to the creditor until the next year. The effect of this on the Final Accounts of an organisation will be as follows: (i) the expense of electricity on the Profit & Loss Account for Year 3 will be increased, resulting in a decrease in net profit, which will in turn decrease owner's capital; (ii) trade creditors on the Balance Sheet at the end of Year 3 will increase, as the amount outstanding for electricity at the year end represents a liability.

Tutorial Questions

2.1 Indicate whether the following transactions will:

• be shown in the Profit & Loss Account as income
• be shown in the Profit & Loss Account as an expense
• not be shown in the Profit & Loss Account

i.   Sales for cash.
ii.   Sales on credit.
iii.   Wages.
iv.   Payment to trade creditors.
v.   Purchase of land.
vi.   Drawings.

2.2   The following information relates to a business.

	£
Owner's capital at start of year	47,000
Sales	24,000
Wages	2,000
Trade debtors	7,500
Trade creditors	1,000
Stock at end of year	2,000
Freehold premises	30,000
Cash & bank	21,500
Loans	20,000
Cost of sales	14,000
Drawings	4,000
Machinery	10,000
Light & heat	500
Postage & stationery	200
Repairs & renewals	300

Required
Prepare the Final Accounts (Profit & Loss Accounts – plus Capital Movements – and Balance Sheet) from the above information.

2.3   The following Final Accounts of a business have been drawn up before the transactions (i–ix) shown below have been accounted for.

Profit & Loss Account for year ended		
	£	£
Sales		24,000
Less Cost of Sales		14,000
Gross Profit		10,000
Less Overhead Expenses		
Wages	2,000	
Light & heat	500	
Postage & stationery	200	
Repairs & renewals	300	3,000
Net Profit		7,000

Capital Movements	£
Net Profit for the period	7,000
Less Drawings during the period	4,000
Retained Profit for the period	3,000
Add Opening Capital and Capital Introduced during the period	47,000
Closing Capital	50,000

Balance Sheet as at	£	£
Fixed Assets		
Freehold Premises		30,000
Machinery		10,000
		40,000
Current Assets		
Stock	2,000	
Trade Debtors	7,500	
Cash & Bank	21,500	
	31,000	
Creditors payable within 1 year		
Trade Creditors	1,000	
Net current assets		30,000
		70,000
Representing		
Creditors payable after 1 year		
Loans		20,000
Equity		
Owner's Capital		50,000
		70,000

The following additional transactions must be accounted for:

i.   Additional long term loans of £25,000 are taken out.
ii. Machinery costing £8,000 is bought and paid for.
iii. Cash drawings of £1,000 are made.
iv. Half the stock shown on the Balance Sheet is sold on credit for £2,500.
v.   Wages of £700 are paid.

vi.   A bill of £150 for electricity is received but is not paid.
vii. Goods are purchased on credit for £3,000.
viii. Cash of £7,500 is received from trade debtors.
ix.   £2,500 is paid to trade creditors.

Required
a.   Indicate the effect of each transaction on the items in the Final Accounts shown above.
b.   Draw up the amended Final Accounts after accounting for all of the above transactions.

2.4   Discuss whether a business which makes a profit of £50,000 is more profitable than a business which makes a profit of £10,000.

The Techniques for Recording Financial Transactions

Basic Rules for Recording Business Transactions

Introduction

Organisations, ranging from multi-national companies to small sports clubs, will need to record their transactions on a regular basis. These records will be needed in order to produce financial statements for a variety of users, e.g. management, the Inland Revenue and the bank manager.

For each transaction it will be necessary to record the following:

- the amount (£)
- the date
- a description of the transaction

Although the examples in this manual will relate to sole traders, i.e. businesses owned by one person, the general principles apply to ALL organisations.

The basic rules for recording business transactions are the same whether a manual accounting system or a computerised system is used.

Business transactions are recorded from the point of view of the business itself, i.e. not from the point of view of the owner (BUSINESS ENTITY CONCEPT).

Recording Business Transactions

The rules for recording business transactions are based on the DUAL ASPECT CONCEPT, i.e. every transaction will affect two items. The effect of the transaction on both items must be recognised in order to record the transaction correctly.

A transaction will have either an increasing (+) effect on an item, or a decreasing (−) effect.

Examples

i.   A machine is bought for cash of £3,000.

The TWO items affected are:

*   Machinery   (+ £3,000)
*   Cash   (– £3,000)

ii.   Goods are sold for cash of £500.

The TWO items affected are:

*   Sales   (+ £500)
*   Cash   (+ £500)

Each item must have its own record, i.e. "account", in the books (ledgers) of the business. The above examples would be recorded in the "cash account", the "machinery account" and the "sales account".

Each account will be divided into two sections. The left section is known as the "debit" and the right section as the "credit". E.g.:

Cash Account	
Debit	Credit

Fig. 12

One side of an account is for increases (+), and the other is for decreases (–). The problem is:

*   Which side of the account should be used for an increase (+)?
*   Which side should be used for a decrease (–)?

To solve this problem, a rule must be memorised.

Double Entry Rule

INCREASES (+) in ASSETS and EXPENSES

Debit	Credit
HERE	

INCREASES (+) in EQUITY (i.e. owner's capital), CREDITOS, INCOME and PROVISIONS

Debit	Credit
	HERE

It follows that DECREASES (−) to an account will be the reverse of the above. I.e.

DECREASES (−) in ASSETS and EXPENSES

Debit	Credit
	HERE

DECREASES (−) in EQUITY (i.e. owner's capital), CREDITORS, INCOME and PROVISIONS

Debit	Credit
HERE	

Fig. 13

Observing this rule means that a transaction should ALWAYS be recorded on the debit side of one account and on the credit side of another account. This provides an arithmetic check on the accuracy of the ledger accounts, as the total debits in the books (ledgers) should always be equal to the total credits.

NOTE

Because of their basic shape, these accounts are sometimes known as "T" accounts.

Examples

i.   A machine is bought for cash for £3,000.

The TWO items affected are:

- Machinery   (+ £3,000)
- Cash   (– £3,000)

The transaction will be recorded on:

- the debit (left) side of the Machinery Account, as the ASSET of Machinery is being increased (+)
- the credit (right) side of the Cash Account, as the ASSET of Cash is being decreased (–)

The transaction will appear in the ledger accounts as follows.

	Machinery Account			
Ref	Debit (= +) (£)		Ref	Credit (= –) (£)
(i)	3,000			

	Cash Account			
Ref	Debit (= +) (£)		Ref	Credit (= –) (£)
			(i)	3,000

Fig. 14

ii.   Goods are sold on credit for £500.

The TWO items affected are:

- Sales   (+ £500)
- Trade Debtors   (+ £500)

The transaction will be recorded on:

- the debit (left) side of the Trade Debtors Account, as the ASSET of Debtors is being increased (+)
- the credit (right) side of the Sales Account, as the INCOME of Sales is being increased (+)

Trade Debtors Account				
Ref	Debit (= +) (£)		Ref	Credit (= −) (£)
(ii)	500			

Sales Account				
Ref	Debit (= −) (£)		Ref	Credit (= +) (£)
			(ii)	500

Fig. 15

Notes

- The transactions have been entered on the correct side of each account.
- The reference column, in practice, will show the date of the transaction, and the name of the other account involved. Showing the name of the other account provides a useful cross reference when checking that entries have been made correctly. It also provides an indication of why the entry has been made, i.e. the reason why that account has been debited or credited will be obvious to a person examining any account.

Example of Recording Business Transactions in the Books of the Cowboys Clothing Co.

The Cowboys Clothing Co. will be used to illustrate how basic transactions are recorded in a business ledger. The accounts involved will be shown after each transaction, with the new entries being shown in **bold** type.

Jan 1.   Jake starts in business, trading as "Cowboys Clothing Co." He puts £30,000 of his own money into a business bank account.

Cash & Bank Account					
	Debit (= +)	£		Credit (= −)	£
Jan 1	**Capital**	**30,000**			

Capital Account					
	Debit (= −)	£		Credit (= +)	£
			Jan 1	**Cash & Bank**	**30,000**

Fig. 16

Notes

- The ASSET of Cash has increased (+), therefore the Cash & Bank Account has been debited. In practice, separate accounts will be kept for each bank account and for cash in hand.
- The increase (+) in EQUITY (owner's capital) has been credited to the Capital Account.
- The reference columns show the date of the transaction and the name of the other account involved in the transaction. In practice, the year of the transaction will also be shown.

Jan 2.   A delivery van is bought for £8,000 and paid for immediately.

Cash & Bank Account					
	Debit (= +)	£		Credit (= –)	£
Jan 1	Capital	30,000	Jan 2	**Motor Vehicles**	**8,000**

Motor Vehicles Account					
	Debit (= +)	£		Credit (= –)	£
Jan 2	**Cash & Bank**	**8,000**			

Fig. 17

Notes

- Debit Motor Vehicles (+ ASSET).
- Credit Cash & Bank (– ASSET).

Jan 5.   Goods for resale are purchased on credit from B. Kidd for £6,000.

Purchases Account					
	Debit (= +)	£		Credit (= –)	£
Jan 5	**Trade Creditors**	**6,000**			

Trade Creditors Account					
	Debit (= –)	£		Credit (= +)	£
			Jan 5	**Purchases**	**6,000**

Fig. 18

Notes

- It is important that purchases of stock and sales of stock are recorded in separate accounts, as one is at cost price and the other is at selling price. As purchases and sales are important elements of the profit calculation, it is essential that only goods for resale are recorded in the Purchases Account and the Sales Account – i.e., these accounts must not be used for recording the acquisition and disposal of fixed assets.
- Debit Purchases (+ EXPENSE). Purchases will always be recorded on the debit side of the Purchases Account, as purchases represent part of the EXPENSE of Cost of Sales.
- Credit Trade Creditors (+ CREDITORS). This transaction has increased the Trade CREDITORS of the business, as the goods have not yet been paid for.
- In practice, a record must also be kept of amounts owed to individual creditors, such as B. Kidd, so that the right amount is paid to the right person at the right time.

Jan 7.   Cash sales are made of £9,500.

Cash & Bank Account					
	Debit (= +)	£		Credit (= –)	£
Jan 1	Capital	30,000	Jan 2	Motor Vehicles	8,000
7	**Sales**	**9,500**			

Sales Account					
	Debit (= –)	£		Credit (= +)	£
			Jan 7	**Cash & Bank**	**9,500**

Fig. 19

Notes

- Debit Cash & Bank (+ ASSET).
- Credit Sales (+ INCOME).

Jan 12.   Cash purchases are made of £10,000.

Cash & Bank Account					
	Debit (= +)	£		Credit (= –)	£
Jan 1	Capital	30,000	Jan 2	Motor Vehicles	8,000
7	Sales	9,500	12	**Purchases**	**10,000**

Purchases Account					
	Debit (= +)	£		Credit (= –)	£
Jan 5	Trade Creditors	6,000			
12	**Cash & Bank**	**10,000**			

Fig. 20

Notes

- Debit Purchases (+ EXPENSE).
- Credit Cash & Bank (- ASSET).

Jan 16. Sales are made on credit to Sundance Ltd for £14,500.

Sales Account					
	Debit (= –)	£		Credit (= +)	£
			Jan 7	Cash & Bank	9,500
			16	**Trade Debtors**	**14,500**

Trade Debtors Account					
	Debit (= +)	£		Credit (= –)	£
Jan 16	**Sales**	**14,500**			

Fig. 21

Notes

- Debit Trade Debtors, as the goods have not yet been paid for (+ ASSET).
- Credit Sales (+ INCOME).
- In practice, a record must also be kept of amounts owed by individual debtors, such as Sundance Ltd, so that the right amount is collected from the right person at the right time.

Jan 21.   Wages are paid of £2,000.

Wages Account					
	Debit (= +)	£		Credit (= −)	£
Jan 21	**Cash & Bank**	**2,000**			

Cash & Bank Account					
	Debit (= +)	£		Credit (= −)	£
Jan 1	Capital	30,000	Jan 2	Motor Vehicles	8,000
7	Sales	9,500	12	Purchases	10,000
			21	**Wages**	**2,000**

Fig. 22

Notes

- Debit Wages (+ EXPENSE).
- Credit Cash & Bank (−ASSET).
- The above transaction is an example of an expense paid for immediately. If, to take a contrary example, an electricity bill is received but not paid immediately, the entries will be:
  Debit Light & Heat (+ EXPENSE).
  Credit Trade Creditors (+ CREDITOR).
- When this electricity bill is paid, the entries will be:
  Debit Trade Creditors (− CREDITOR).
  Credit Cash & Bank (− ASSET).
  N.B. The records must show that the debt to the electricity company has been settled, not that additional electricity expense has been incurred.

Jan 25.   The debtor Sundance Ltd pays £7,000.

Cash & Bank Account					
	Debit (= +)	£		Credit (= −)	£
Jan 1	Capital	30,000	Jan 2	Motor Vehicles	8,000
7	Sales	9,500	12	Purchases	10,000
25	**Trade Debtors**	**7,000**	21	Wages	2,000

Trade Debtors Account					
	Debit (= +)	£		Credit (= −)	£
Jan 16	Sales	14,500	**Jan 25**	**Cash & Bank**	**7,000**

Fig. 23

Notes

- Debit Cash & Bank (+ ASSET).
- Credit Trade Debtors (– ASSET).
- In practice, the receipt of £7,000 must also be shown in the individual debtor's account, i.e. that of Sundance Ltd.

Jan 31.   A payment of £5,000 is made to the creditor B. Kidd.

Cash & Bank Account					
	Debit (= +)	£		Credit (= –)	£
Jan 1	Capital	30,000	Jan 2	Motor Vehicles	8,000
7	Sales	9,500	12	Purchases	10,000
25	Trade Debtors	7,000	21	Wages	2,000
			31	**Trade Creditors**	**5,000**

Trade Creditors Account					
	Debit (= –)	£		Credit (= +)	£
Jan 31	**Cash & Bank**	**5,000**	Jan 5	Purchases	6,000

Fig. 24

Notes

- Debit Trade Creditors (– CREDITOR).
- Credit Cash & Bank (– ASSET).
- In practice, the payment of £5,000 must also be shown in the individual creditor's account, i.e. that of B. Kidd.

The Trial Balance

It is important that a book-keeping system incorporates controls to ensure that the records are accurate. One of these controls, which is a check on the arithmetic accuracy of the ledger accounts, is the Trial Balance.

As each transaction involves a debit entry and a credit entry of the same value, it follows that at all times the total of the debit entries in the ledger should equal the total of the credit entries. The aim of the Trial Balance is to prove that for every debit entry a corresponding credit entry has been made.

As one side of a ledger account records increases (+) and the other side records decreases (−), it follows that the difference between the two sides represents the value on the account at a particular date, i.e. the balance.

For example, if total cash receipts amount to £46,500 and total cash payments amount to £25,000, the value on the cash account, i.e. the balance, will be £21,500. Balancing off an account will simplify the figures in the account. Only the balance on the account will be carried forward, i.e. in this example the £21,500 will be used as a starting point when recording future transactions.

The mechanics of balancing off a ledger account are as follows:

1. Leaving a line blank, rule a total box on each side of the account. The total boxes must be level with each other. This is demonstrated by the Cash & Bank Account of the Cowboys Clothing Co.

Cash & Bank Account					
	Debit	£		Credit	£
Jan 1	Capital	30,000	Jan 2	Motor Vehicles	8,000
7	Sales	9,500	12	Purchases	10,000
25	Trade Debtors	7,000	21	Wages	2,000
	(Blank Line →)		31	Trade Creditors	5,000
				(Blank Line →)	
	(Total box →)			(Total box →)	

Fig. 25

2. Add up the debit side of the account (= £46,500).
3. Add up the credit side of the account (= £25,000).
4. Enter the GREATER value in EACH total box (= £46,500).
5. Enter the shortfall – the closing balance to be carried down ("c/d") of £21,500 – to make both sides equal.
6. The balance must be brought down ("b/d") on the OPPOSITE side, BELOW the total box.

Cash & Bank Account					
	Debit	£		Credit	£
Jan 1	Capital	30,000	Jan 2	Motor Vehicles	8,000
7	Sales	9,500	12	Purchases	10,000
25	Trade Debtors	7,000	21	Wages	2,000
			31	Trade Creditors	5,000
			Jan 31	**Balance c/d**	**21,500**
		46,500			**46,500**
Feb 1	**Balance b/d**	**21,500**			

Fig. 26

Notes

- The balancing off of the account has netted the total value of all the entries on the account for the period.
- As the debit side exceeded the credit side, the balance of £21,500 is a debit balance, i.e. a net debit.
- The cash transactions for the next period will be added to/subtracted from the balance brought down (b/d), i.e. the next period will start with this balance, £21,500 on the debit side.
- According to the Cash and Bank Account, the Cowboys Clothing Co. should have £21,500 cash at the end of this period/beginning of next period, i.e. 31st January/1st February. This must be compared with actual cash in hand and at bank, to verify the accuracy of this record.
- The double entry rule is reinforced by the balancing-off process:

BALANCES

Debit	Credit
Asset	Equity
Expense	Creditor
	Income
	Provision

Fig. 27

The Trial Balance of the Cowboys Clothing Co.

The Trial Balance will list all the balances in the ledgers, at a point in time, to prove that the net debits recorded equal the net credits recorded.

The balances in the ledgers of Cowboys Clothing Co. are shown below. (For clarity, the dates and cross references have been omitted.)

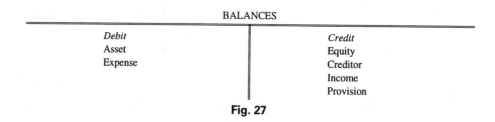

Cash & Bank Account					Trade Creditors Account			
Ref	Debit (£)	Ref	Credit (£)		Ref	Debit (£)	Ref	Credit (£)
	30,000		8,000			5,000		6,000
	9,500		10,000		c/d	1,000		
	7,000		2,000					
			5,000			6,000		6,000
		c/d	21,500				b/d	1,000
	46,500		46,500					
b/d	21,500							

Capital Account			
Ref	Debit (£)	Ref	Credit (£)
			30,000
c/d	30,000		
	30,000		30,000
		b/d	**30,000**

Sales Account			
Ref	Debit (£)	Ref	Credit (£)
			9,500
			14,500
c/d	24,000		
	24,000		24,000
		b/d	**24,000**

Motor Vehicles Account			
Ref	Debit (£)	Ref	Credit (£)
	8,000		
		c/d	8,000
	8,000		8,000
b/d	**8,000**		

Trade Debtors Account			
Ref	Debit (£)	Ref	Credit (£)
	14,500		7,000
		c/d	7,500
	14,500		14,500
b/d	**7,500**		

Purchases Account			
Ref	Debit (£)	Ref	Credit (£)
6,000			
10,000			
		c/d	16,000
	16,000		16,000
b/d	**16,000**		

Wages Account			
Ref	Debit (£)	Ref	Credit (£)
	2,000		
		c/d	2,000
	2,000		2,000
b/d	**2,000**		

Fig. 28

The Trial Balance will be as follows:

Cowboys Clothing Co.

Trial Balance as at 31st January

	Dr (£)	Cr (£)
Cash & Bank	21,500	
Capital		30,000
Motor Vehicles	8,000	
Purchases	16,000	
Trade Creditors		1,000
Sales		24,000
Trade Debtors	7,500	
Wages	2,000	
	55,000	55,000

Fig. 29

Notes

- The Trial Balance is a list of all the balances in the ledger at one moment in time, in this example as at 31st January.
- The importance of the Trial Balance is that it proves that for every debit entry in the ledger there is a credit entry of the same value. It is a good indication that the recording has been made correctly.
- Some errors will **not** show up in the Trial Balance, i.e. it will still balance. These include: transactions missed out entirely; entries made on the correct side but in the wrong account, e.g. the purchase of a machine, a fixed asset, debited to the purchases account instead of to the machinery account.
- A Trial Balance should be drawn up regularly to locate errors in the recording system promptly.
- A Trial Balance should always be extracted to indicate the accuracy of the records, before the information is used to draw up the Profit and Loss Account and the Balance Sheet.

Tutorial Questions

3.1   Which of the following is the correct terminology for the right-hand side of a ledger account?

i.   Debit.
ii.   Credit.
iii.   Negative.
iv.   Positive.

3.2   Is it true to say that the debit side of a ledger account always records an increase in value?

3.3   Is it true to say that a decrease in an asset or an expense will be recorded on the credit side of a ledger account?

3.4   Is it true to say that a decrease in equity or a creditor will be recorded on the credit side of a ledger account?

3.5   Discuss the reasons for keeping accounting records.

3.6 Identify which accounts should be debited and which should be credited to record the following transactions.

i.   The owner starts a business by introducing cash.
ii.   A vehicle is bought and paid for immediately.
iii. Goods for resale are bought on credit.
iv.   Goods are sold on credit.
v.   Wages are paid.
vi.   Cash is paid to trade creditors.
vii. Cash is received from trade debtors.

3.7 The following transactions relate to a new business.

May 1   The owner starts a business by introducing cash of £15,000.
3   A vehicle costing £9,000 is bought and paid for.
8   Goods for resale costing £2,500 are bought on credit from Guy.
9   Cash purchases are made of £500.
10   Goods are sold on credit to James for £3,500.
15   Wages of £200 are paid.
16   Cash sales are made of £1,200
18   Stock is bought for £1,500 on credit from Scott.
20   A vehicle costing £8,000 is bought from Rocket Motors. A deposit of £2,000 is paid immediately. The balance will be paid in August.
21   An electricity bill for £100 is received (but not paid).
25   An invoice from Travel Co. Ltd. for £120 is received.
26   Sales of £2,000 are made on credit to Catherine.
27   £1,800 is paid to the trade creditor Guy.
28   £1,400 is received from the trade debtor James.
31   The electricity bill is paid.

Required

a.   Draw up the ledger accounts to record the above transactions.
b.   Balance off the accounts and extract a Trial Balance as at 31st May.
c.   Show a breakdown of the Trade Debtors figure, identifying the amount outstanding from each individual debtor.
d.   Show a breakdown of the Trade Creditors figure, identifying the amount owing to each individual creditor.

RECORDING TRANSACTIONS OF AN ESTABLISHED BUSINESS

Introduction

In Tutorial 3, all the examples dealt with a new business. In established businesses, the ledger accounts will already contain balances arising from transactions previously recorded.

Example of Recording Business Transactions in the Books of A. Trader Co.

An explanation of the necessary entries in the ledger will be given after each transaction. The ledger accounts, together with a Trial Balance, will be shown at the end of the tutorial.

It is assumed that A. Trader Co. is an established business and that the accounts in the business ledgers already contain the following balances brought down (b/d) from the previous period.

A. Trader Co.		
Trial Balance as at 31st May	*Dr (£)*	*Cr (£)*
Cash & Bank	60,000	
Capital		80,000
Drawings	2,000	
Machinery	54,000	
Motor Vehicles	70,000	
Loans		50,000
Purchases	500,000	
Trade Creditors		45,000
Sales		735,000
Trade Debtors	95,000	
Wages	90,000	
Light & Heat	14,000	
Rent & Insurance	25,000	
	910,000	910,000

Fig. 30

The transactions for the month of June can now be recorded in the ledgers of A. Trader Co.

1. *Machines are bought for £4,000 and paid for immediately*

- Debit Machinery (+ ASSET)
- Credit Cash & Bank (– ASSET)

2. *A cash loan for £20,000 is taken out*

- Debit Cash & Bank (+ ASSET)
- Credit Loans (+ CREDITORS)

3. *Additional machinery is bought for £6,000 using loan finance*

- Debit Machinery (+ ASSET)
- Credit Loans (+ CREDITORS)

4. *A motor vehicle is bought for £16,000. A cash deposit of £3,000 is paid immediately. Loan finance is used for the remainder*

- Debit Motor Vehicles £3,000 + £13,000 (+ ASSET)
- Credit Cash & Bank £3,000 (– ASSET)
- Credit Loans £13,000 (+ CREDITORS)

5. *Loan creditors are repaid £10,000*

- Debit Loans (– CREDITORS)
- Credit Cash & Bank (– ASSET)

6. *The owner makes cash drawings of £500*

- Debit Drawings (– EQUITY)
  (*Note*: It is usual to use a separate drawings account to record day to day drawings, rather than use the capital account)
- Credit Cash & Bank (– ASSET)

7. *Additional capital of £9,000 is introduced by the owner*

- Debit Cash & Bank (+ ASSET)
- Credit Capital (+ EQUITY)

The accounts recording the above transactions are shown below.

Cash & Bank Account

Ref	Debit (£)	Ref	Credit (£)
b/d	60,000		
		1	4,000
2	20,000		
		4	3,000
		5	10,000
		6	500
	9,000		
7		c/d	71,500
	89,000		89,000
b/d	71,500		

Loans Account

Ref	Debit (£)	Ref	Credit (£)
		b/d	50,000
		2	20,000
		3	6,000
		4	13,000
5	10,000		
c/d	79,000		
	89,000		89,000
		b/d	79,000

Machinery Account

Ref	Debit (£)	Ref	Credit (£)
b/d	54,000		
1	4,000		
3	6,000		
		c/d	64,000
	64,000		64,000
b/d	64,000		

Drawings Account

Ref	Debit (£)	Ref	Credit (£)
b/d	2,000		
6	500		
		c/d	2,500
	2,500		2,500
b/d	2,500		

Motor Vehicles Account

Ref	Debit (£)	Ref	Credit (£)
b/d	70,000		
1	3,000		
3	13,000		
		c/d	86,000
	86,000		86,000
b/d	86,000		

Capital Account

Ref	Debit (£)	Ref	Credit (£)
		b/d	80,000
		7	9,000
c/d	89,000		
	89,000		89,000
		b/d	89,000

Fig. 31

Note

In practice, the reference columns will show dates and cross references. To be compatible with the software which accompanies this manual, the reference columns will show the transaction numbers instead of the dates and cross references.

After the above transactions have been recorded, the Trial Balance will be as follows:

A. Trader Co.		
Trial Balance as at 30th June	Dr (£)	Cr (£)
Cash & Bank	71,500	
Capital		89,000
Drawings	2,500	
Machinery	64,000	
Motor Vehicles	86,000	
Loans		79,000
Purchases	500,000	
Trade Creditors		45,000
Sales		735,000
Trade Debtors	95,000	
Wages	90,000	
Light & Heat	14,000	
Rent & Insurance	25,000	
	948,000	948,000

Fig. 32

Note

It will be assumed throughout this manual that all loans are Long Term Liabilities, i.e. they will be listed on the Balance Sheet as Creditors payable after 1 year. If any of the loans are repayable within one year of the Balance Sheet date, they should be listed on the Balance Sheet as Creditors payable within 1 year.

Tutorial Questions

4.1   Below is the Trial Balance of A. Trader Co. as at 30th June.

The following transactions take place during July.

1.   A motor vehicle is bought for £14,000 and paid for immediately.
2.   A cash loan for £10,000 is taken out.
3.   Additional machinery is bought for £9,000 using loan finance.
4.   A machine is bought for £18,000. A cash deposit of £5,000 is paid immediately. Loan finance is used for the remainder.
5.   Cash of £5,000 is introduced by the owner.
6.   Loans of £30,000 are repaid.
7.   The owner makes cash drawings of £2,500.
8.   A van worth £7,000 is introduced by the owner.
9.   The owner draws a cheque on the business bank account to pay his son's school fees of £2,000.

A. Trader Co.		
Trial Balance as at 30th June.	*Dr (£)*	*Cr (£)*
Cash & Bank	71,500	
Capital		89,000
Drawings	2,500	
Machinery	64,000	
Motor Vehicles	86,000	
Loans		79,000
Purchases	500,000	
Trade Creditors	95,000	45,000
Sales		735,000
Trade Debtors		
Wages	90,000	
Light & Heat	14,000	
Rent & Insurance	25,000	
	948,000	948,000

Required

Record the transactions for July in the books of A. Trader Co. and draw up the Trial Balance as at 31st July.

4.2   Discuss whether the owner of a business should make drawings equal to profits.

4.3   A friend has asked for your help in preparing a business plan for his new business.

Required

a.   Identify the type of expenditure that is likely to be incurred during the first year of a business.

b.   Discuss the various sources of finance which may be available to a business.

LOAN INTEREST

Introduction

A business may take out loans to finance its operations. Normally, interest will be payable on loans. Interest payable is a business expense and is calculated by reference to:

- the amount borrowed
- the rate of interest (normally expressed as % per annum)

Example

A business takes out a loan of £10,000 at an interest rate of 8% per annum.
The interest expense for one year will be:

$$£10,000 \times \frac{8}{100} = £800$$

Recording Interest Paid

When interest is paid, the following entries must be made in the ledgers of the business:

- Debit Interest Payable (+ EXPENSE)
- Credit Cash & Bank (− ASSET)

The interest in the above example will be recorded as follows:

Cash & Bank Account			
Ref	Debit (£)	Ref	Credit (£)
			800

Interest Payable Account			
Ref	Debit (£)	Ref	Credit (£)
	800		

Fig. 33

Notes

- Interest must not be entered in the loan account itself. The payment of interest does not represent a repayment of the amount borrowed.
- Interest payable will appear as a debit balance on the Trial Balance and must be included as an expense on the Profit & Loss Account.

Interest Due but not yet Paid

The Profit & Loss Account must show all expenses incurred in the accounting period whether or not these expenses have been paid (ACCRUALS CONCEPT).

Interest due at the end of the accounting period, but not yet paid, must be added to interest paid in order to account in full for the interest expense. Also, the interest outstanding at the end of the period must be recognised as a liability (therefore included in Trade Creditors).

Example

1.   On the first day of the accounting year, a business takes out a long term loan of £20,000 at an annual rate of interest of 10% (i.e. the annual interest will be £20,000 ×
$$\frac{10}{100} = £2,000)$$

- Debit Cash & Bank £20,000 (+ ASSET)
- Credit Loans £20,000 (+ CREDITORS)

2.   During the year, £900 interest is paid on the loan

- Debit Interest Payable £900 (+ EXPENSE)

- Credit Cash & Bank £900 (–ASSET)

3.   At the year end, the expense of interest outstanding must be accounted for (£2,000 – £900 = £1,100)

- Debit Interest Payable £1,100 (+ EXPENSE)
- Credit Trade Creditors £1,100 (+ CREDITORS)

	Cash & Bank Account					Interest Payable Account		
Ref	Debit (£)	Ref	Credit (£)		Ref	Debit (£)	Ref	Credit (£)
1	20,000				2	900		
		2	900		3	1,100		
		c/d	19,100				c/d	2,000
	20,000		20,000			2,000		2,000
b/d	19,100				b/d	2,000		

	Loans Account					Trade Creditors Account		
Ref	Debit (£)	Ref	Credit (£)		Ref	Debit (£)	Ref	Credit (£)
		1	20,000				3	1,100
c/d	20,000				c/d	1,100		
	20,000		20,000			1,100		1,100
		b/d	20,000				b/d	1,100

Fig. 34

The above will appear in the Trial Balance as follows:

Trial Balance as at end of Year		
	Dr (£)	Cr (£)
Cash & Bank	19,100	
Loans		20,000
Interest Payable	2,000	
Trade Creditors		1,100
	21,100	21,100

Fig. 35

52   Loan Interest

When the Final Accounts are prepared for the year, the EXPENSE of Interest Payable (£2,000) will be transferred to the Profit & Loss Account to calculate net profit. On the Balance Sheet, Loans (£20,000) will be listed under Creditors payable after 1 year, while Trade Creditors, which will include outstanding loan interest (£1,100), will be listed under Creditors payable within 1 year.

Note

If a business lends money, INCOME called "interest receivable" will be earned.

Tutorial Questions

5.1   What is the % rate of interest per annum on a loan of £30,000 where the annual interest payable is £2,400?

5.2   A business takes out a 5 year loan of £100,000, at an interest rate of 10% per annum:

a.   Calculate the interest expense for one year.
b.   What is the balance on the loan account after the interest has been paid?
c.   If £8,000 interest has been paid during the year, what will be shown on the Balance Sheet for loans and loan interest?

5.3 a.   Record the following in the ledgers of a new business and extract a Trial Balance.

1.   On the first day of business a long term loan of £60,000 is taken out. The annual rate of interest is 7%.
2.   During the year, £2,100 interest is paid on the loan.
3.   At the year end, account for interest outstanding.

b.   How much loan interest will be shown in the Profit & Loss Account?

5.4   A business has opened a bank deposit account. How will the interest on the deposit account be shown in the Profit & Loss Account?

THE PRINCIPLES OF DEPRECIATION

Introduction

A business acquires fixed assets, such as machines, primarily for use within the business rather than for resale. Fixed assets are normally used for more than one accounting period. The value of most fixed assets will diminish over time.

Example

At the beginning of Year 1, a business buys a machine for £21,000 cash. It is estimated that the machine will be used for 3 years, when it will have no scrap value.
The cost of £21,000 must be spread over the life of the machine. This process is known as "depreciation". Depreciation must be recognised as:

- a business expense which must be charged against profits
- a reduction in the book value of the fixed asset, for which a provision must be set up

The Profit & Loss Account for one year must only be charged with one year's expenses (ACCRUALS CONCEPT). Clearly the whole £21,000 is not an expense of any one year. The £21,000 must be shared between the 3 years of use of the machine.

Recording Depreciation

The above example will be used to illustrate the recording of depreciation in the business ledgers. In this example, it will be assumed that total depreciation of £21,000 will be apportioned equally over the life of the machine (the straight line method), i.e.:

$$\frac{£21,000}{3 \text{ years}} = £7,000 \text{ per annum}$$

The entries in the ledgers in Year 1

1.   To record the acquisition of the machine

- Debit Machinery at Cost (+ ASSET)
- Credit Cash & Bank (–ASSET)

2.   To record the depreciation expense for Year 1

- Debit Depreciation Expense (+ EXPENSE)
- Credit Provision for Depreciation of Machinery (+ PROVISION)

Cash & Bank Account			
Ref	Debit (£)	Ref	Credit (£)
		1	21,000

Machinery at Cost Account			
Ref	Debit (£)	Ref	Credit (£)
1	21,000		
		c/d	21,000
	21,000		21,000
b/d	21,000		

Depreciation Expense Account			
Ref	Debit (£)	Ref	Credit (£)
2	7,000		
		c/d	7,000
	7,000		7,000
b/d	7,000		

Provision for Depreciation of Machinery Account			
Ref	Debit (£)	Ref	Credit (£)
		2	7,000
c/d	7,000		
	7,000		7,000
		b/d	7,000

Fig. 36

The above will appear in the Trial Balance at the end of the year as follows:

Trial Balance as at end of Year 1		
	Dr (£)	Cr (£)
Machinery at Cost	21,000	
Depreciation Expense	7,000	
Provision for Depreciation of Machinery		7,000

Fig. 37

When the Final Accounts are prepared for the year, the depreciation expense (debit of £7,000) will be transferred to the Profit & Loss Account as an expense in order to calculate net profit.

Depreciation Expense Account			
Ref	Debit (£)	Ref	Credit (£)
T.B.	7,000	to Year 1 P&L	7,000
		Balance c/d	0
	7,000		7,000
Balance b/d	0		

Fig. 38

The balances remaining on the Machinery at Cost Account and on the Provision for Depreciation of Machinery Account will appear on the Balance Sheet as follows:

Balance Sheet as at end of Year 1			
Fixed Assets	Cost (£)	Accum.Dep. (£)	Net Book Value (£)
Machinery	21,000	7,000	14,000

Fig. 39

NOTES

- It is normal accounting practice to keep separate accounts for: (i) the cost of each type of fixed asset; (ii) the provision for depreciation of each type of fixed asset.
- The balance on an asset's Provision for Depreciation Account will increase each year, i.e. the total provision will accumulate over the life of the asset. In this example,

the total depreciation provided by the end of Year 1 is £7,000. By the end of Year 2 another £7,000 will have been provided, increasing the provision to £14,000.

• The net book value is the difference between the original cost of the asset and its accumulated depreciation. The net book value is calculated on the Balance Sheet by netting off the balances from the two ledger accounts: (i) Fixed Asset at Cost Account; (ii) Provision for Depreciation Account.

• The net book value of a fixed asset represents the portion of the cost of the fixed asset which has not yet been recognised as an expense. The net book value will not necessarily be the same as the market value of the asset.

Year 2

At the start of Year 2, the balance on the Machinery at Cost Account and on the Provision for Depreciation Account will be brought forward from Year 1.

At the end of Year 2, another £7,000 depreciation must be accounted for. This represents the depreciation expense for Year 2 and a further reduction in the book value of the machine.

	Machinery at Cost Account			
Ref	Debit (£)		Ref	Credit (£)
b/d	21,000			

	Provision for Depreciation of Machinery Account			
Ref	Debit (£)		Ref	Credit (£)c/d
			b/d	7,000
			Year 2	7,000
			exp.	
c/d	14,000			
	14,000			14,000
			b/d	14,000

	Depreciation Expense Account			
Ref	Debit (£)		Ref	Credit (£)
b/d	0			
Year 2	7,000			
			c/d	7,000
	7,000			7,000
b/d	7,000			

Fig. 40

The above will appear in the Trial Balance at the end of Year 2 as follows:

Trial Balance as at end of Year 2		
	Dr (£)	Cr (£)
Machinery at Cost	21,000	
Depreciation Expense	7,000	
Provision for Depreciation of Machinery		14,000

Fig. 41

When the Final Accounts are prepared for the year, the expense of depreciation (debit of £7,000) will be transferred to the Profit & Loss Account as an expense for Year 2 in order to calculate net profit for Year 2.

Depreciation Expense Account			
Ref	Debit (£)	Ref	Credit (£)
T.B.	7,000	to Year 2 P&L	7,000
		Balance c/d	0
	7,000		7,000
Balance b/d	0		

Fig. 42

The balances remaining on the Machinery at Cost Account and on the Provision for Depreciation of Machinery Account will appear on the Balance Sheet at the end of Year 2 as follows:

Balance Sheet as at end of Year 2			
Fixed Assets	Cost (£)	Accum.Dep. (£)	Net Book Value (£)
Machinery	21,000	14,000	7,000

Fig. 43

Year 3

At the start of Year 3, the balance on the Machinery at Cost Account and on the Provision for Depreciation Account will be brought forward from Year 2.

At the end of Year 3, another £7,000 depreciation must be accounted for. This represents the depreciation expense for Year 3 and a further reduction in the book value of the machine.

Machinery at Cost Account			
Ref	Debit (£)	Ref	Credit (£)
b/d	21,000		

Provision for Depreciation of Machinery Account			
Ref	Debit (£)	Ref	Credit (£) c/d
		b/d	14,000
		Year 3 exp.	7,000
c/d	21,000		
	21,000		21,000
		b/d	21,000

Depreciation Expense Account			
Ref	Debit (£)	Ref	Credit (£)
b/d	0		
Year 3	7,000		
		c/d	7,000
	7,000		7,000
b/d	7,000		

Fig. 44

The above will appear in the Trial Balance at the end of Year 3 as follows:

Trial Balance as at end of Year 3		
	Dr (£)	Cr (£)
Machinery at Cost	21,000	
Depreciation Expense	7,000	
Provision for Depreciation of Machinery		21,000

Fig. 45

When the Final Accounts are prepared for the year, the depreciation expense (debit of £7,000) will be transferred to the Profit & Loss Account as an expense for Year 3 in order to calculate net profit for Year 3.

Depreciation Expense Account			
Ref	Debit (£)	Ref	Credit (£)
T.B.	7,000	to Year 3 P&L	7,000
		Balance c/d	0
	7,000		7,000
Balance b/d	0		

Fig. 46

The balances remaining on the Machinery at Cost Account and on the Provision for Depreciation of Machinery Account will appear on the Balance Sheet at the end of Year 3 as follows:

Balance Sheet as at end of Year 3			
Fixed Assets	Cost (£)	Accum.Dep. (£)	Net Book Value (£)
Machinery	21,000	21,000	Nil

Fig. 47

Tutorial Questions

6.1   A business buys a machine costing £50,000 at the start of Year 1. It is estimated that the machine will be used for 5 years and will have no scrap value. If the business uses the straight line method to depreciate its machines:

a.   How much is the depreciation charge per annum?
b.   What will be the annual % rate of depreciation?
c.   What will be the balance on the Provision for Depreciation of Machinery Account at the end of Year 3?
d.   What will be the net book value of the machine at the end of Year 3?
e.   Discuss whether the net book value of the machine, as shown on the Balance Sheet, will be the same as its market value.

6.2   A business buys a machine costing £50,000 at the start of Year 1. It is estimated that the machine will be used for 5 years and will have no scrap value. The business uses the straight line method to depreciate its machines.

Required

a.   Draw up the ledger accounts to record the above in the ledgers of the business for the first 3 years.

b.   Draw up the Fixed Assets section of the Balance Sheet at the end of Year 3.

DEPRECIATION ADJUSTMENTS

Introduction

In Tutorial 6, the recording of depreciation of a machine was demonstrated. In practice, an organisation may have many machines. Normally, the figures in the Machinery at Cost Account and the Provision for Depreciation of Machinery Account will relate to all the machines owned by the organisation.

Depreciation Methods

Depreciation seeks to allocate a portion of the net cost of a fixed asset as an expense to the Profit & Loss Account. There are many methods of calculating the depreciation expense. The straight line method of depreciation allocates cost equally over the life of the asset. Other methods, e.g. the reducing balance method, recognise that asset values may not diminish by the same amount each year.

It is important that an organisation adopts an accounting policy for depreciating its fixed assets and applies that policy consistently. The accounting entries for depreciation will be the same regardless of the method chosen to calculate the depreciation charge.

The straight line method is almost always used in practice and will, therefore, be used in all the examples in this manual and in the accompanying software.

Example

A firm owns Fixtures which originally cost £40,000. The accounting policy for depreciating Fixtures is 10% using the straight line method.
The depreciation to be shown as an expense in the Profit & Loss Account each year will be:

$$£40,000 \times \frac{10}{100} = £4,000$$

Depreciation Adjustments

Depreciation adjustments may be necessary because there is an element of prediction in judging the life of an asset. Occasionally firms will need to make a one-off adjustment to the depreciation provision to reflect the reality of a situation. Under these circumstances, the Provision for Depreciation Account will have to be increased or reduced, with a corresponding entry in the Depreciation Expense Account. Depreciation is recorded as follows:

- Debit Depreciation Expense Account (+ EXPENSE)
- Credit Provision for Depreciation Account (+ PROVISION)

It follows that if the balance on the Provision for Depreciation Account is too low, a further amount must be debited to the Depreciation Expense Account and credited to the Provision for Depreciation Account. Conversely, if the balance on the Provision for Depreciation Account is too high, an amount must be credited to the Depreciation Expense Account and debited to the Provision for Depreciation Account.

Example

A computer, which was bought for £5,000, was originally expected to be in use for 5 years. The depreciation charge was £1,000 per annum.
At the end of Year 3 the computer was shown on the draft Balance Sheet as follows:

Balance Sheet as at end of Year 3			
Fixed Assets	*Cost (£)*	*Accum. Dep. (£)*	*Net Book Value (£)*
Computer	5,000	*3,000	2,000

* 3 years' depreciation at £1,000 per annum

Fig. 48

During the review of the draft Final Accounts for Year 3, it was noted that the computer would become obsolete by the end of Year 4. The Final Accounts for Year 3 are to be amended to reflect this new information. An adjustment must be made to the Provision for Depreciation Account as follows:

Annual depreciation based on a life of **4** years $\quad \dfrac{£5,000}{4 \text{ years}} = £1,250$

Accumulated depreciation to end of Year 3 $\quad £1,250 \times 3 \text{ years} = £3,750$
Accumulated depreciation already provided $\qquad\qquad\qquad\qquad £3,000$
Adjustment (extra depreciation required) $\qquad\qquad\qquad\qquad\quad £750$

Debit Depreciation Expense £750 (+ EXPENSE)
Credit Provision for Depreciation £750 (+ PROVISION)

The extra depreciation expense of £750 in Year 3 will decrease the profit by £750.

Depreciation Expense Account			
Ref	Debit (£)	Ref	Credit (£)
Year 3 **adjustment**	750	to Year 3 P&L	750
		Balance c/d	0
	750		750
Balance b/d	0		

Provision for Depreciation of Computer Account			
Ref	Debit (£)	Ref	Credit (£)
		Balance b/d	3,000
		Year 3 **adjustment**	750
Balance c/d	3,750		
	3,750		3,750
		Balance b/d	3,750

Fig. 49

Note

The depreciation expense on the revised Profit & Loss Account for Year 3 will be £1,750, calculated as follows:

Depreciation based on the original accounting policy	£1,000
Depreciation adjustment	£750
	£1,750

The revised Balance Sheet at the end of Year 3 will be as follows:

Balance Sheet as at end of Year 3			
Fixed Assets	Cost (£)	Accum.Dep. (£)	Net Book Value (£)
Computer	5,000	3,750	1,250

Fig. 50

Tutorial Questions

7.1   What entries will be necessary to adjust the balance on the Provision for Depreciation of Fixtures Account from £7,000 to £9,000?

7.2   What entries will be necessary to adjust the balance on the Provision for Depreciation of Motor Vehicles Account from £40,000 to £35,000?

7.3   What will be the effect of the adjustments made in questions 7.1 and 7.2 on:

- Profits?
- Owner's Capital?
- Net Assets?

7.4   The following is an extract from the draft accounts of a business at the end of Year 3.

Balance Sheet as at end of Year 3			
Fixed Assets	*Cost (£)*	*Accum.Dep. (£)*	*Net Book Value (£)*
Machinery	50,000	30,000	20,000

On reviewing the draft Final Accounts, it is decided that the balance on the Provision for Depreciation of Machinery Account should be amended to 65% of the cost of the asset.

Required

a.   Record the adjustment in the ledgers of the business.
b.   Show the amended Balance Sheet extract.
c.   What will be the depreciation expense charged to the Profit & Loss Account for Year 3, if originally annual depreciation was calculated at 20% on cost?

7.5   Discuss whether a business should reduce its depreciation charge for an accounting period where it is predicted that profits will be lower than normal.

DISCOUNTS

Introduction

Many businesses sell goods on credit terms (sales to trade debtors). It may be several weeks before the trade debtors settle their accounts, i.e. before the cash is received.

Although offering credit terms may be an incentive for customers to trade with the business, it is important to collect the cash from trade debtors as quickly as possible so that the cash can be put to use by the business, e.g.:

- to invest in a deposit account and earn interest (+ income)
- to pay off a bank overdraft, which will result in less interest to pay (– expense)
- to buy more fixed assets in order to expand the business
- to buy more stock
- to pay creditors

In order to collect the cash from debtors as quickly as possible, a business may offer discount to its debtors for prompt payment, i.e. it will allow debtors to pay less than the total sum outstanding if they settle their accounts within a certain time period.

Recording Discount Allowed

When a customer is allowed to deduct discount from the amount owed to the business, the cash received by the business will be lower than the amount of the debt being settled. The difference (discount allowed) must be recognised as a business EXPENSE.

Example

1. A business sells goods on credit for £10,000. The business will allow the debtor 5% discount if payment is received within one month

- Debit Trade Debtors £10,000 (+ ASSET)
- Credit Sales £10,000 (+ INCOME)

Note: At this stage the potential discount is ignored

2.   *The debtor settles the account within a month and claims the discount allowed*

- Debit Cash & Bank £9,500, i.e. £10,000 × 95% (+ ASSET)
- Credit Trade Debtors £9,500 (– ASSET)

3.   *The business agrees the discount of £500, i.e. £10,000 × 5%*

- Debit Discount Allowed £500 (+ EXPENSE)
- Credit Trade Debtors £500 (– ASSET)

Note: The discount allowed reduces the ASSET of debtors. It does **not** reduce the sales INCOME

The ledger accounts will appear as follows:

		Sales Account			
Ref	Debit (£)		Ref	Credit (£)	
c/d	10,000		1	10,000	
	10,000			10,000	
			b/d	10,000	

		Cash & Bank Account			
Ref	Debit (£)		Ref	Credit (£)	
2	9,500		c/d	9,500	
	9,500			9,500	
b/d	9,500				

		Trade Debtors Account			
Ref	Debit (£)		Ref	Credit (£)	
1	10,000				
			2	9,500	
			3	500	
			c/d	0	
	10,000			10,000	
b/d	0				

		Discount Allowed Account			
Ref	Debit (£)		Ref	Credit (£)	
3	500				
			c/d	500	
	500			500	
b/d					

Fig. 51

The above will appear in the Trial Balance as follows:

Trial Balance as at		
	Dr (£)	*Cr (£)*
Sales		10,000
Trade Debtors	0	
Cash & Bank	9,500	
Discount Allowed	500	
	10,000	10,000

Fig. 52

When the Final Accounts are prepared, the Sales figure of £10,000 will be transferred to the Profit & Loss Account as INCOME. The Discount Allowed of £500 will be treated as an EXPENSE in the Profit & Loss Account.

Discount Received

Discount received is the opposite of discount allowed. It is the amount a business may deduct for prompt payment to its trade creditors.

Recording Discount Received

When a business deducts discount from the amount owed to its trade creditors, the cash paid will be lower than the amount being settled. The difference (discount received) must be recognised as INCOME.

Example

1. A business buys goods on credit for £8,000. The business may receive 4% discount if payment is made within 25 days

- Debit Purchases £8,000 (+ EXPENSE)
- Credit Trade Creditors £8,000 (+ CREDITORS)

Note: At this stage the potential discount is ignored

2. The business pays the trade creditor within 25 days

- Debit Trade Creditors £7,680, i.e. £8,000 × 96% (– CREDITORS)

- Credit Cash & Bank £7,680 (– ASSET)

3. *The business claims the discount of £320, i.e. £8,000 × 4%*

- Debit Trade Creditors £320 (– CREDITORS)
- Credit Discount Received £320 (+ INCOME)

Note: The discount received reduces the amount due to CREDITORS. It does **not** reduce the Purchases figure

The ledger accounts will appear as follows:

	Purchases Account		
Ref	Debit (£)	Ref	Credit (£)
1	8,000	c/d	8,000
	8,000		8,000
b/d	8,000		

	Cash & Bank Account		
Ref	Debit (£)	Ref	Credit (£)
c/d	7,680	2	7,680
	7,680		7,680
		b/d	7,680

	Trade Creditors Account		
Ref	Debit (£)	Ref	Credit (£)
		1	8,000
2	7,680		
3	320		
c/d	0		
	8,000		8,000
		b/d	0

	Discount Received Account		
Ref	Debit (£)	Ref	Credit (£)
		3	320
c/d	320		
	320		320
		b/d	320

Fig. 53

The above will appear in the Trial Balance as follows:

Trial Balance as at		
	Dr (£)	Cr (£)
Purchases	8,000	
Trade Creditors		0
Cash & Bank		7,680
Discount Received		320
	8,000	8,000

Fig. 54

When the Final Accounts are prepared, the Purchases figure of £8,000 will be used to calculate Cost of Sales. The Discount Received of £320 will be treated as INCOME in the Profit & Loss Account.

Using the figures from the two examples above, and assuming there is no opening or closing stock, the Profit & Loss Account would include the following:

Profit & Loss Account for	£	£
Sales		10,000
Less Cost of Sales		8,000
Gross Profit		2,000
Other Income		
Discount Received		320
		2,320
Less Overhead Expenses		
Discount Allowed	500	
Rent etc.	0	
Net Profit		

Fig. 55

NOTE

This Tutorial is concerned with discount for prompt payment, sometimes known as "cash discount". Cash discount does **not** affect the amount recorded in sales or purchases; it is always recorded separately in the discount allowed and received accounts.

Trade Discount

Trade discount may be given when large quantities of goods are bought, i.e. trade discount is part of the negotiation of the purchase/sales price of the goods themselves. Trade discount must not be confused with cash discount.

Tutorial Questions

8.1 The balance on the account of a trade creditor is £3,000; 5% discount may be deducted for prompt payment.

Required
Assuming payment is made on time:

a. Calculate the amount of discount to be deducted.
b. Identify the accounting entries necessary to record the above matters.
c. What effect will the discount have on the profit for the period?

8.2 A new business will allow its trade debtors to deduct 3% discount if they settle their accounts within 28 days. The following transactions take place during the first two months of trading.

Jan 3   Goods are sold on credit to Becky for £1,000
   14   Goods are sold on credit to Hazel for £800
   20   Goods are sold on credit to Bruno for £2,000
   30   Becky settles her account
Feb 5   Bruno settles his account
   25   Hazel settles her account

Required

a. Identify the accounting entries necessary to record the above matters.
b. What will be shown on the Profit & Loss Account for sales and for discount allowed?

8.3 The following details relate to a business which has been trading for several years.

	Dr (£)	Cr (£)
Ged & Co.		
Trial Balance as at		
Cash & Bank	33,000	
Capital		101,000
Drawings	7,000	
Machinery	91,000	
Motor Vehicles	107,000	
Loans		81,000
Purchases	500,000	
Trade Creditors		43,000
Discount Allowed	5,000	
Discount Received		2,000
Sales		735,000
Trade Debtors	90,000	
Wages	90,000	
Light & Heat	14,000	
Rent & Insurance	25,000	
	962,000	962,000

The following additional transactions need to be recorded.

1. Sales are made on credit for £20,000.
2. Cash of £18,000 is paid to trade creditors. Discount of £450 has been deducted.
3. Purchases are made on credit for £40,000.
4. A trade debtor, who owes £16,000 to the business, settles his account after deducting 3% discount.

Required

a. Record the above transactions in the ledgers of the business.
b. Extract an amended Trial Balance.

BAD DEBTS

Introduction

Most businesses sell goods on credit terms, i.e. to trade debtors. Offering credit terms is an incentive for customers to trade with a business. It must be recognised, however, that there is a risk that some debtors will fail to pay their debts, i.e. that the debts may be bad.

Recording Bad Debts

When a debt is deemed to be bad, it can no longer be recognised as an ASSET. A bad debt is an EXPENSE incurred by a business which has traded on credit terms with a debtor who cannot pay his debt in full.

Example

1. *A business sells goods on credit for £5,000*

- Debit Trade Debtors £5,000 (+ ASSET)
- Credit Sales £5,000 (+ INCOME)

2. *The debtor is declared bankrupt and the debt is to be written off as bad*

- Debit Bad Debts Expense £5,000 (+ EXPENSE)
- Credit Trade Debtors £5,000 (– ASSET)

Note: The bad debt reduces the ASSET of debtors. It does **not** reduce the sales INCOME The ledger accounts will appear as follows:

Sales Account				
Ref	Debit (£)	Ref	Credit (£)
c/d	5,000		
		1	5,000
	5,000		5,000
		b/d	5,000

Bad Debts Expense Account				
Ref	Debit (£)	Ref	Credit (£)
2	5,000		
		c/d	5,000
	5,000		5,000
b/d	5,000		

Trade Debtors Account				
Ref	Debit (£)	Ref	Credit (£)
1	5,000		
		2	5,000
		c/d	0
	5,000		5,000
b/d	0		

Fig. 56

The above will appear in the Trial Balance as follows:

Trial Balance as at		
	Dr (£)	Cr (£)
Sales		5,000
Trade Debtors	0	
Bad Debts Expense	5,000	

Fig. 57

When the Final Accounts are prepared, the Sales figure of £5,000 will be transferred to the Profit & Loss Account as INCOME. The Bad Debts Expense of £5,000 will be treated as an EXPENSE in the Profit & Loss Account.

The CURRENT ASSET of Debtors on the Balance Sheet must not include any debts which are known to be bad.

Notes

- A business should seek to establish the credit worthiness of its customers before trading on credit terms.
- A business should try to recover its debts, i.e. writing off a debt as bad should be a last resort.
- A debt should not be written off as bad unless proper authorisation has been obtained from a senior member of staff within the business.

Provision for Bad Debts

In addition to writing off debts identified as bad during the accounting period, a business may need to create a "provision" for bad debts. This provision will be necessary if it is considered that there may be doubtful debts still contained in the Debtors figure, after writing off any specific bad debts.

The creation of a provision for bad debts enables the Debtors figure on the Balance Sheet to be reduced to net realisable value, in accordance with the PRUDENCE CONCEPT. The balance on the Provision for Bad Debts Account must be adjusted annually, as the value of Debtors is reassessed.

RULE

Debit   Bad Debts Expense Account
Credit   Provision for Bad Debts Account
With   *Increase* in provision for the period

Recording Provision for Bad Debts

The following example relates to a business in its first year of trading.

Example

1.   Goods are sold on credit to various customers for £96,000

- Debit Trade Debtors £96,000 (+ ASSET)
- Credit Sales £96,000 (+ INCOME)

2.   One of the debtors is declared bankrupt and his debt of £5,000 is to be written off as bad

- Debit Bad Debts Expense £5,000 (+ EXPENSE)
- Credit Trade Debtors £5,000 (– ASSET)

3.   Some of the debtors pay the business £30,000

- Debit Cash & Bank £30,000 (+ ASSET)
- Credit Trade Debtors £30,000 (– ASSET)

Note: The balance on the Trade Debtors Account is now £61,000

4.   At the end of the accounting period, it is considered that 2% of the remaining debts may be bad, i.e. £61,000 × 2% = £1,220

- Debit Bad Debts Expense £1,220 (+ EXPENSE)
- Credit Provision for Bad Debts £1,220 (+ PROVISION)

Note: This is the first year of trading, therefore there is no balance brought forward from the previous year on the Provision for Bad Debts Account. The **increase** in the Provision is, therefore, £1,220

The ledger accounts will appear as follows:

Sales Account

Ref	Debit (£)	Ref	Credit (£)
c/d	96,000	1	96,000
	96,000		96,000
		b/d	96,000

Bad Debts Expense Account

Ref	Debit (£)	Ref	Credit (£)
2	5,000		
4	1,220	c/d	6,220
	6,220		6,220
b/d	6,220		

Trade Debtors Account

Ref	Debit (£)	Ref	Credit (£)
1	96,000		
		2	5,000
		3	30,000
		c/d	61,000
	96,000		96,000
b/d	61,000		

Cash & Bank Account

Ref	Debit (£)	Ref	Credit (£)
3	30,000		
		c/d	30,000
	30,000		30,000
b/d	30,000		

Provision for Bad Debts Account				
Ref	Debit (£)		Ref	Credit (£)
c/d	1,220		4	1,220
	1,220			1,220
			b/d	1,220

Fig. 58

The above will appear in the Trial Balance as follows:

Trial Balance as at end of Year 1		
	Dr (£)	Cr (£)
Sales		96,000
Trade Debtors	61,000	
Bad Debts Expense	6,220	
Cash & Bank	30,000	
Provision for Bad Debts		1,220

Fig. 59

When the Final Accounts are prepared, the Sales figure of £96,000 will be transferred to the Profit & Loss Account as income. The Bad Debts Expense of £6,220 will be treated as an expense in the Profit & Loss Account. This expense comprises the specific bad debt of £5,000 and the increase in the provision for bad debts of £1,220.

The Current Asset of debtors will be shown on the Balance Sheet at the end of Year 1 as follows:

Balance Sheet as at end of Year 1		
	£	£
Current Assets		
Stock		0
Trade Debtors	61,000	
Less Provision for Bad Debts	1,220	59,780
Cash & Bank		30,000

Fig. 60

NOTE

The purpose of the Provision for Bad Debts Account is to provide an amount which will reduce the asset of Trade Debtors on the Balance Sheet to net realisable value. This is achieved by subtracting the balance on the Provision for Bad Debts Account from the balance on the Trade Debtors Account.

The following example relates to the above business at the end of its second year of trading.

	Trial Balance as at end of Year 2	
	Dr (£)	Cr (£)
Sales		127,000
Trade Debtors	85,000	
Bad Debts Expense	**3,000**	
Cash & Bank	50,000	
Provision for Bad Debts		**1,220**

Fig. 61

Notes

- The balance on the Provision for Bad Debts Account of £1,220 is the balance brought forward from Year 1, i.e. before the adjustment for Year 2 has been made.
- The balances on the other accounts are the result of Year 2 transactions.

1.   Additional bad debts of £1,200 are to be written off

- Debit Bad Debts Expense £1,200 (+ EXPENSE)
- Credit Trade Debtors £1,200 (− ASSET)

2.   A debt of £400, previously written off as bad, is now deemed to be recoverable

- Debit Trade Debtors £400 (+ ASSET)
- Credit Bad Debts Expense £400 (− EXPENSE)

Note: The balance on the Trade Debtors Account is now £84,200

3.   At the end of the accounting period, it is considered that 2% of the remaining debts may be bad, i.e. £84,200 × 2% = £1,684, i.e. an increase of £464

- Debit Bad Debts Expense £464 (+ EXPENSE)
- Credit Provision for Bad Debts £464 (+ PROVISION)

The ledger accounts will appear as follows:

Trade Debtors Account			
Ref	Debit (£)	Ref	Credit (£)
b/d	85,000		
		1	1,200
2	400		
		c/d	84,200
	85,400		85,400
b/d	84,200		

Provision for Bad Debts Account			
Ref	Debit (£)	Ref	Credit (£)
			c/d
c/d	1,684	3	1,220
			464
	1,684		1,684
		b/d	1,684

Bad Debts Expense Account			
Ref	Debit (£)	Ref	Credit (£)
b/d	3,000		
1	1,200		
		2	400
3	464	c/d	4,264
	4,664		4,664
b/d	4,264		

Fig. 62

After the above have been accounted for, the Trial Balance will be as follows:

Trial Balance as at end of Year 2		
	Dr (£)	Cr (£)
Sales		127,000
Trade Debtors	84,200	
Bad Debts Expense	4,264	
Cash & Bank	50,000	
Provision for Bad Debts		1,684

Fig. 63

When the Final Accounts are prepared, the Bad Debts Expense of £4,264, which includes the increase in the provision for bad debts, will be treated as an expense in the Profit & Loss Account.

The Current Asset of debtors will be shown on the Balance Sheet at the end of Year 2 as follows:

Balance Sheet as at end of Year 2		
	£	£
Current Assets		
Stock		0
Trade Debtors	84,200	
Less Provision for Bad Debts	1,684	82,516
Cash & Bank		50,000

Fig. 64

Reduction in Provision for Bad Debts

The **balance** on the Provision for Bad Debts Account must be adjusted annually, as the value of debtors is reassessed. This may result in a **reduction** in the balance on the Provision for Bad Debts Account.

RULE

Debit   Provision for Bad Debts Account (– PROVISION)
Credit   Bad Debts Expense Account (– EXPENSE)
With   *Decrease* in provision for the period

Credit Control

A good accounting system will provide a detailed analysis of Trade Debtors. This analysis will give information on the status of each individual debtor, indicating the age of each debt. This information may be used for a variety of purposes:

- triggering debt collection procedures for overdue amounts
- re-assessing credit worthiness of customers
- calculating a realistic provision for bad debts

Tutorial Questions

9.1   What accounting entries are necessary to write off a bad debt?

9.2   What accounting entries are necessary when a debt previously written off as bad is now deemed to be recoverable?

9.3   The following ledger accounts relate to Bob's business:

Trade Debtors Account							
Ref	Debit (£)		Ref	Credit (£)			
b/d	188,000						
			c/d				
b/d							

Provision for Bad Debts Account				
Ref	Debit (£)		Ref	Credit (£)
			b/d	7,000
c/d				
			b/d	

Bad Debts Expense Account				
Ref	Debit (£)		Ref	Credit (£)
b/d	5,000			
			c/d	
b/d				

Required

Complete the above ledger accounts assuming that there are additional bad debts of £1,000 and that the closing balance on the Provision for Bad Debts Account should be 5% of the closing Debtors figure.

Trial Balance as at		
	Dr (£)	Cr (£)
Sales		430,000
Trade Debtors	175,000	
Bad Debts Expense	6,000	
Cash & Bank	80,000	
Provision for Bad Debts		1,800

9.4   The following is an extract from the Trial Balance of Barbara's business. The following must be accounted for.

1.   It is discovered that a debtor, who owes £5,000, has absconded to South America without settling his account.

2. Cash of £800 is received in payment of a debt which had previously been written off as bad.
3. A company which owes the business £10,000 has gone into liquidation. Unsecured creditors will receive only 30p in the pound.
4. At the end of the accounting period, the balance on the Provision for Bad Debts is to be revised to £1,200.

Required
Record the above in the ledgers of the business and show the amended Trial Balance extract.

9.5 Discuss what action a business should take if a customer does not settle his account on the due date.

RETURNS

Introduction

Sometimes a business will return purchases to the supplier, e.g. if the goods are faulty. Similarly, goods which have been sold to a customer may be returned to the business.

- returns of purchases (goods returned outwards to the supplier) must be subtracted from Purchases
- returns of sales (goods returned inwards from customers) must be subtracted from Sales

Recording Returns Outwards (Purchases Returns)

When purchases are returned to the supplier, the ledgers must show:

- a decrease in Purchases
- an increase in Cash (if a cash refund is obtained immediately)
- a decrease in Trade Creditors (if there is no immediate cash refund)

   I.e.

If a cash refund is obtained immediately

- Debit Cash & Bank (+ ASSET)
- Credit Purchases (– EXPENSE)

If a cash refund is not obtained immediately

- Debit Trade Creditors (- CREDITORS)
- Credit Purchases (– EXPENSE)

Example

1.   A business purchases goods for cash for £1,000

- Debit Purchases £1,000 (+ EXPENSE)
- Credit Cash & Bank £1,000 (– ASSET)

2.   Purchases to the value of £200 are returned and a cash refund is obtained immediately

- Debit Cash & Bank £200 (+ ASSET)
- Credit Purchases £200 (– EXPENSE)

3.   Goods are bought on credit for £12,000

- Debit Purchases £12,000 (+ EXPENSE)
- Credit Trade Creditors £12,000 (+ CREDITORS)

4.   Purchases to the value of £500 are returned to the suppliers; no immediate cash refund is obtained

- Debit Trade Creditors £500 (– CREDITORS)
- Credit Purchases £500 (– EXPENSE)

The ledger accounts will appear as follows:

Purchases Account			
Ref	Debit (£)	Ref	Credit (£)
1	1,000		
		2	200
3	12,000		
		4	500
		c/d	12,300
	13,000		13,000
b/d	12,300		

Cash & Bank Account			
Ref	Debit (£)	Ref	Credit (£)
		1	1,000
2	200		
c/d	800		
	1,000		1,000
		b/d	800

Trade Creditors Account			
Ref	Debit (£)	Ref	Credit (£)
		3	12,000
4	500		
c/d	11,500		
	12,000		12,000
		b/d	11,500

Fig. 65

The above will appear in the Trial Balance as follows:

Trial Balance as at ......

	Dr (£)	Cr (£)
Purchases	12,300	
Cash & Bank		800
Trade Creditors		11,500

Fig. 66

When the Final Accounts are prepared for the year, the net purchases figure of £12,300 will be used in the calculation of Cost of Sales.

Notes

- As purchases are made at cost price, the returns outwards (purchases returns) are normally valued at cost.
- In some book-keeping systems, returns outwards are recorded in a separate account instead of being credited to the Purchases Account.

Recording Returns Inwards (Sales Returns)

When sales are returned by a customer, the ledgers must show:

- a decrease in Sales
- a decrease in Cash (if a cash refund is given immediately)
- a decrease in Trade Debtors (if there is no immediate cash refund)

I.e.
If a cash refund is given immediately

- Debit Sales (– INCOME)
- Credit Cash & Bank (– ASSET)

If a cash refund is not given immediately

- Debit Sales (– INCOME)
- Credit Trade Debtors (– ASSET)

Example

1. A business sells goods for cash for £15,000

- Debit Cash & Bank £15,000 (+ ASSET)
- Credit Sales £15,000 (+ INCOME)

2. Sales to the value of £900 are returned and a cash refund is given immediately

- Debit Sales £900 (– INCOME)
- Credit Cash & Bank £900 (– ASSET)

3. Goods are sold on credit for £23,000

- Debit Trade Debtors £23,000 (+ ASSET)
- Credit Sales £23,000 (+ INCOME)

4. Sales to the value of £7,000 are returned by the customers; no immediate cash refund is given

- Debit Sales £7,000 (– INCOME)
- Credit Trade Debtors £7,000 (– ASSET)

The ledger accounts will appear as follows:

Sales Account				
Ref	Debit (£)	Ref	Credit (£)	
		1	15,000	
2	900			
		3	23,000	
4	7,000			
c/d	30,100			
	38,000		38,000	
		b/d	30,100	

Cash & Bank Account				
Ref	Debit (£)	Ref	Credit (£)	
1	15,000			
		2	900	
		c/d	14,100	
	15,000		15,000	
b/d	14,100			

Trade Debtors Account				
Ref	Debit (£)	Ref	Credit (£)	
3	23,000			
		4	7,000	
		c/d	16,000	
	23,000		23,000	
b/d	16,000			

Fig. 67

The above will appear in the Trial Balance as follows:

Trial Balance as at		
	Dr (£)	*Cr (£)*
Sales		30,100
Cash & Bank	14,100	
Trade Debtors	16,000	

Fig. 68

When the Final Accounts are prepared for the year, the net sales figure of £30,100 will be transferred to the Profit & Loss Account to calculate profit.

Notes

- As sales are made at selling price, the returns inwards (sales returns) are normally valued at selling price.
- In some book-keeping systems, returns inwards are recorded in a separate account instead of being debited to the Sales Account.

Invoices and Credit Notes

Supporting documentation will be required for most business transactions. When a business sells goods, a document called a "sales invoice" will list all the details of the transaction:

- name and address of the business (usually pre-printed)
- invoice number
- name and address of customer
- full details of the goods and the prices
- terms, e.g. any discounts for prompt payment
- total amount due

The sales invoice, in the customer's own records, will be treated as a purchase invoice.

If goods are returned to a business, the business may issue a credit note. Credit notes are the opposite of invoices and are usually printed in red. A credit note may also be issued where an allowance is to be made to a customer in the event of a disagreement over the goods. Returns and allowances will be credited to a customer's account (– ASSET), hence the term "credit note".

Business documents, such as invoices and credit notes, provide evidence of transactions and are an important part of the record system.

Tutorial Questions

10.1 What will be the accounting entries to record the following?

a. Returns outwards where a cash refund is obtained immediately.
b. Goods returned to a supplier and a credit note obtained.

10.2 What will be the accounting entries to record the following?

a. Cash immediately refunded to customers for goods returned.
b. A credit note is issued for returns inwards.

10.3 The following is an extract from the Trial Balance of Frances's business.

Trial Balance as at	Dr (£)	Cr (£)
Sales		180,000
Trade Debtors	46,000	
Purchases	66,000	
Cash & Bank	34,100	
Trade Creditors		22,800

The following must be accounted for:

1. Goods are bought on credit for £4,000.
2. A customer returns goods to the value of £1,000 and a credit note is issued.
3. Goods are returned to a supplier and a cash refund of £900 is obtained.
4. Cash of £1,500 is refunded to a customer who has returned goods.
5. A supplier sends a credit note to the value of £600 for goods returned.

Required
Record the above in the ledgers of the business and show the amended Trial Balance extract.

10.4 A business buys goods for £1 per unit and sells them at £1.50 per unit. Assuming that all transactions are for cash, what will be the accounting entries to record the following?

a. Purchases of 1,000 units.
b. Sales of 700 units.
c Returns outwards of 50 units.
d. Returns inwards of 40 units.

DISPOSALS OF FIXED ASSETS

Introduction

Fixed assets are normally used by a business for more than one accounting period, and their value will diminish over time. The loss of value of a fixed asset is known as "depreciation". The recording of depreciation was dealt with in Tutorial 6. Depreciation must be recognised as:

* a business expense which must be charged against profits
* a reduction in the book value of the fixed asset, for which a provision must be set up

Depreciation is usually based on:

* cost of the asset
* estimated useful life

Firms frequently dispose of a fixed asset before the end of its useful life, e.g. because they wish to use a more up to date machine to remain competitive. Equally, even though an asset may have been fully depreciated, it may still have a sales value. For example, a machine tool which is no longer suitable for a very precise application, such as the manufacture of aerospace parts, may be useful for less precise applications.

It is unusual for the sales proceeds of a fixed asset to equal the net book value of the asset.

When a firm disposes of a fixed asset, a special set of entries is required in the ledgers.

Example

A business owns many vehicles which are depreciated at 20% per annum on cost.
The balances on the Vehicles at Cost Account and on the Provision for Depreciation of Vehicles Account appear on the Balance Sheet at the end of Year 3 as follows:

Balance Sheet as at end of Year 3			
Fixed Assets	*Cost (£)*	*Accum.Dep. (£)*	*Net Book Value (£)*
Vehicles	230,000	78,000	152,000

Fig. 69

At the beginning of Year 4, one of the vehicles, which was bought at the beginning of Year 1 for £30,000, is sold for £11,500. The net book value of the vehicle disposed of must be compared with the proceeds of sale. Net book value can be calculated as follows:

	£
Cost	30,000
Less accumulated depreciation to date	*18,000
Net book value at start of Year 4	12,000

*£30,000 × 20% × 3 years = £18,000

The net book value of the vehicle (£12,000) is greater than its sales value (£11,500). There has been a loss on disposal of £500, due to the vehicle having been underdepreciated during the 3 years of its use.

It is important that the loss of £500 is correctly dealt with in the Profit & Loss Account for Year 4.

Recording Disposals of Fixed Assets

The above example will be used to illustrate the entries required on disposal of a fixed asset. The Disposals Account is used to deal with this type of transaction. The following entries must be made in the ledgers:

1.   Identify the cost of the vehicle being sold (£30,000). Transfer this to the Disposals Account:

  • Debit Disposals Account £30,000
  • Credit Vehicles at Cost Account £30,000

2.   Calculate the accumulated depreciation provided on the asset being sold (£18,000). Transfer this to the Disposals Account:

  • Debit Provision for Depreciation of Vehicles Account £18,000
  • Credit Disposals Account £18,000

Note: At this stage the balance on the Disposals Account will represent the net book value of the vehicle.

3.   Record the sales proceeds in the Disposals Account (£11,500):

- Debit Cash Account (or Debtors if cash is not received immediately) £11,500
- Credit Disposals Account £11,500

Note: The balance now on the Disposals Account represents a profit or loss on disposal and this is shown eventually in the Profit & Loss Account.

	Vehicles at Cost Account			
Ref	Debit (£)		Ref	Credit (£)
b/d	230,000			
			1	30,000
			c/d	200,000
	230,000			230,000
b/d	200,000			

	Provision for Depreciation of Vehicles Account			
Ref	Debit (£)		Ref	Credit (£)
			b/d	78,000
2	18,000			
c/d	60,000			
	78,000			78,000
			b/d	60,000

	Disposals Account			
Ref	Debit (£)		Ref	Credit (£)
1	30,000		2	18,000
			3	11,500
			c/d	500
	30,000			30,000
b/d	500			

Fig. 70

The above will appear in the Trial Balance after the disposal, as follows:

Trial Balance		
	Dr (£)	*Cr (£)*
Vehicles at cost	200,000	
Provision for Depreciation of Vehicles		60,000
Disposals	500	

Fig. 71

Recording the Depreciation of Fixed Assets Remaining after a Disposal

In the above example, the balance on the Vehicles at Cost Account (£200,000) now represents the cost of the vehicles remaining after the disposal has been accounted for. The balance on the Provision for Depreciation of Vehicles Account (£60,000) represents the accumulated depreciation to the end of Year 3 of the vehicles remaining after the disposal has been accounted for.

4. Year 4's expense of depreciation of the remaining vehicles must now be calculated as follows: £200,000 × 20% = £40,000

    - Debit Depreciation Expense Account £40,000
    - Credit Provision for Depreciation of Vehicles Account £40,000

The ledger accounts relating to vehicles for Year 4 are as follows:

Vehicles at Cost Account				
Ref	Debit (£)		Ref	Credit (£)
b/d	230,000			
			1	30,000
			c/d	200,000
	230,000			230,000
b/d	200,000			

Provision for Depreciation of Vehicles Account			
Ref	Debit (£)	Ref	Credit (£)
		b/d	78,000
2	18,000		
c/d	60,000		
	78,000		78,000
		b/d	60,000
c/d	100,000	4	40,000
	100,000		100,000
		b/d	100,000

Disposals Account			
Ref	Debit (£)	Ref	Credit (£)
1	30,000	2	18,000
		3	11,500
		c/d	500
	30,000		30,000
b/d	500		

Depreciation Expense Account			
Ref	Debit (£)	Ref	Credit (£)
4	**40,000**		
		c/d	40,000
	40,000		40,000
b/d	40,000		

Fig. 72

After accounting for depreciation for Year 4, the Trial Balance will be as follows:

Trial Balance as at end of Year 4	Dr (£)	Cr (£)
Vehicles at cost	200,000	
Provision for Depreciation of Vehicles		100,000
Disposals	500	
Depreciation Expense	40,000	

Fig. 73

The depreciation expense and the loss on disposal will be charged to the Profit & Loss Account for Year 4 as follows:

	Depreciation Expense Account			
Ref	Debit (£)		Ref	Credit (£)
T.B.	40,000			
			to Year 4 P&L	40,000
			Balance c/d	0
	40,000			40,000
Balance b/d	0			

	Disposals Account			
Ref	Debit (£)		Ref	Credit (£)
T.B.	500			
			to Year 4 P&L	500
			Balance c/d	0
	500			500
Balance b/d	0			

Profit & Loss Account for Year 4		
	£	£
Sales		X
Less Cost of Sales		X
Gross Profit		X
Less Expenses		
Wages etc.	X	
Depreciation	40,000	
Loss on Disposal	500	X
Net Profit		X

Fig. 74

Note

In this example, the adjustment on disposal was an expense (debit). This increases the total expenses on the Profit & Loss Account. A gain on disposal (credit) will decrease the total expenses on the Profit & Loss Account.

The Balance Sheet as at the end of Year 4 will show the following balances:

Balance Sheet as at end of Year 4			
Fixed Assets	Cost (£)	Accum. Dep. (£)	Net Book Value (£)
Vehicles	200,000	100,000	100,000

Fig. 75

Tutorial Questions

11.1   What accounting entries will be necessary to record the following?

a.   A cheque received for the sale of an old motor vehicle.
b.   The sales proceeds of an old machine sold on credit terms.

11.2   What will be the effect on profit of the disposal of a fixed asset which has a net book value of £10,000 where the sales proceeds are:

a.   £9,000?
b.   £10,500?

11.3   Give the reasons why the sales proceeds of a fixed asset are rarely the same as its net book value at the date of disposal.

11.4   The following is an extract from the Trial Balance of Simon's business at the end of Year 8.

Trial Balance as at end of Year 8		
	Dr (£)	Cr (£)
Machines at Cost	54,000	
Provision for Depreciation of Machines to end of year 7		16,000
Cash & Bank	12,000	

It is Simon's accounting policy to depreciate machines by 10% per annum using the straight line method. The following must be accounted for:

1. A machine, which cost £4,000 at the start of Year 6, has been sold for cash of £3,000 at the start of Year 8.
2. The depreciation expense for machines for Year 8.

Required

a. Record the above in the ledgers of the business
b. Show how the above matters will appear in the Final Accounts of Simon's business for Year 8.

Constructing Final Accounts

THE INTER-RELATIONSHIP BETWEEN THE LEDGER ACCOUNTS AND THE FINAL ACCOUNTS

Introduction

The Final Accounts of a business comprise:

- a Profit & Loss Account for the accounting period
- a Balance Sheet as at the end of the accounting period

The details of transactions are recorded in the ledger accounts as and when they occur. The arithmetic accuracy of the accounts is checked by the Trial Balance. The Trial Balance is an intermediate stage in the production of the Final Accounts.

Profit is calculated in the Profit & Loss Account by selecting the relevant account balances. The Balance Sheet is constructed in a similar way.

Most of the information required to draw up the Profit & Loss Account is contained in the Trial Balance. There are, however, certain adjustments which must be made to the basic information, contained in the Trial Balance, before it can be used in the profit calculation.

The first adjustment is needed in order to calculate cost of sales.

The ledger account of purchases will record the cost of goods bought. In practice, not all goods bought during the period will have been sold by the end of that period, therefore purchases will not exactly equal cost of sales. Opening and closing stock will account for the difference.

In the examples used in this Tutorial it will be assumed that there is no opening or closing stock and, therefore, Purchases will be the only item to be transferred to the Cost of Sales Account.

Example

The following Trial Balance has been drawn up after all the period's transactions have been recorded in the ledgers.

Trial Balance as at		
	Dr (£)	Cr (£)
Cash & Bank	21,500	
Capital		30,000
Motor Vehicles	8,000	
Purchases	16,000	
Trade Creditors		1,000
Sales		24,000
Trade Debtors	7,500	
Wages	2,000	
	55,000	55,000

Fig. 76

According to the Trial Balance (T.B.), the balance on the Purchases Account at the end of the period is £16,000. This must be transferred to the Cost of Sales Account before the Profit & Loss Account can be drawn up.

Purchases Account				
Ref	Debit (£)		Ref	Credit (£)
T.B.	16,000			
			to Cost of Sales A/c	**16,000**
			Balance c/d	0
	16,000			16,000
Balance b/d	0			

Cost of Sales Account				
Ref	Debit (£)		Ref	Credit (£)
from Purchases A/c	**16,000**			
			Balance c/d	16,000
	16,000			16,000
Balance b/d	16,000			

Fig. 77

The Trial Balance will now appear as follows:

Trial Balance as at		
	Dr (£)	Cr (£)
Cash & Bank	21,500	
Capital		30,000
Motor Vehicles	8,000	
Purchases	0	
Cost of Sales	**16,000**	
Trade Creditors		1,000
Sales		24,000
Trade Debtors	7,500	
Wages	2,000	
	55,000	55,000

Fig. 78

Assuming there are no other adjustments, the Final Accounts may now be drawn up as follows.

Profit & Loss Account

As explained in Tutorial 2, the Profit & Loss Account matches income against expenses for one accounting period, in accordance with the ACCRUALS CONCEPT. The income and expenses, relating to the accounting period, are transferred to the Profit & Loss Account. In the software which accompanies this manual, the Profit & Loss Account items will be transferred from the Trial Balance. In practice, however, the transfers to the Profit & Loss Account will be made from the ledger accounts themselves. The transfers from the ledger accounts to the Profit & Loss Account, for the above example, are shown below:

Sales Account				
Ref	Debit (£)		Ref	Credit (£)
to P&L Account Balance c/d	**24,000** 0		T.B.	24,000
	24,000			24,000
			Balance b/d	0

Fig. 79

Cost of Sales Account			
Ref	Debit (£)	Ref	Credit (£)
from Purchases a/c	16,000	Balance c/d	**16,000**
	16,000		16,000
Balance b/d	16,000	to P&L Account	16,000
		Balance c/d	0
	16,000		16,000
Balance b/d	0		

Wages Account			
Ref	Debit (£)	Ref	Credit (£)
T.B.	2,000	to P& L Account	**2,000**
		Balance c/d	0
	2,000		2,000
Balance b/d	0		

Profit & Loss Account for Period ended		
	£	£
Sales		24,000
Less Cost of Sales		16,000
Gross Profit		8,000
Less Overhead Expenses		
Wages	2,000	
Rent etc.	0	2,000
Net Profit		6,000

Fig. 79

The net profit, as explained in Tutorial 1, will increase the owner's capital. The changes in the owner's capital during the period can be summarised as follows:

Capital Movements	£
Net Profit for the period	6,000
Less Drawings during the period	0
Retained Profit for the period	6,000
Add Opening Capital and Capital Introduced during the period	30,000
Closing Capital	36,000

Fig. 80

The above changes must also be reflected in the Capital Account in the ledger.

Capital Account				
Ref	Debit (£)	Ref	Credit (£)
		T.B.	30,000
from drawings a/c	0	**from P&L a/c (profit)**	**6,000**
Balance c/d	36,000		
	36,000		36,000
		Balance b/d	36,000

Fig. 81

The Trial Balance will now show the following balances:

Trial Balance as at		
	Dr (£)	*Cr (£)*
Cash & Bank	21,500	
Capital (updated balance)		36,000
Motor Vehicles	8,000	
Trade Creditors		1,000
Trade Debtors	7,500	
	37,000	37,000

Fig. 82

The account balances representing income and expenses are **not** shown in the above Trial Balance, as the amounts have been transferred to the Profit & Loss Account.

The account balances remaining in the ledger, after the Profit & Loss Account has been drawn up, are assets, liabilities and equity. These will be used to draw up the Balance Sheet.

Balance Sheet

The balances representing assets, liabilities and equity at the end of the accounting period will appear on the Balance Sheet as at the end of the period. These balances remain in the ledger accounts and will be brought forward as the opening balances at the start of the next accounting period.

Balance Sheet as at		
	£	£
Fixed Assets		
Motor Vehicles		8,000
		8,000
Current Assets		
Stock	0	
Trade Debtors	7,500	
Cash & Bank	21,500	
Creditors payable within 1 year	29,000	
Trade Creditors	1,000	
Net current assets		28,000
		36,000
Representing		
Creditors payable after 1 year		
Loans		0
Equity		
Owner's Capital		36,000
		36,000

Fig. 83

Tutorial Questions

12.1 Indicate which of the following items will be shown on the Profit & Loss Account and which will be shown on the Balance Sheet:

i.   Cash & Bank.
ii. Rent.
iii. Trade Debtors.

iv. Loans.

v. Wages.

vi. Loan Interest.

vii. Trade Creditors.

12.2 Should machinery be shown in the Profit & Loss Account?

12.3 The following balances appear in the ledgers of Michael's business after the transactions for Year 6 have been recorded:

	Cash & Bank Account			
Ref	Debit (£)	Ref	Credit (£)
b/d	30,000		

	Purchases Account			
Ref	Debit (£)	Ref	Credit (£)
b/d	40,000		

	Capital Account			
Ref	Debit (£)	Ref	Credit (£)
		b/d 58,000	

	Trade Creditors Account			
Ref	Debit (£)	Ref	Credit (£)
		b/d	6,000

	Machinery Account			
Ref	Debit (£)	Ref	Credit (£)
b/d	8,000		

	Sales Account			
Ref	Debit (£)	Ref	Credit (£)
		b/d	95,000

	Trade Debtors Account			
Ref	Debit (£)	Ref	Credit (£)
b/d	14,500		

	Loans Account			
Ref	Debit (£)	Ref	Credit (£)
		b/d	15,000

	Wages Account			
Ref	Debit (£)	Ref	Credit (£)
b/d	25,000		

	Motor Vehicles Account			
Ref	Debit (£)	Ref	Credit (£)
b/d	35,000		

Light & Heat Account			
Ref	Debit (£)	Ref	Credit (£)
b/d	9,500		

Drawings Account			
Ref	Debit (£)	Ref	Credit (£)
b/d	12,000		

Cost of Sales Account			
Ref	Debit (£)	Ref	Credit (£)
b/d	0		

Required

a. Extract a Trial Balance as at the end of Year 6.
b. Assuming there is no opening or closing stock, transfer Purchases to Cost of Sales.
c. Draw up the Profit & Loss Account for Year 6, showing the transfers from the relevant ledger accounts. (Ignore depreciation of fixed assets.)
d. Show the changes in owner's capital in the Capital Account.
e. Draft the Balance Sheet as at the end of Year 6.

COST OF SALES

Introduction

The Profit & Loss Account matches the cost of goods **sold** against sales income in order to calculate gross profit. The ledger account of purchases will record the cost of goods **bought**. In practice, not all goods purchased during the period will have been sold by the end of that period, therefore purchases will not exactly equal cost of sales. Opening and closing stock will account for the difference and will need to be taken into consideration when calculating cost of sales. The following example relates to a business in its first month of trading.

Example

During January:
Purchases are made of 100 identical units of stock at £1 each; sales are made of 55 of the units for £1.60 each, i.e. at a gross profit of £0.60 per unit (i.e. a gross profit margin per unit of $\frac{£0.60}{£1.60} \times 100 = 37.5\%$).

The accounting records of the business will show:

- Purchases (100 @ £1.00) £100
- Sales (55 @ £1.60) £88

In the calculation of gross profit, it would be wrong to compare the cost of buying 100 units with the revenue from selling only 55 units. It is a more accurate calculation of profit to match the cost of buying 55 units with the income from selling 55 units. So the cost of the unsold items (45 units) is removed from cost of sales, i.e. the closing stock of 45 units must be accounted for in order to calculate cost of sales.

Calculation of Cost of Sales for January	Units	Cost per unit £	Total Cost £
Purchases	100	1.00	100
Less Closing stock	45	1.00	45
= Cost of sales	55	1.00	55

Fig. 84

The Profit & Loss Account for January may now be drawn up.

Profit & Loss Account for January	Units	£ per unit	Total £
Sales	55	1.60	88
Less Cost of Sales	55	1.00	55
Gross Profit	55	0.60	33
Less Overhead expenses Rent, wages, etc.			
Net Profit			

Fig. 85

NOTE

The gross profit margin for January is $\underline{£33} \times 100 = 37.5\%$.
$$£88$$
The following details relate to the second month of trading of the above business.

During February:
Purchases are made of 90 units of stock at £1 each = £90
Sales are made of 120 units at £1.60 each = £192

NOTE

In the calculation of cost of sales for February, it must be remembered that the business already has 45 units of stock left over from January, i.e. January's closing stock is February's opening stock.

Calculation of Cost of Sales for February	Units	Cost per unit £	Total Cost £
Opening stock	45	1.00	45
Add Purchases	90	1.00	90
(Goods available for sale)	135	1.00	135
Less Closing stock	15	1.00	15
= Cost of sales (goods actually sold)	120	1.00	120

Fig. 86

TION = Fig. 86

The Profit & Loss Account for February will show the following:

Profit & Loss Account for February	Units	£ per unit	Total £
Sales	120	1.60	192
Less Cost of Sales	120	1.00	120
Gross Profit	120	0.60	72
Less Overhead expenses Rent, wages, etc.			
Net Profit			

Fig. 87

Notes

- The cost of 120 units has been **matched** against the selling price of 120 units, in accordance with the ACCRUALS CONCEPT.
- The gross profit has remained constant at £0.60 per unit (37.5% of sales). Any unexpected deviation from the standard gross profit % will provide an indicator of possible problems, e.g. theft of stock and/or cash.
- Profit has only been recognised on the goods **sold** (realised), in accordance with the PRUDENCE CONCEPT and the REALISATION CONCEPT.
- The current asset of closing stock has been valued at cost, i.e. the potential profit of the goods not yet sold has not been recognised, in accordance with **prudence** and **realisation**.
- In practice, stock should physically be counted, compared with the firm's stock records and valued at the **lower** of cost and net realisable value, in accordance with the PRUDENCE CONCEPT and accounting standards. If for any reason, e.g. damage, stock is worth less than its original cost price, this loss must be recognised immediately. The current asset of stock must be written down to net realisable value: i.e. estimated sales proceeds *less* anticipated expenses in order to sell the goods.

Entries in the Ledger for Cost of Sales

The Trial Balance of the above business will show the following at the end of February **before** cost of sales is calculated.

Trial Balance as at 28th February		
	Dr (£)	*Cr (£)*
Opening Stock	45	
Purchases	90	
Cost of Sales	0	
Sales		192
Closing stock	0	
etc.		

Fig. 88

Transactions involving purchases and sales will have been recorded in the ledgers throughout February. February's opening stock will already be in the ledgers, as it will have been brought forward from January's transactions, i.e. it is January's closing stock. Closing stock at the end of February will be entered into the ledger system when accounting for February's cost of sales.

In order to prepare the Final Accounts, closing stock must now be ascertained and the cost of sales must be calculated. In this example, closing stock at the end of February is 15 units, which cost £1 each, i.e. £15.

The EXPENSE of cost of sales is calculated by adding opening stock and purchases and subtracting closing stock. The accounting entries are as follows:

i.   Transfer the opening stock to the Cost of Sales Account

- Debit Cost of Sales
- Credit Opening Stock

ii.   Transfer purchases to the Cost of Sales Account

- Debit Cost of Sales
- Credit Purchases

iii.   Account for closing stock

- Debit Closing Stock
- Credit Cost of Sales

Opening Stock Account			
Ref	Debit (£)	Ref	Credit (£)
T.B.	45	i. to Cost of Sales	45
		Balance c/d	0
	45		45
Balance b/d	0		

Purchases Account			
Ref	Debit (£)	Ref	Credit (£)
T.B.	90	ii. to Cost of Sales	90
		Balance c/d	0
	90		90
Balance b/d	0		

Cost of Sales Account			
Ref	Debit (£)	Ref	Credit (£)
T.B.	0		
i. from Opening Stock	45		
ii. from Purchases	90	iii. to Closing Stock	15
		Balance c/d	120
	135		135
Balance b/d	120		

Closing Stock Account			
Ref	Debit (£)	Ref	Credit (£)
T.B.	0		
iii. from Cost of Sales	15	Balance c/d	15
	15		15
Balance b/d	15		

Fig. 89

NOTE

The Closing Stock Account for February will be the Opening Stock Account for March. After the calculation of cost of sales, the Trial Balance will appear as follows:

Trial Balance as at 28th February	Dr (£)	Cr (£)
Opening Stock	0	
Purchases	0	
Cost of Sales	120	
Sales		192
Closing Stock	15	
etc.		

Fig. 90

When the Final Accounts are prepared for February, the Sales and the Cost of Sales will be transferred to the Profit & Loss Account to calculate gross profit.

Profit & Loss Account for February	Units	£ per unit	Total £
Sales	120	1.60	192
Less Cost of sales	120	1.00	120
Gross Profit	120	0.60	72
Less Overhead expenses Rent, wages, etc.			
Net Profit			

Fig. 91

The closing stock will be shown on the Balance Sheet as follows:

Balance Sheet as at 28th February *Current Assets*	£
Stock	15

Fig. 92

Tutorial Questions

13.1 Mandy commences in business at the start of Year 1. She buys goods for £3.00 per unit and sells them at £5.00 per unit. During Year 1, Mandy buys 1,600 units and sells 1,200 units. During Year 2, Mandy buys 1,800 units and sells 1,900 units.

Required

a. Calculate the gross profit margin (%) per unit.
b. Calculate the gross profit for Year 1 and for Year 2.
c. Calculate the gross profit margin for Year 1 and for Year 2.
d. Show the ledger accounts for Sales, Purchases, Cost of Sales and Stock, assuming that all purchases and sales are on credit terms.

13.2 Refer back to Mandy's business in question 13.1 above.

a. Calculate the gross profit and the gross profit margin for Year 2, assuming that a physical stock count reveals that there are only 120 units of stock remaining at the end of Year 2.
b. Comment on your answer.

13.3 Cathy sells sweaters which she buys for £30 each and sells for £38 each. At the end of her financial year, Cathy has 45 sweaters in stock, 40 of which are in good condition and 5 are slightly damaged. Cathy's brother, who has a market stall, will buy the damaged sweaters for £15 each if Cathy sends them to him. It will cost Cathy a total of £20 to send the sweaters to her brother.

Required
Calculate the value of closing stock to be shown on the Balance Sheet of Cathy's business at the end of the financial year.

13.4 The following Trial Balance has been extracted from the ledgers of John's business at the end of Year 4.

Trial Balance as at 30th June Year 4	Dr (£)	Cr (£)
Capital at 1st July Year 3		62,600
Drawings	11,075	
Trade Debtors	5,844	
Trade Creditors		2,730
Sales		80,870
Stock at 1st July Year 3	4,637	
Purchases	41,050	
Postage & Stationery	1,940	
Light & Heat	1,620	
Wages	15,039	
Insurance	1,085	
Cash & Bank	4,790	
Fixtures & Fittings	6,120	
Freehold Premises	53,000	
	146,200	146,200

Required

Prepare the Final Accounts for Year 4, assuming stock at 30th June Year 4 to be valued at £5,700. Ignore depreciation of fixed assets.

MISPOSTINGS

Introduction

For every debit entry in the ledger there should be a credit entry of the same value. The arithmetic accuracy of the ledger can be proved by drawing up a Trial Balance. Some errors will, however, not show up in the Trial Balance, i.e. the Trial Balance will still balance. These errors include:

- Transactions entirely missed out (omissions)
- Entries made on the correct side but in the wrong account (mispostings), e.g. the purchase of a fixed asset, such as a machine, debited to the Purchases Account instead of to the Machinery Account

Entries to Correct Mispostings

Errors in the ledgers should be corrected using the double entry rule, i.e. a debit entry **and** a credit entry will be required to correct an error. E.g.: when a machine was bought for cash, the following entries were made in the ledgers.

- Debit Purchases Account (this is an error, as the debit entry should be in the Machinery Account (+ FIXED ASSET))
- Credit Cash & Bank Account (this is correct)

To correct the above misposting, the following entries must be made.

- Debit Machinery Account (to record the acquisition of the fixed asset)
- Credit Purchases Account (to cancel the original misposting)

Example

The following Trial Balance has been drawn up at the year end before the Final Accounts have been prepared.

Trial Balance as at year end		
	Dr (£)	Cr (£)
Cash & Bank	144,000	
Capital		80,000
Drawings	2,000	
Machinery at Cost	54,000	
Provision for Depreciation of Machinery		14,000
Loans		50,000
Purchases	500,000	
Cost of Sales	0	
Trade Creditors		45,000
Sales		735,000
Trade Debtors	95,000	
Wages	90,000	
Light & Heat	14,000	
Travel	25,000	
	924,000	924,000

Fig. 93

The following errors in the ledgers need to be corrected.

1. The purchase of a machine costing £5,000 has been debited to the Purchases Account instead of to the Machinery at Cost Account. (Ignore depreciation of this machine)

- Debit Machinery at Cost (+ ASSET)
- Credit Purchases (to cancel the original misposting)

2. An amount of £800 for electricity has been debited to the Wages Account

- Debit Light & Heat (+ EXPENSE)
- Credit Wages (to cancel the original misposting)

3. A loan of £10,000 has been credited to the Sales Account

- Debit Sales (to cancel the original misposting)
- Credit Loans (+ CREDITORS)

4. A bill for £3,000 for a holiday of the owner of the business has been debited to the Travel Account

- Debit Drawings (– EQUITY)
- Credit Travel (to cancel the original misposting)

5. A payment of £8,000 to trade creditors has been debited to the purchases account

- Debit Trade Creditors (– CREDITORS)
- Credit Purchases (to cancel the original misposting)

6. A payment of £900 for electricity has been debited to the Light & Heat Account. When the bill was received 2 weeks earlier, it was correctly recorded in the Light & Heat and Trade Creditors Accounts

- Debit Trade Creditors (– CREDITORS)
- Credit Light & Heat (to cancel the original misposting)

The accounts correcting the above mispostings are shown below.

Machinery at Cost Account			
Ref	Debit (£)	Ref	Credit (£)
T.B.	54,000		
1	5,000		
		c/d	59,000
	59,000		59,000
b/d	59,000		

Light & Heat Account			
Ref	Debit (£)	Ref	Credit (£)
T.B.	14,000		
2	800	1	
		6	900
		c/d	13,900
	14,800		14,800
b/d	13,900		

Purchases Account			
Ref	Debit (£)	Ref	Credit (£)
T.B.	500,000		
		1	5,000
		5	8,000
		c/d	487,000
	500,000		500,000
b/d	487,000		

Wages Account			
Ref	Debit (£)	Ref	Credit (£)
T.B.	90,000		
		2	800
		c/d	89,200
	90,000		90,000
b/d	89,200		

Loans Account			
Ref	Debit (£)	Ref	Credit (£)
		T.B.	50,000
		3	10,000
c/d	60,000		
	60,000		60,000
		b/d	60,000

Sales Account			
Ref	Debit (£)	Ref	Credit (£)
		T.B.	735,000
3	10,000		
c/d	725,000		
	735,000		735,000
		c/d	725,000

Drawings Account			
Ref	Debit (£)	Ref	Credit (£)
T.B.	2,000		
4	3,000		
		c/d	5,000
	5,000		5,000
b/d	5,000		

Travel Account			
Ref	Debit (£)	Ref	Credit (£)
T.B.	25,000		
		4	3,000
		c/d	22,000
	25,000		25,000
b/d			

Trade Creditors Account			
Ref	Debit (£)	Ref	Credit (£)
		T.B.	45,000
5	8,000		
6	900		
c/d	36,100		
	45,000		45,000
		b/d	36,100

Fig. 94

After the above transactions have been recorded, the Trial Balance will be as follows:

Trial Balance as at year end		
	Dr (£)	Cr (£)
Cash & Bank	144,000	
Capital		80,000
Drawings	5,000	
Machinery at Cost	59,000	
Provision for Depreciation of Machinery		14,000
Loans		60,000
Purchases	487,000	
Cost of Sales	0	
Trade Creditors		36,100
Sales		725,000
Trade Debtors	95,000	
Wages	89,200	
Light & Heat	13,900	
Travel	22,000	
	915,100	915,100

Fig. 95

NOTE

The Final Accounts will be drawn up using the amended figures per the above Trial Balance.

Suspense Account

In the above example, the original Trial Balance was in balance despite the existence of mispostings. Other book-keeping errors, however, will result in the Trial Balance failing to balance. E.g. a machine, costing £540 and bought for cash, is recorded as follows:

- Debit Machinery £540
- Credit Cash & Bank £450 (i.e. a misposting of £90)

The Debit side of the resulting Trial Balance will be greater than the Credit side by £90.

A "Suspense Account" will be opened to record the difference in the Trial Balance. In this example, the Suspense Account will show a credit balance of £90. The error must be corrected using the double entry rule as follows:

- Debit Suspense Account £90 (to clear the Suspense Account)
- Credit Cash & Bank Account £90 (to correct the original misposting)

The ledger accounts will appear as follows:

Machinery Account			
Ref	Debit (£)	Ref	Credit (£)
Cash	540	Balance c/d	540
	540		540
Balance b/d	540		

Cash & Bank Account			
Ref	Debit (£)	Ref	Credit (£)
Balance c/d	450	Machinery	450
	450		450
Balance c/d		Balance b/d	450
	540	Suspense A/c	90
	540		540
		Balance b/d	540

Suspense Account			
Ref	Debit (£)	Ref	Credit (£)
Cash A/c	90	Difference per T.B.	90
Balance c/d	0		
	90		90
		Balance b/d	0

Fig. 96

NOTES

- The above misposting was due to transposing the figures. Differences arising from transposition errors will always be divisible by 9.
- Errors involving Suspense Accounts are not dealt with in the software which accompanies this manual.

Controls

To ensure that the accounting records are accurate, it is important that a book-keeping system incorporates controls. The Trial Balance is one of these controls. Other controls may include:

- *Physical comparison of assets with the accounting records* – e.g. cash in hand compared with the balance on the Cash Account; verification that fixed assets agree with Fixed Asset Accounts
- *Reconciliations* – e.g. bank statement compared with the Bank Account in the ledger; supplier's statement compared with the account of the individual creditor in the ledger
- *Control accounts* – e.g. the balances on the individual debtors' accounts are listed and totalled, and this total is compared with the balance on the Total Trade Debtors Account in the ledger; the balances on the individual creditors' accounts are listed and totalled, and this total is compared with the balance on the Total Trade Creditors Account in the ledger
- *Analytical review* – when the Final Accounts are produced, the figures may be compared with those of previous periods and with budgeted results, e.g. sales forecast compared with actual turnover; gross profit margin of the previous period compared with the gross profit margin of this period

Tutorial Questions

14.1   What will be the accounting entries to correct the following mispostings?

a.   A motor vehicle, costing £14,000, has been debited to the Purchases Account.
b.   Wages of £2,000 have been debited to the Travel Expenses Account.
c.   The receipt of £90 cash from Elsie, a trade debtor, has not been recorded.
d.   Credit purchases of £3,500 have been recorded as follows: Debit Purchases Account; Credit Bank Account.

14.2   Discuss how the errors in question 14.1 may have come to light.

14.3   The following Trial Balance (below) for Steve's business has been drawn up at the year end before the Final Accounts have been prepared.

The following errors in the ledgers have now come to light.

i.   An amount of £300 for rates has been debited to the Wages Account.
ii.   A loan of £10,000 has been credited to the Sales Account. Assume the loan has been taken out on the first day of the year at 8% per annum interest and that no interest has been accounted for on this loan.
iii. The owner of the business has paid himself a "salary" of £6,000 which has been debited to the Wages Account.

Trial Balance as at year end		
	Dr (£)	Cr (£)
Cash & Bank	66,000	
Capital		40,000
Drawings	1,000	
Motor Vehicles at Cost	24,000	
Provision for Depreciation of Motor Vehicles		7,000
Depreciation Expense	6,000	
Loans		25,000
Loan Interest	3,000	
Purchases		22,500
Trade Creditors		367,500
Sales	250,000	
Trade Debtors	47,500	
Wages	45,000	
Rates & Insurance	19,500	
	462,000	462,000

iv. The purchase of a motor vehicle costing £5,000 has been debited to the Purchases Account instead of to the Motor Vehicles at Cost Account. Assume that the vehicle was bought on the first day of the year and that the accounting policy for depreciation of motor vehicles is 25% straight line.

Required

a. Record the correction of the above mispostings in the ledgers of Steve's business.
b. Draw up the Trial Balance after the correcting entries have been made.

14.4   The following Trial Balance (below) for Angela's business has been drawn up at the year end before the Final Accounts have been prepared.

The following errors in the ledgers have now come to light.

i.   Postage of £70, paid for immediately, has been recorded as follows:
     Debit Postage & Stationery Account £70; Credit Cash & Bank Account £700.
ii. Cash purchases of £200 have been recorded as follows:
     Credit Cash & Bank Account £200; Credit Sales Account £200.

Required

a. Record the correction of the above mispostings in the ledgers of Angela's business.
b. Draw up the Trial Balance after the correcting entries have been made.

Trial Balance as at year end		
	Dr (£)	*Cr (£)*
Cash & Bank	30,470	
Capital		20,000
Drawings	500	
Fixtures & Fittings at Cost	13,500	
Provision for Depreciation of Fixtures & Fittings		3,500
Depreciation Expense	3,000	
Loans		12,500
Loan Interest	1,500	
Purchases	125,000	
Trade Creditors		11,250
Sales		183,750
Trade Debtors	23,750	
Wages	22,500	
Rates & Insurance	3,500	
Postage & Stationery	6,250	
SUSPENSE ACCOUNT	1,030	
	462,000	462,000

ACCRUALS

Introduction

The division of the life of a business into accounting periods creates the problem of deciding where this year's transactions cut-off and next year's transactions begin. E.g. the Profit & Loss Account of a business for Year 3 should include income and expenses for Year 3 only; the Balance Sheet at the end of Year 3 should show assets, liabilities and capital as at that date only.

THE LIFE OF
ANY BUSINESS
(YEARS)

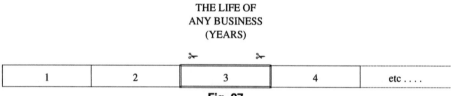

Fig. 97

Profit is calculated by matching income earned during an accounting period with expenses incurred during that period. This is known as the ACCRUALS CONCEPT.

Income and expenses will be recognised during an accounting period even though the cash may be received or paid in a different period.

The application of the ACCRUALS CONCEPT is fundamental to the preparation of the Profit & Loss Account and is the reason for accounting for the following.

- **accrued expenses**
- **accrued income**
- stock
- depreciation
- prepayments

Accrued Expenses

Accrued expenses are expenses incurred during the accounting period for which a bill has not been received by the end of the period, e.g. electricity, which is normally billed quarterly.

In the profit calculation income earned is matched with expenses incurred during the accounting period. An estimate must, therefore, be made for any expenses incurred which are not yet recorded in the ledgers, i.e. accrued expenses.

The term "accruals" is often used instead of "accrued expenses", although accounting for accrued expenses is only one of many applications of the ACCRUALS CONCEPT.

In this Tutorial, and in the software accompanying this manual, the term "accruals" will be used for accrued expenses.

Recording Expenses

There are three ways in which an expense is recorded in the ledgers, e.g. electricity:

1. If the electricity bill has been paid immediately:

*   Debit Light & Heat (+ EXPENSE)
*   Credit Cash & Bank (– ASSET)

2. If the electricity bill is not paid immediately:

*   Debit Light & Heat (+ EXPENSE)
*   Credit Trade Creditors (+ CREDITORS)

Note: The above entries, as explained in previous tutorials, will be made during the accounting period before a Trial Balance is drawn up.

3. If at the end of the accounting period electricity has been used for which a bill has not been received, the expense must be accrued:

*   Debit Light & Heat (+ EXPENSE)
*   Credit Trade Creditors (+ CREDITORS)

Note: A Trial Balance will be normally drawn up before accounting for accruals. Accruals are adjustments to the balances in the ledger which must be made before the Final Accounts are drawn up.

Example

The following Trial Balance has been drawn up for Karen's Business at the end of Year 1.

	Dr (£)	Cr (£)
Karen's Business		
Trial Balance as at end of Year 1		
Cash & Bank	144,000	
Capital		80,000
Drawings	2,000	
Machinery at Cost	54,000	
Provision for Depreciation of Machinery		14,000
Loans		50,000
Purchases	500,000	
Cost of Sales	0	
Trade Creditors		45,000
Sales		735,000
Trade Debtors	95,000	
Wages	90,000	
Light & Heat	14,000	
Travel	25,000	
	924,000	924,000

Fig. 98

The following adjustments for accrued expenses at the end of Year 1 must be made.

1.   Wages £300

• Debit Wages (+ EXPENSE)
• Credit Trade Creditors (+ CREDITORS)

2.   2 months electricity estimated at £80 per month (£160)

• Debit Light & Heat (+ EXPENSE)
• Credit Trade Creditors (+ CREDITORS)

The ledger accounts will be as follows:

Wages Account			
Ref	Debit (£)	Ref	Credit (£)
T.B. 1	90,000 300	c/d	90,300
	90,300		90,300
b/d	90,300	Yr 1 P&L c/d	90,300 0
	90,300		90,300
b/d	0		

Trade Creditors Account			
Ref	Debit (£)	Ref	Credit (£)
		T.B. 1 2	45,000 300 160
c/d	45,460		
	45,460		45,460
		b/d	45,460

Light & Heat Account			
Ref	Debit (£)	Ref	Credit (£)
T.B. 2	14,000 160	c/d	14,160
	14,160		14,160
b/d	14,160	Yr 1 P&L c/d	14,160 0
	14,160		14,160
b/d	0		

Fig. 99

After the accruals have been accounted for, but before the Final Accounts are drawn up, the Trial Balance will be as follows:

Karen's Business

Trial Balance as at end of Year 1

	Dr (£)	Cr (£)
Cash & Bank	144,000	
Capital		80,000
Drawings	2,000	
Machinery at Cost	54,000	
Provision for Depreciation of Machinery		14,000
Loans		50,000
Purchases	500,000	
Cost of Sales	0	
Trade Creditors		**45,460**
Sales		735,000
Trade Debtors	95,000	
Wages	**90,300**	
Light & Heat	**14,160**	
Travel	25,000	
	924,460	924,460

Fig. 100

Notes

- The Final Accounts will be drawn up using the adjusted figures per the above Trial Balance.
- In the Balance Sheet, the Trade Creditors figure will be £45,460. An alternative presentation of the Balance Sheet is to show accruals separately, i.e.

Creditors due within 1 year	£
Trade Creditors	45,000
Accruals	460
	45,460

- Accounting for accrued expenses frequently involves making estimates, e.g. the amount of electricity used in the last 2 months of the year is **estimated** to be £160. Provided the estimate is reasonably accurate, decisions based on the resulting profit calculation will not be affected.

Accrued Expenses at the Start of an Accounting Period

The estimate for an expense owing at the end of a year, i.e. an accrued expense, will be accounted for as follows:

- Debit Expense Account
- Credit Trade Creditors

When the Final Accounts for the year are drawn up, the balance on the expense account (which includes the accrual) is transferred to the Profit & Loss Account. This results in a nil balance on the expense account at the start of the next year.

Using the example of Karen's business (above), it was estimated, at the end of Year 1, that the electricity used in the last two months of Year 1 amounted to £160.
The following information relates to Year 2.
An electricity bill for £250 is received for electricity consumed during the last two months of Year 1 and the first month of Year 2. The electricity bill will be recorded as follows:

- Debit Light & Heat £250
- Credit Trade Creditors £250

As £160 has already been accounted for at the end of Year 1, the following adjustment must be made for the opening accrual at the start of Year 2 to avoid double counting.

- Debit Trade Creditors £160
- Credit Light & Heat £160

The ledger accounts will show the following.

Light & Heat Account				
Ref	Debit (£)	Ref	Credit (£)
Year 1 T.B.	14,000	Year 1 P&L	14,160
Trade Creditors (Accrual at end of Yr. 1)	160	Balance c/d	0
	14,160		14,160
Year 2 Balance b/d	0	Trade Creditors (Accrual at start of Yr. 2)	160
Trade Creditors	250	Balance c/d	90
	250		250
Balance b/d	90		

Trade Creditors Account			
Ref	Debit (£)	Ref	Credit (£)
		Year 1 T.B.	45,000
		Accruals at end of Yr. 1:	
		Wages	300
Balance c/d	45,460	Light & Heat	160
	45,460		45,460
Accruals at start of Yr. 2:		Year 2 Balance b/d	45,460
Wages	300		
Light & Heat	160		
		Light & Heat	250
Balance c/d	45,250		
	45,710		45,710
		Balance b/d	45,250

Fig. 101

The balance on the Light & Heat Account (£90) represents the electricity charge for the first month of Year 2. The balance on the Trade Creditors Account of £45,250 includes £250 represented by the electricity bill.

NOTE

The reversing entries to account for opening accruals will not be shown in the software which accompanies this manual.

Accrued Income

Accrued income is income earned for which a bill has not been raised by the business. This must be accounted for at the end of the accounting period so that the Profit & Loss Account shows the total income earned during the period and the Balance Sheet shows all amounts due to the business at the end of the period.

The accounting entries to record accrued income will be as follows, using the example of rent receivable:

• Debit Trade Debtors with the amount due from tenant (+ ASSET)
• Credit Rent Receivable (+ INCOME)

Tutorial Questions

15.1   Motor expenses of £6,000 are shown on the Trial Balance of a business at the end of an accounting period. It is estimated that a further £50 is outstanding for repairs to a vehicle.

Required

a.   Calculate the charge for motor expenses to be shown in the Profit & Loss Account for the year.
b.   What will be shown on the Balance Sheet for motor expenses?
c.   What accounting entries will be necessary to record the accrued motor expenses?

15.2   As estimates are rarely accurate, discuss whether a business should account for accrued expenses.

15.3   The following details relate to Anne's business.

Trial Balance as at 31st December Year 6	Dr (£)	Cr (£)
Cash & Bank	30,470	
Capital		20,000
Drawings	1,830	
Fixtures & Fittings at Cost	13,500	
Provision for Depreciation of Fixtures & Fittings		4,000
Depreciation Expense	3,000	
10% Loans		12,000
Loan Interest	500	
Purchases	125,700	
Trade Creditors		11,250
Sales		183,750
Trade Debtors	23,750	
Wages	22,500	
Rates & Insurance	3,500	
Postage & Stationery	6,250	
	231,000	231,000

The following accrued expenses must be accounted for at 31st December Year 6.

i.   Wages £600.
ii.   Stationery £75.
iii. Outstanding Loan Interest £700.

Required

Assuming there is no opening or closing stock, prepare the Final Accounts for the year ended 31st December Year 6.

PREPAYMENTS

Introduction

The ACCRUALS CONCEPT dictates that profit is calculated by matching income earned during an accounting period with expenses incurred during that period, irrespective of the timing of cash flows. The application of the ACCRUALS CONCEPT is fundamental to the preparation of the Profit & Loss Account and is the reason for accounting for the following.

- accrued expenses
- accrued income
- stock
- depreciation
- **prepayments**

Prepayments

Prepayments are amounts paid for expenses incurred in advance of the accounting period to which they relate. E.g.: on 1st October Year 1, a business pays £120 for insurance for the next 12 months. If the financial year ends on 31st December, the prepaid portion can be calculated as follows: 9/12ths of £120 = £90, i.e.:

	£
3 months (October–December) relate to Year 1	30
9 months (January–September) relate to Year 2	90
	120

The profit calculation matches income earned with expenses incurred during the accounting period. In the above example, although £120 has been paid, only £30 must be recognised as an expense in the Profit & Loss Account of Year 1. The prepayment of £90 will be shown on the Balance Sheet as a Debtor, as it represents 9 months' insurance cover owed to the business at 31st December Year 1.

Recording Prepayments

Example

The following Trial Balance has been drawn up for Karen's Business at the end of Year 1.

	Dr (£)	Cr (£)
Karen's Business		
Trial Balance as at end of Year 1		
Cash & Bank	144,000	
Capital		80,000
Drawings	2,000	
Machinery at Cost	54,000	
Provision for Depreciation of Machinery		14,000
Loans		50,000
Purchases	500,000	
Cost of Sales	0	
Trade Creditors		45,000
Sales		735,000
Trade Debtors	95,000	
Wages	90,000	
Light & Heat	14,000	
Travel	25,000	
	924,000	924,000

Fig. 102

The following transaction has not yet been recorded.

1.   On 1st October Year 1, the business pays £120 for insurance for the next 12 months (£10 per month)

- Debit Insurance (+ EXPENSE)
- Credit Cash & Bank (– ASSET)

The ledger accounts will show the following.

Insurance Account					Cash & Bank Account			
Ref	Debit (£)	Ref	Credit (£)		Ref	Debit (£)	Ref	Credit (£)
b/d	0				b/d	144,000		
1	120						1	120
		c/d	120				c/d	143,880
	120		120			144,000		144,000
b/d	120				b/d	143,880		

Fig. 103

NOTE

The above entries will be made **during** the accounting period.

The Trial Balance drawn up at 31st December will show the following.

Trial Balance as 31st December Year 1		
	Dr (£)	Cr (£)
Cash & Bank	143,880	
Capital		80,000
Drawings	2,000	
Machinery at Cost	54,000	
Provision for Depreciation of Machinery		14,000
Loans		50,000
Purchases	500,000	
Cost of Sales	0	
Trade Creditors		45,000
Sales		735,000
Trade Debtors	95,000	
Insurance	**120**	
Wages	90,000	
Light & Heat	14,000	
Travel	25,000	
	924,000	924,000

Fig. 104

NOTE

The Trial Balance will normally be drawn up **before** accounting for prepayments. Prepayments are adjustments to the balances in the ledger which must be made before the Final Accounts are drawn up.

The adjustment for prepaid insurance will be made as follows:

2.   *Insurance prepaid at 31st December Year 1 amounts to £90 (9 months at £10)*

- Debit Trade Debtors (+ ASSET)
- Credit Insurance (– EXPENSE)

	Insurance Account					Trade Debtors Account			
Ref	Debit (£)	Ref	Credit (£)		Ref	Debit (£)	Ref	Credit (£)
1	120				b/d	95,000		
		c/d	120		2	90		
							c/d	95,090
	120		120			95,090		95,090
b/d	120	2	**90**		b/d	95,090		
		c/d	30					
	120		120					
b/d	30							
		Yr 1 P&L	30					
		c/d	0					
	30		30					
b/d	0							

Fig. 105

After the prepayments have been accounted for, but before the Final Accounts have been drawn up, the Trial Balance will be as follows:

The following prepayments must be accounted for at 31st August Year 8.

Rates £400.
Insurance £150.

Required

Assuming there is no opening or closing stock, prepare the Final Accounts for the year ended 31st August Year 8.

THE CONCEPTUAL FRAMEWORK OF ACCOUNTING

Introduction

The objective of the Final Accounts of an organisation is to provide information to a range of users about the resources of the organisation; in particular:

- the financial position of the organisation at the start of the period
- the financial position of the organisation at the end of the period
- an analysis of changes during the period
- the financial adaptability of the organisation
- an indicator for the future prospects of the organisation

Financial information is of vital importance to all organisations. Essentially, in order to be of maximum benefit to the users, financial information should be:

- relevant and concise
- reasonably accurate but timely, i.e. it is preferable for information to be 98% accurate but produced in time for decision making, rather than 100% accurate but available too late to be of use
- comprehensible, which may be made more difficult by legal constraints

In recent years, many more people have become involved in the financial aspects of organisations. For example, many more people are budget holders in the organisation in which they work.

Users of Financial Information

Financial information is of interest to many different user groups. The main user groups and their particular areas of interest are listed below.

User Groups	Areas of Interest
Investors	Risk
	Return
Employees	Employment stability
	Wage negotiations
Lenders	Payment of interest
	Repayment of capital
Suppliers	Ability of organisation to pay its creditors
	Continuity of trade
Customers	Continuity of trade
Government	Statistics
	Profitability
	Taxation policy
General Public	Prosperity
	Employment prospects
	Activities
Management	All aspects

It is acknowledged that the financial statements cannot meet all the needs of all the user groups. There are, however, needs which are common to all the groups. Most users will be interested in the profitability and liquidity of an organisation.

As there are many different users of financial information, it is essential that the financial statements of all organisations are drawn up in adherence to the same fundamental ACCOUNTING CONCEPTS.

Accounting Concepts

An accounting concept is a rule, adopted as a guide to action, which rests on general acceptance (consensus) rather than some basic, undeniable truth. The following are the basic accounting concepts which underpin the preparation of the financial statements of an organisation.

Business entity concept

The business entity concept dictates that a distinction is drawn between the owner and his business, i.e. the Final Accounts of an organisation are drawn up from the perspective of the organisation itself.

Accounting separately for personal and business transactions facilitates the assessment of the success or failure of the business.

This distinction between a sole trader and his business is not recognised in law. The result of this is that a sole trader will be liable personally for all the debts of the business, i.e. a sole trader does not have limited liability.

If, however, a business is a limited company, its owners, i.e. the shareholders, will enjoy limited liability.

Limited companies will not be dealt with in this manual.

Dual aspect concept

The dual aspect concept recognises that each transaction will have a dual effect on the business, i.e. each transaction will affect TWO items within the business.

Dual aspect is the basis of the Accounting Equation, i.e. Net Assets = Capital.

The double entry book-keeping system is based on duality, i.e. the recording of both sides of each transaction.

Periodicity concept

All organisations must produce financial statements periodically, usually at least once a year. This is known as the periodicity concept.

The division of the life of a business into accounting periods creates the problem of deciding where this year's transactions cut-off and next year's transactions begin. E.g. the Profit & Loss Account of a business for Year 3 should include income and expenses for Year 3 only; the Balance Sheet at the end of Year 3 should show assets, liabilities and capital as at that date only.

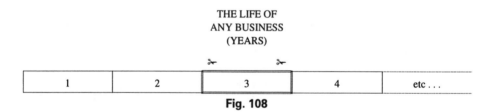

THE LIFE OF
ANY BUSINESS
(YEARS)

Fig. 108

The true profitability of an organisation can only be measured at the end of its life. As profits must be reported on an annual basis, there is a need for profit measurement rules. The aim of these measurement rules is to avoid distortions in the Final Accounts of each year.

Accruals concept

The accruals concept requires that profit is calculated by matching income earned during an accounting period with expenses incurred during that period.

Income and expenses will be recognised during an accounting period even though the cash may be received or paid in a different period.

The application of the accruals concept is fundamental to the preparation of the Profit & Loss Account and is the reason for accounting for the following:

- accrued expenses
- accrued income
- stock
- depreciation
- prepayments

Going concern concept

The going concern concept assumes that an organisation will continue in operational existence for the foreseeable future. This means that the Final Accounts will be drawn up on the assumption that there is no intention or necessity to liquidate or to curtail significantly the scale of operations.

If an organisation is a "going concern", the asset values on the Balance Sheet need not reflect the amounts which would be realised were the assets to be sold immediately, rather than in the normal course of business.

Historical cost concept

The historical cost concept is used as a basis of valuation for transactions. The original acquisition cost (historical cost) is objective and verifiable.

The application of the historical cost concept results in the inclusion of only those items which can be measured in monetary terms (**money measurement concept**). The exclusion of factors which have no historical cost and, therefore, cannot easily be measured in monetary terms, is an obvious deficiency of financial statements. For example, the Final Accounts of an organisation will list Fixed Assets such as premises and machinery, but will not include its workforce or its management team.

Over time, changing price levels (inflation) will have a distorting effect on financial statements drawn up using the historical cost concept. The greatest distortions arise from accounting for fixed assets. Traditionally, the recording of fixed assets has been at historical cost, with depreciation based on historical cost. The net book value of fixed assets on the Balance Sheet will, therefore, merely represent unexpired costs of different vintages, and not the current values of the assets. The reported profits will be overstated, as the depreciation expense, based on outdated historical cost, will be inadequate.

The valuation of fixed assets is an area of considerable controversy and debate. Many would advocate the use of current values rather than valuations based on historical cost.

Prudence (conservatism) concept

The prudence/conservatism concept states that revenues and profits should not be anticipated. Losses, however, should be provided for as soon as they arise or are likely to arise.

An element of uncertainty will surround many business transactions. Potential profits and potential losses must, therefore, be judged on a prudent basis.

The **realisation concept** dictates that revenues and profits must be recognised only when they are realised in the form of cash or assets which are expected to be converted into cash (e.g. debtors).

The application of the prudence and realisation concepts may be illustrated by stock transactions. When goods are purchased for resale, the potential profit must be ignored until a sale has been made, i.e. the stock has been exchanged for debtors or cash. Stock must be valued at the lower of cost and net realisable value for inclusion in the Final Accounts, judging each item of stock separately.

Consistency

The consistency concept dictates that the accounting treatment of like items should be consistent both within an accounting period and from one period to the next.

The consistency concept aids the comparison of the financial results of one accounting period with those of successive accounting periods.

There are many areas of accounting where a choice of method is available. An organisation must adopt, and consistently apply, an accounting policy in areas such as:

- depreciation of fixed assets
- stock valuation

Financial Reporting Regulation

The fundamental accounting concepts allow for a variety of alternative accounting practices to co-exist.

Unincorporated businesses, such as sole traders, can usually prepare their financial statements in any form they choose. In the interest of credibility, however, it is desirable that financial statements show what is generally understood to be a "true and fair view" of the financial position of the organisation and its performance.

The over-riding priority when preparing the financial statements of a limited company is to give a "true and fair view".

The preparation of the financial statements of companies is constrained by a mass of rules and regulations in the form of legislation and accounting standards.

Legislation

The Companies Acts.

Accounting standards

The prime objective of accounting standards is to narrow the areas of difference and variety in accounting practice and to promote "truth and fairness" in financial reporting.

Originally, the accountancy professional bodies were responsible for issuing accounting standards. These were designated "Statements of Standard Accounting Practice" (SSAPs).

Accounting standards are now issued by the Accounting Standards Board. These are designated as "Financial Reporting Standards" (FRSs). Some SSAPs are still in force, as they have not yet been replaced by FRSs.

Appendices

ANSWERS TO TUTORIAL QUESTIONS

Tutorial 1

1.1

i.	Cash at bank	Current Asset
ii.	Bank overdraft	Creditor payable within 1 year
iii.	Office equipment	Fixed Assets
iv.	Trade debtors	Current Assets
v.	Trade creditors	Creditors payable within 1 year
vi.	Owner's capital	Equity
vii.	5 year loan to the business	Creditor payable after 1 year

1.2a

i.   Cash +£15,000; Capital +£15,000
ii.   Vehicles +£9,000; Cash –£9,000
iii. Stock +£2,500; Trade creditors +£2,500
iv.   Trade debtors +£3,500; Capital +£3,500
      Stock –£2,500; Capital –£2,500
v.   Cash –£200; Capital –£200
vi.   Cash –£1,800; Trade creditors –£1,800
vii. Cash +£1,400; Trade debtors –£1,400

1.2b

Balance Sheet as at	£	£
Fixed Assets		
Motor Vehicles		9,000
		9,000
Current Assets		
Stock	—	
Trade Debtors	2,100	
Cash & Bank	5,400	
	7,500	
Creditors Payable within 1 year		
Trade Creditors	700	
Net Current Assets		6,800
		15,800
Representing		
Equity		
Owner's Capital		15,800
		15,800

1.3a

i.   Loans +£20,000; Cash & bank +£20,000
ii. Machinery +£5,000; Cash & bank –£5,000
iii. Motor vehicles +£12,000; Trade creditors +£12,000
iv. Trade debtors +£27,000; Capital +£27,000
       Stock –£15,000; Capital –£15,000
v.   Cash –£2,000; Capital –£2,000
vi. Trade creditors +£600; Capital –£600
vii. Stock +£13,000; Trade creditors +£13,000
viii. Cash +£30,000; Trade debtors –£30,000
ix. Cash –£18,000; Trade creditors –£18,000

1.3b

```
                              Any Business

                     Balance Sheet as at 31st January

                                               £              £

Fixed Assets
Machinery                                                 125,000
Motor Vehicles                                             42,000

Current Assets                                            167,000
Stock                                       13,000
Trade Debtors                                5,000
Cash & Bank                                 25,500
                                            _____
Creditors payable within 1 year             43,500
Trade Creditors                             16,600
                                            _____
Net current assets                                        26,900
                                                         _____
                                                         193,900

Representing
Creditors payable after 1 year
Loans                                                     60,000
Equity
Owner's Capital                                          133,900
                                                         _____
                                                         193,900
```

1.3c   The owner's equity has increased by £9,400, i.e. £133,900 – £124,500. In this example the change is due solely to profit:

	£	£
Sales income *(iv)*		27,000
Less Cost of sales *(iv)*		15,000
Profit on sale of goods (Gross profit)		12,000
Less other expenses		
Wages *(v)*	2,000	
Motor expenses *(vi)*	600	2,600
Net profit		9,400

NOTE

Owner's equity will also increase if the owner introduces additional capital, i.e. personal assets, into the business. Conversely, equity will decrease if the owner withdraws business assets for personal use (drawings).

1.4a The business Balance Sheet must only show business assets – BUSINESS ENTITY rule.

1.4b Stock is usually valued at HISTORICAL COST. Historical cost is usually the basis of recording transactions, as it is objective and verifiable. Stock is not valued at selling price, as selling price includes a potential profit element and the PRUDENCE and REALISATION concepts dictate that profit should not be recognised until an actual sale has been made.

1.4c To assess the liquidity of a business a number of factors must be considered. These factors include:

- speed of stock turnover
- speed of collection of debts
- timescale of payments to creditors
- availability of additional funding

1.4d It is **not** true to say that the owner of the business is worth £124,500 at 31st December. Firstly, the equity on the business Balance Sheet only represents the owner's investment in **that** business – BUSINESS ENTITY concept. Secondly, as the value of the items on a Balance Sheet is usually based on HISTORICAL COST, the Balance Sheet rarely reflects the current value of the business.

1.5 Interested parties (user groups) include:

- loan creditors (including banks)
- trade creditors
- customers
- competitors
- employees
- government (including the Inland Revenue)
- investment analysts

Tutorial 2

2.1

i.	Sales for cash	Income
ii.	Sales on credit	Income

iii.	Wages	Expense
iv.	Payment to trade creditors	not P&L item
v.	Purchase of land	not P&L item
vi.	Drawings	not P&L item

2.2

Profit & Loss Account for year ended	£	£
Sales		24,000
Less Cost of Sales		14,000
Gross Profit		10,000
Less Overhead Expenses		
Wages	2,000	
Light & heat	500	
Postage & stationery	200	
Repairs & renewals	300	3,000
Net Profit		7,000

Capital Movements	£
Net Profit for the period	7,000
Less Drawings during the period	4,000
Retained Profit for the period	3,000
Add Opening Capital and Capital Introduced during the period	47,000
Closing Capital	50,000

Balance Sheet as at ......

	£	£
Fixed Assets		
Freehold Premises		30,000
Machinery		10,000
		40,000
Current Assets		
Stock	2,000	
Trade Debtors	7,500	
Cash & Bank	21,500	
	31,000	
Creditors payable within 1 year		
Trade Creditors	1,000	
Net current assets		30,000
		70,000
Representing		
Creditors payable after 1 year		
Loans		20,000
Equity		
Owner's Capital		50,000
		70,000

2.3a

i.   Cash & bank +£25,000; Loans +£25,000
ii. Machinery +£8,000; Cash & bank –£8,000
iii. Drawings +£1,000; Cash & bank –£1,000
     (*Note:* Closing capital will decrease as a result of the drawings)
iv. Sales +£2,500; Trade debtors +£2,500
     Stock –£1,000; Cost of sales +£1,000
     (*Note:* This transaction will result in an increase in gross profit, net profit and closing capital)
v.   Wages +£700; Cash & bank –£700
     (*Note:* This transaction will result in a decrease in net profit and closing capital)
vi. Light & heat +£150; Trade creditors +£150
     (*Note:* This transaction will result in a decrease in net profit and closing capital)
vii Stock +£3,000; Trade creditors +£3,000
viii. Cash & bank +£7,500; Trade debtors –£7,500
ix. Cash & bank –£2,500; Trade creditors –£2,500

2.3b

Profit & Loss Account for year ended		
	£	£
Sales		26,500
Less Cost of Sales		15,000
Gross Profit		11,500
Less Overhead Expenses		
Wages	2,700	
Light & heat	650	
Postage & stationery	200	
Repairs & renewals	300	3,850
Net Profit		7,650

Capital Movements	
	£
Net Profit for the period	7,650
Less Drawings during the period	5,000
Retained Profit for the period	2,650
Add Opening Capital and Capital Introduced during the period	47,000
Closing Capital	49,650

Balance Sheet as at		
	£	£
Fixed Assets		
Freehold Premises		30,000
Machinery		18,000
		48,000
Current Assets		
Stock	4,000	
Trade Debtors	2,500	
Cash & Bank	41,800	
	48,300	
Creditors payable within 1 year		
Trade Creditors	1,650	
Net current assets		46,650
		94,650
Representing		
Creditors payable after 1 year		
Loans		45,000
Equity		
Owner's Capital		49,650
		94,650

2.4 Profitability is not the same as profit. Profitability is the return on the resources employed in the business. The resources employed in the business which earned a profit of £50,000 may have been £500,000, giving a return of 10%. The resources employed in the business which earned a profit of £10,000 may have been £40,000, giving a return of 25%.

Tutorial 3

3.1 i. Credit.

3.2 It is **not** true to say that the debit side of a ledger account always records an increase in value. Increases in equity, creditors, income and provisions will be recorded on the credit side of the ledger account.

3.3 It **is** true to say that a decrease in an asset or an expense will be a credit entry.

3.4   It is **not** true to say that a decrease in equity or a creditor will be a credit entry.

3.5   Accounting records are necessary to:

- aid memory
- provide evidence of transactions
- record debtors and creditors
- control assets and liabilities
- provide management information
- provide information from which to draw up Final Accounts
- satisfy legal requirements, e.g. taxation

3.6

i.   Debit Cash & Bank; Credit Capital
ii.   Debit Motor Vehicles; Credit Cash & Bank
iii.   Debit Purchases; Credit Trade Creditors
iv.   Debit Trade Debtors; Credit Sales
v.   Debit Wages; Credit Cash & Bank
vi.   Debit Trade Creditors; Credit Cash & Bank
vii.   Debit Cash & Bank; Credit Trade Debtors

3.7a

Cash & Bank Account						
	Debit	£		Credit	£
May 1	Capital	15,000	May 3	Motor Vehicles	9,000
16	Sales	1,200	9	Purchases	500
28	Trade Debtors	1,400	15	Wages	200
			20	Motor Vehicles	2,000
			27	Trade Creditors	1,800
			31	Trade Creditors	100
			31	Balance c/d	4,000
		17,600			17,600
June 1	Balance b/d	4,000			

Capital Account

	Debit	£		Credit	£
May 31	Balance c/d	15,000	May 1	Cash & Bank	15,000
		15,000			15,000
			June 1	Balance b/d	15,000

Motor Vehicles Account

	Debit	£		Credit	£
May 3	Cash & Bank	9,000			
20	Cash & Bank	2,000			
20	Trade Creditors	6,000	May 31	Balance c/d	17,000
		17,000			17,000
June 1	Balance b/d	17,000			

Purchases Account

	Debit	£		Credit	£
May 8	Trade Creditors	2,500			
9	Cash & Bank	500			
18	Trade Creditors	1,500	May 31	Balance c/d	4,500
		4,500			4,500
June 1	Balance b/d	4,500			

Trade Creditors Account

	Debit	£		Credit	£
May 27	Cash & Bank	1,800	May 8	Purchases	2,500
31	Cash & Bank	100	18	Purchases	1,500
			20	Motor Vehicles	6,000
			21	Light & Heat	100
			25	Travelling Expenses	120
31	Balance c/d	8,320			
		10,220			10,220
			June 1	Balance b/d	8,320

	Sales Account					
	Debit	£			Credit	£
			May 10	Trade Debtors		3,500
			16	Cash & Bank		1,200
			26	Trade Debtors		2,000
May 31	Balance c/d	6,700				
		6,700				6,700
			June 1	Balance b/d		6,700

	Trade Debtors Account					
	Debit	£			Credit	£
May 10	Sales	3,500	May 28	Cash & Bank		1,400
26	Sales	2,000				
			31	Balance c/d		4,100
		5,500				5,500
June 1	Balance b/d	4,100				

	Wages Account					
	Debit	£			Credit	£
May 15	Cash & Bank	200	May 31	Balance c/d		200
		200				200
June 1	Balance b/d	200				

	Light & Heat Account					
	Debit	£			Credit	£
May 21	Trade Creditors	100	May 31	Balance c/d		100
		100				100
June 1	Balance b/d	100				

	Travelling Expenses Account				
	Debit	£		Credit	£
May 25	Trade Creditors	120			
			May 31	Balance c/d	120
		120			120
June 1	Balance b/d	120			

3.7 b

Trial Balance as at 31st May		
	Dr (£)	Cr (£)
Cash & Bank	4,000	
Capital		15,000
Motor Vehicles	17,000	
Purchases	4,500	
Trade Creditors		8,320
Sales		6,700
Trade Debtors	4,100	
Wages	200	
Light & Heat	100	
Travelling Expenses	120	
	30,020	30,020

3.7c

Trade Debtors			£
James	£3,500 – £1,400	=	2,100
Catherine	£2,000 – 0	=	2,000
Total equal to balance on Trade Debtors Account			4,100

3.7d

Trade Creditors			£
Guy	£2,500 – £1,800	=	700
Scott	£1,500 – 0	=	1,500
Rocket Motors	£6,000 – 0	=	6,000
Travel Co. Ltd	£120 – 0	=	120
Total equal to balance on Trade Creditors Account			8,320

Tutorial 4

4.1

	Cash & Bank Account		
Ref	Debit (£)	Ref	Credit (£)
b/d	71,500	1	14,000
2	10,000	4	5,000
5	5,000	6	30,000
		7	2,500
		9	2,000
		c/d	33,000
	86,500		86,500
b/d	33,000		

	Machinery Account		
Ref	Debit (£)	Ref	Credit (£)
b/d	64,000		
· 3	9,000		
4	5,000		
4	13,000		
		c/d	91,000
	91,000		91,000
b/d	91,000		

	Motor Vehicles Account		
Ref	Debit	Ref	Credit
b/d	86,000		
1	14,000		
8	7,000		
		c/d	107,000
	107,,000		107,000
	107,000		

	Loans Account		
Ref	Debit (£)	Ref	Credit (£)
6	30,000	b/d	79,000
		2	10,000
		3	9,000
		4	13,000
c/d	81,000		
	111,000		111,000
		b/d	81,000

	Drawings Account		
Ref	Debit (£)	Ref	Credit (£)
b/d	2,500		
7	2,500		
9	2,000		
		c/d	7,000
	7,000		7,000
b/d	7,000		

	Capital Account		
Ref	Debit (£)	Ref	Credit (£)
		b/d	89,000
		5	5,000
		8	7,000
c/d	101,000		
	101,000		101,000
		b/d	101,000

	A. Trader Co.	
	Trial Balance as at 31st July	
	Dr (£)	Cr (£)
Cash & Bank	33,000	
Capital		101,000
Drawings	7,000	
Machinery	91,000	
Motor Vehicles	107,000	
Loans		81,000
Purchases	500,000	
Trade Creditors		45,000
Sales		735,000
Trade Debtors	95,000	
Wages	90,000	
Light & Heat	14,000	
Rent & Insurance	25,000	
	962,000	962,000

4.2 Profits increase owner's capital, drawings decrease owner's capital. Profit, therefore, represents the amount which can be withdrawn from the business without decreasing capital, i.e. the net worth of the business. If drawings do not exceed profits, the capital of the business will be maintained in monetary terms. In times of inflation, however, maintenance of capital at its monetary value will fail to maintain the real value of the net assets which represent the capital. An increase in the net worth of the business in real terms represents growth. A business will, therefore, need to "plough back" profits, i.e. retain profits for survival and growth.

4.3a Finance will be required for:

- purchase of fixed assets, e.g. premises, machinery, etc.
- payment for stock purchases and expenses, e.g. wages
- customers to be allowed a period of credit, i.e. trade debtors

4.3b Sources of finance:

- *Owner's capital* – In the case of a sole trader, this may be constrained by personal wealth. In the case of a partnership or a limited company, more than one entrepreneur will share the capital contributions. However, multiple ownership will dilute control and also profit share.

- *Loan capital* – There is risk involved in borrowing. Interest on loans is a business expense which must be paid even if the business is not profitable. Loan repayments must be made on time, therefore sufficient cash resources must be available. On the other hand, loan creditors are not entitled to a share of profits.
- *Trade creditors* allow the business to buy stock and to incur expenses without an immediate cash outflow.

Tutorial 5

5.1 8%.

5.2

a. £10,000.

b. £100,000.

c. Outstanding interest of £2,000 will be shown as Creditors payable within 1 year. The loan of £100,000 will be shown as Creditors payable after 1 year.

5.3a

Cash & Bank Account				
Ref	Debit (£)	Ref	Credit (£)
1	60,000		
		2	2,100
		c/d	57,900
	60,000		60,000
b/d	57,900		

Interest Payable Account				
Ref	Debit (£)	Ref	Credit (£)
2	2,100		
3	2,100		
		c/d	4,200
	4,200		4,200
b/d	4,200		

Loans Account				
Ref	Debit (£)	Ref	Credit (£)
		1	60,000
c/d	60,000		
	60,000		60,000
		b/d	60,000

Trade Creditors Account				
Ref	Debit (£)	Ref	Credit (£)
		3	2,100
c/d	2,100		
	2,100		2,100
		b/d	2,100

Trial Balance as at end of Year		
	Dr (£)	Cr (£)
Cash & Bank	57,900	
Loans		60,000
Interest Payable	4,200	
Trade Creditors		2,100
	62,100	62,100

5.3b   The interest expense for the year to be shown on the Profit & Loss Account is £4,200.

5.4   Interest received will be shown in the Profit & Loss Account as other income, after gross profit has been calculated.

Tutorial 6

6.1

a.   £10,000 per annum.

b.   20% per annum.

c.   £30,000.

d.   £20,000.

e.   Net book value is rarely the same as market value. Net book value usually represents the cost of the fixed asset which has not yet been expensed to the Profit & Loss Account i.e. the unexpired portion of the asset's original (historical) cost. In this question, the net book value at the end of Year 3 is calculated by reference to a transaction which occurred 3 years previously, while market value is the amount that the machine could be sold for if it were sold at the end of Year 3. As fixed assets are not acquired with the primary intention of resale, it may be argued that market value is not relevant. Conversely it may be argued that Balance Sheets based on historical cost are not meaningful to the users of the accounts.

6.2a

Machinery at Cost Account			
Ref	Debit (£)	Ref	Credit (£)
Cash & Bank	50,000	Balance c/d	50,000
	50,000		50,000
Balance b/d	50,000		

Depreciation Expense Account			
Ref	Debit (£)	Ref	Credit (£)
Prov for Dep'n	10,000	to Year 1 P&L	10,000
		Balance c/d	0
	10,000		10,000
Balance b/d	0		
Prov for Dep'n	10,000	to Year 2 P&L	10,000
		Balance c/d	0
	10,000		10,000
Balance b/d	0		
Prov for Dep'n	10,000	to Year 3 P&L	10,000
		Balance c/d	0
	10,000		10,000
Balance b/d	0		

Provision for Depreciation of Machinery Account			
Ref	Debit (£)	Ref	Credit (£)
		Yr. 1 Dep'n exp.	10,000
Balance c/d	10,000		
	10,000		10,000
		Balance b/d	10,000
		Yr. 2 Dep'n exp.	10,000
Balance c/d	20,000		
	20,000		20,000
		Balance b/d	20,000
		Yr. 3 Dep'n exp	10,000
Balance c/d	30,000		
	30,000		30,000
		Balance b/d	30,000

6.2b

Balance Sheet as at end of Year 3			
Fixed Assets	Cost (£)	Accum.Dep. (£)	Net Book Value (£)
Machinery	50,000	30,000	20,000

Tutorial 7

7.1

Debit Depreciation Expense Account £2,000
Credit Provision for Depreciation of Fixtures Account £2,000

7.2

Debit Provision for Depreciation of Motor Vehicles Account £5,000
Credit Depreciation Expense Account £5,000

7.3

	7.1	7.2
Profit	–£2,000	+£5,000
Capital	–£2,000	+£5,000
Net Assets	–£2,000	+£5,000

7.4a

Depreciation Expense Account				
Ref	Debit	Ref	Credit
Extra Yr. 3 Prov for Dep'n	2,500		
		to Year 3 P&L	2,500
		Balance c/d	0
	2,500		2,500
Balance b/d	0		

Provision for Depreciation of Machinery Account				
Ref	Debit	Ref	Credit	
		Balance b/d	30,000	
		Extra Yr. 3 Dep'n exp.	2,50	
Balance c/d	32,500			
	32,500		32,500	
		Balance b/d	32,500	

7.4b

Amended Balance Sheet as at end of Year 3			
Fixed Assets	Cost (£)	Accum. Dep. (£)	Net Book Value (£)
Machinery	50,000	32,500	17,500

7.4c Year 3 Profit & Loss Account will show £12,500 for the expense of depreciation, i.e.:

Original charge	£50,000 @ 20% =	£10,000	
Adjustment		£2,500	
		£12,500	

7.5 The purpose of depreciation is to allocate the cost of a fixed asset over its useful life, not to manipulate profits. Depreciation should be calculated objectively without reference to the level of profits. A business should adopt and consistently apply an accounting policy for depreciation. It is prudent to account for depreciation of fixed assets in order to maintain the capital of the business.

Tutorial 8

8.1

a. Discount received = £150.

b. Debit Trade Creditors £2,850; Credit Cash & Bank £2,850.
Debit Trade Creditors £150; Credit Discount Received £150.

c. Profit will be increased by £150 discount received.

8.2a

Jan 3   Debit Trade Debtors £1,000; Credit Sales £1,000
  14   Debit Trade Debtors £800; Credit Sales £800
  20   Debit Trade Debtors £2,000; Credit Sales £2,000
  30   Debit Cash & Bank £970; Credit Trade Debtors £970
        Debit Discount Allowed £30; Credit Trade Debtors £30
Feb 5   Debit Cash & Bank £1,940; Credit Trade Debtors £1,940
        Debit Discount Allowed £60; Credit Trade Debtors £60
  25   Debit Cash & Bank £800; Credit Trade Debtors £800
        (*Note:* No discount may be deducted by Hazel)

8.2b   The Profit & Loss Account will show:

Sales (income)   £3,800
Discounts Allowed (expense)   £90

8.3a

Purchases Account			
Ref	Debit (£)	Ref	Credit (£)
b/d	500,000		
3	40,000	c/d	540,000
	540,000		540,000
b/d	540,000		

Sales Account			
Ref	Debit (£)	Ref	Credit (£)
c/d	755,000	b/d	735,000
		1	20,000
	755,000		755,000
		b/d	755,000

Trade Creditors Account			
Ref	Debit (£)	Ref	Credit (£)
2	18,000	b/d	43,000
2	450	3	40,000
c/d	64,550		
	83,000		83,000
		b/d	64,550

Discount Allowed			
Ref	Debit (£)	Ref	Credit (£)
b/d	5,000		
4	480	c/d	5,480
	5,480		5,480
b/d	5,480		

Cash & Bank Account

Ref	Debit (£)	Ref	Credit (£)
b/d	33,000	2	18,000
4	15,520	c/d	30,520
	48,520		48,520
b/d	30,520		

Trade Debtors Account

Ref	Debit (£)	Ref	Credit (£)
b/d	90,000	4	15,520
1	20,000	4	480
		c/d	94,000
	110,000		110,000
b/d	94,000		

Discount Received Account

Ref	Debit (£)	Ref	Credit (£)
		b/d	2,000
c/d	2,450	2	450
	2,450		2,450
		b/d	2,450

8.3b

Ged & Co.
Amended Trial Balance as at ......

	Dr (£)	Cr (£)
Cash & Bank	30,520	
Capital		101,000
Drawings	7,000	
Machinery	91,000	
Motor Vehicles	107,000	
Loans		81,000
Purchases	540,000	
Trade Creditors		64,550
Discount Allowed	5,480	
Discount Received		2,450
Sales		755,000
Trade Debtors	94,000	
Wages	90,000	
Light & Heat	14,000	
Rent & Insurance	25,000	
	1,004,000	1,004,000

Tutorial 9

9.1   Debit Bad Debts Expense; Credit Trade Debtors.

9.2   Debit Trade Debtors; Credit Bad Debts Expense.

9.3

Trade Debtors Account			
Ref	Debit (£)	Ref	Credit (£)
b/d	188,000		1,000
		c/d	187,000
	188,000		188,000
b/d	187,000		

Provision for Bad Debts Account			
Ref	Debit (£)	Ref	Credit (£)
		b/d	7,000
c/d	9,350		2,350
	9,350		9,350
		b/d	9,350

Bad Debts Expense Account			
Ref	Debit (£)	Ref	Credit (£)
b/d	5,000		
	1,000		
	2,350	c/d	8,350
	8,350		8,350
b/d	8,350		

9.4

Trade Debtors Account			
Ref	Debit (£)	Ref	Credit (£)
b/d	175,000	1	5,000
		3	7,000
		c/d	163,000
	175,000		175,000
b/d	163,000		

Provision for Bad Debts Account			
Ref	Debit (£)	Ref	Credit (£)
4	600	b/d	1,800
c/d	1,200		
	1,800		1,800
		b/d	1,200

Bad Debts Expense Account			
Ref	Debit (£)	Ref	Credit (£)
b/d	6,000	2	800
1	5,000	4	600
3	7,000	c/d	16,600
	18,000		18,000
b/d	16,600		

Cash & Bank Account			
Ref	Debit (£)	Ref	Credit (£)
b/d	80,000		
2	800	c/d	80,800
	80,800		80,800
b/d	80,800		

Trial Balance as at	Dr (£)	Cr (£)
Sales		430,000
Trade Debtors	163,000	
Bad Debts Expense	16,600	
Cash & Bank	80,800	
Provision for Bad Debts		1,200

9.5 Failure to collect debts on time will adversely affect the cash flow of the business. The risk of bad debts increases with the age of the debt: as soon as a debt becomes overdue appropriate action should be initiated to collect the cash. This may include: sending a reminder; a personal call to the debtor; legal proceedings. The risk of incurring a bad debt must be weighed against the risk of losing a customer by inappropriate action.

Tutorial 10

10.1

a. Debit Cash & Bank; Credit Purchases.

b. Debit Trade Creditors; Credit Purchases.

10.2

a. Debit Sales; Credit Cash & Bank.

b. Debit Sales; Credit Trade Debtors.

10.3

Trade Debtors Account			
Ref	Debit (£)	Ref	Credit (£)
b/d	46,000	2	1,000
		4	1,500
		c/d	43,500
	46,000		46,000
b/d	43,500		

Cash & Bank Account			
Ref	Debit (£)	Ref	Credit (£)
b/d	34,100	4	1,500
3	900	c/d	33,500
	35,000		35,000
b/d	33,500		

Purchases Account			
Ref	Debit (£)	Ref	Credit (£)
b/d	66,000	3	900
1	4,000	5	600
		c/d	68,500
	70,000		70,000
b/d	68,500		

Sales Account			
Ref	Debit (£)	Ref	Credit (£)
2	1,000	b/d	180,000
4	1,500		
c/d	177,500		
	180,000		180,000
		b/d	177,500

Trade Creditors Account			
Ref	Debit (£)	Ref	Credit (£)
5	600	b/d	22,800
c/d	26,200	1	4,000
	26,800		26,800
		b/d	26,200

Trial Balance as at		
	Dr (£)	Cr (£)
Sales		177,500
Trade Debtors	43,500	
Purchases	68,500	
Cash & Bank	33,500	
Trade Creditors		26,200

10.4

a. Debit Purchases £1,000; Credit Cash & Bank £1,000.

b. Debit Cash & Bank £1,050; Credit Sales £1,050.

c. Debit Cash & Bank £50; Credit Purchases £50.

d. Debit Sales £60; Credit Cash & Bank £60.

Tutorial 11

11.1

a. Debit Cash & Bank; Credit Disposals.

b. Debit Debtors; Credit Disposals.

11.2

a. Profit – £1,000 (underdepreciation).

b. Profit + £500 (overdepreciation).

11.3 The sales proceeds of an asset will depend upon:

- condition of the asset at the date of disposal
- market forces at the date of disposal

The net book value of a fixed asset represents its unexpired cost, i.e. cost less accumulated depreciation to date. An accounting policy for the depreciation of a fixed asset is based on evidence available at the time the asset is acquired:

- historical cost of the asset
- estimated useful life
- estimated scrap value

In practice, the actual life and actual scrap value of an asset will rarely be the same as the estimates made at the time the asset was acquired.

11.4a

Machines at Cost Account				
Ref	**Debit (£)**		**Ref**	**Credit (£)**
T.B.	54,000			
			Disposals	4,000
			Balance c/d	50,000
	54,000			54,000
Balance b/d	50,000			

Provision for Depreciation of Machines Account				
Ref	**Debit (£)**		**Ref**	**Credit (£)**
			T.B.	16,000
Disposals	800			
			Year 8 Depreciation	
Balance c/d	20,200		Expense	5,000
	21,000			21,000
			Balance b/d	20,200

Disposals Account				
Ref	**Debit (£)**		**Ref**	**Credit (£)**
Machines at Cost	4,000			
			Provision for	
			Depreciation	800
			Cash at Bank	3,000
			Balance c/d	200
	4,000			4,000
Balance b/d	200			
			to Year 8 P&L	200
			Balance c/d	0
	200			200
Balance b/d	0			0

Cash & Bank Account			
Ref	Debit (£)	Ref	Credit (£)
T.B.	12,000		
Disposals	3,000	Balance c/d	15,000
	15,000		15,000
Balance b/d	15,000		

Depreciation Expense Account			
Ref	Debit (£)	Ref	Credit (£)
Provision for Depreciation	5,000	Balance c/d	5,000
	5,000		5,000
Balance b/d			

11.4b

Profit & Loss Account for Year 8		
	£	£
Sales		X
Less Cost of Sales		X
Gross Profit		X
Less Expenses		
Wages etc.	X	
Depreciation	5,000	X
Loss on Disposal	200	
Net Profit		X

Balance Sheet as at end of Year 8			
Fixed Assets	Cost (£)	Accum.Dep. (£)	Net Book Value (£)
Machines	50,000	20,200	29,800

Tutorial 12

12.1

i. Cash & Bank	Balance Sheet (Current Asset)
ii. Rent	P&L Account (may be Income or Expense)
iii. Trade Debtors	Balance Sheet (Current Asset)
iv. Loans	Balance Sheet (Liabilities/Creditors)
v. Wages	P&L Account (Expense)
vi. Loan Interest	P&L Account (may be Income or Expense)
vii. Trade Creditors	Balance Sheet (Liabilities/Creditors)

12.2 The entire cost of a fixed asset should not be charged to the Profit & Loss Account of any one year. The expenditure on fixed assets will benefit **all** the accounting periods that the asset is in use. Accounting for depreciation is the means by which fixed assets are "expensed" to the Profit & Loss Account over the years of their useful life. Depreciation allocates the cost of a fixed asset to the Profit & Loss Account over several years to prevent the distorting effect of charging the entire cost of an asset to a single accounting period.

12.3a

Michael's Business

Trial Balance as at end of Year 6

	Dr (£)	Cr (£)
Cash & Bank	30,000	
Capital		58,000
Machinery	8,000	
Purchases	40,000	
Trade Creditors		6,000
Sales		95,000
Trade Debtors	14,500	
Wages	25,000	
Light & Heat	9,500	
Loans		15,000
Motor Vehicles	35,000	
Drawings	12,000	
Cost of Sales	0	
	174,000	174,000

12.3b, c, d

Cash & Bank Account

Ref	Debit (£)	Ref	Credit (£)
b/d	30,000		
		c/d	30,000
	30,000		30,000
b/d	30,000		

Machinery Account

Ref	Debit (£)	Ref	Credit (£)
b/d	8,000		
		c/d	8,000
	8,000		8,000
b/d	8,000		

Capital Account

Ref	Debit (£)	Ref	Credit (£)d.
c/d	12,000	b/d	58,000
	66,500	d	20,500
	78,500		78,500
		b/d	66,500

Purchases Account

Ref	Debit (£)	Ref	Credit (£)
b/d	40,000		
		b.	40,000
		c/d	0
	40,000		40,000
b/d	0		

Trade Creditors Account

Ref	Debit (£)	Ref	Credit (£)
c/d	6,000	b/d	6,000
	6,000		6,000
		b/d	6,000

Loans Account

Ref	Debit (£)	Ref	Credit (£)
		b/d	15,000
c/d	15,000		
	15,000		15,000
		b/d	15,000

Sales Account

Ref	Debit (£)	Ref	Credit (£)
		b/d	95,000
c.	95,000		
c/d	0		
	95,000		95,000
		b/d	0

Motor Vehicles Account

Ref	Debit (£)	Ref	Credit (£)
b/d	35,000		
		c/d	35,000
	35,000		35,000
b/d	35,000		

	Trade Debtors Account		
Ref	Debit (£)	Ref	Credit (£)
b/d	14,500		
		c/d	14,500
	14,500		14,500
b/d	14,500		

	Drawings Account		
Ref	Debit (£)	Ref	Credit (£)
b/d	12,000		
		d.	12,000
		c/d	0
	12,000		12,000
b/d	0		

	Wages Account		
Ref	Debit (£)	Ref	Credit (£)
b/d	25,000		
		c.	25,000
		c/d	0
	25,000		25,000
b/d	0		

	Cost of Sales Account		
Ref	Debit (£)	Ref	Credit (£)
b/d	0		
b.	40,000	c/d	40,000
	40,000		40,000
b/d	40,000		
		c.	40,000
		c/d	0
	40,000		40,000
b/d	0		

	Light & Heat Account		
Ref	Debit (£)	Ref	Credit (£)
b/d	9,500		
		c.	9,500
		c/d	0
	9,500		9,500
b/d	0		

Michael's Business		
Profit & Loss Account for Year 6		
	£	£
Sales		95,000
Less Cost of Sales		40,000
Gross Profit		55,000
Less Overhead Expenses		
Wages	25,000	
Light & Heat	9,500	34,500
Net Profit		20,500

Capital Movements	
	£
Net Profit for the period	20,500
Less Drawings during the period	12,000
Retained Profit for the period	8,500
Add Opening Capital and Capital Introduced during the period	58,000
Closing Capital	66,500

12.3e

Michael's Business		
Balance Sheet as at end of Year 6		
	£	£
Fixed Assets		
Machinery		8,000
Motor Vehicles		35,000
		43,000
Current Assets		
Stock	0	
Trade Debtors	14,500	
Cash & Bank	30,000	
	44,500	
Creditors payable within 1 year		
Trade Creditors	6,000	
Net current assets		38,500
		81,500
Representing		
Creditors payable after 1 year		
Loans		15,000
Equity		
Owner's Capital		66,500
		81,500

Tutorial 13

13.1a   Gross profit margin per unit; $\underline{£2.00} \times 100 = 40\%$.
$£5.00$

13.1b

Mandy's Business *Profit & Loss Account for Year 1*	Units	£ per unit	Total £
Sales	1,200	5.00	6,000
Less Cost of sales	1,200	3.00	3,600
Gross Profit	1,200	2.00	2,400

Mandy's Business *Profit & Loss Account for Year 2*	Units	£ per unit	Total £
Sales	1,900	5.00	9,500
Less Cost of sales	1,900	3.00	5,700
Gross Profit	1,900	2.00	3,800

13.1c Gross profit margin:

Year 1 $\dfrac{£2,400}{£6,000} \times 100 = 40\%$

Year 2 $\dfrac{£3,800}{£9,500} \times 100 = 40\%$

13.1d

		Sales Account		
Ref	Debit (£)		Ref	Credit (£)
			Trade Debtors	6,000
to Year 1 P&L	6,000			
Balance c/d	0			
	6,000			6,000
			Balance b/d	0
to Year 2 P&L	9,500		Trade Debtors	9,500
Balance c/d	0			
	9,500			9,500
			Balance b/d	0

Purchases Account				
Ref	Debit (£)		Ref	Credit (£)
Trade Creditors	4,800		Year 1 Cost of Sales	4,800
			Balance c/d	0
	4,800			4,800
Balance b/d	0			
Trade Creditors	5,400		Year 2 Cost of Sales	5,400
			Balance c/d	0
	5,400			5,400
Balance b/d	0			

Cost of Sales Account				
Ref	Debit (£)		Ref	Credit (£)
Purchases (Year 1)	4,800		Stock (Yr 1 closing), i.e. 400 units × £3.00	1,200
			Year 1 P&L (cost of sales)	3,600
			Balance c/d	0
	4,800			4,800
Balance b/d	0			
Stock (Yr 2 opening)	1,200		Stock (Yr 2 closing), i.e. 300 units × £3.00	900
Purchases (Year 2)	5,400		Year 2 P&L (cost of sales)	5,700
			Balance c/d	0
	6,600			6,600
Balance b/d	0			

Stock Account				
Ref	Debit (£)	Ref	Credit (£)
Cost of Sales (Yr 1 closing stock)	1,200	Balance c/d	1,200
	1,200		1,200
Balance b/d	1,200	Cost of Sales (Yr 2 opening stock)	1,200
Cost of Sales (Yr 2 closing stock)	900	Balance c/d	900
	2,100		2,100
Balance b/d	900		

13.2a

Workings	£
Opening stock	1,200
Add Purchases	5,400
	6,600
Less Closing stock (120 units)	360
Cost of Sales (Year 2)	6,240

Mandy's Business	
Profit & Loss Account for Year 2	
	£
Sales	9,500
Less Cost of sales	6,240
Gross Profit	3,260

Gross profit margin
Year 2 $\dfrac{£3,260}{£9,500} \times 100 = 34\%$

13.2b   The reduction in gross profit of £540 is the result of the missing stock (180 units × £3.00), i.e. the sales income from 1,900 units has been matched with costs relating to 2,080 units. If a business does not keep detailed stock records, the reduction in the gross profit margin (%) may be the first indication of problems such as missing stock or missing cash (sales proceeds).

13.3

Stock in good condition at cost 40 × £30		= £1,200
Damaged stock at net realisable value:		
Estimated sales proceeds 5 × £15 =	£75	
Less transport costs	£20	= £55
Closing stock valued at lower of cost and net realisable value		= £1,255

13.4

Workings	£
Opening stock	4,637
Add Purchases	41,050
	45,687
Less Closing stock	5,700
Cost of Sales	39,987

John's Business

Profit & Loss Account for Year 4

	£	£
Sales		80,870
Less Cost of Sales		39,987
Gross Profit		40,883
Less Overhead Expenses		
Wages	15,039	
Light & Heat	1,620	
Postage & Stationery	1,940	
Insurance	1,085	19,684
Net Profit		21,199

Capital Movements	£
Net Profit for the period	21,199
Less Drawings during the period	11,075
Retained Profit for the period	10,124
Add Opening Capital	62,600
Closing Capital	72,724

	£	£
John's Business		
Balance Sheet as at end of Year 4		
Fixed Assets		
Freehold Premises		53,000
Fixtures & Fittings		6,120
		59,120
Current Assets		
Stock	5,700	
Trade Debtors	5,844	
Cash & Bank	4,790	
	16,334	
Creditors payable within 1 year		
Trade Creditors	2,730	
Net current assets		13,604
		72,724
Representing		
Equity		
Owner's Capital		72,724
		72,724

Tutorial 14

14.1

a.   Debit Motor Vehicle Account £14,000; Credit Purchases Account £14,000. (*Note:* The depreciation expense for the year must include depreciation of the above vehicle.)

b.   Debit Wages Account £2,000; Credit Travel Expenses Account £2,000.

c.   Debit Cash Account £90; Credit Trade Debtors Account £90.

d.   Debit Bank Account £3,500; Credit Trade Creditors Account £3,500.

14.2

a.   Actual motor vehicles compared with the Motor Vehicles Accounts in the ledger; stock records; gross profit margin.

b.   Comparison of detailed payroll records with Wages Account; comparison of wages and travel expenses with equivalent amounts for previous period.

c. Complaint from Elsie when asked to settle her account; comparison of actual cash with balance on Cash Account (provided cash has not been misappropriated).

d. Reconciliation of bank statement with Bank Account in ledger; request by supplier for payment; reconciliation of supplier's statement with that trade creditor's account in ledger.

14.3a *Steve's Business*

Rates & Insurance A/c			
T.B.	19,500		
i.	300	c/d	19,800
	19,800		19,800
b/d	19,800		

Drawings A/c			
T.B.	1,000		
iii.	6,000	c/d	7,000
	7,000		7,000
b/d	7,000		

Wages A/c			
T.B.	45,000	i.	300
		iii.	6,000
		c/d	38,700
	45,000		45,000
b/d	38,700		

Motor Vehicles at Cost A/c			
T.B.	24,000		
iv.	5,000	c/d	29,000
	29,000		29,000
b/d	29,000		

Loans A/c			
c/d		T.B.	25,000
	35,000	ii.	10,000
	35,000		35,000
		b/d	35,000

Purchases A/c			
T.B.	250,000	iv.	5,000
i.		c/d	245,000
	250,000		250,000
b/d	245,000		

Sales A/c			
ii	10,000	T.B.	367,500
c/d	357,500		
	367,500		367,500
		b/d	357,500

Provision for Depreciation of Motor Vehicles A/c			
c/d		T.B.	7,000
	8,250	iv.	1,250
	8,250		8,250
		b/d	8,250

Loan Interest A/c			
T.B.	3,000		
ii.	800	c/d	3,800
	3,800		3,800
b/d	3,800		

Depreciation Expense A/c			
T.B.	6,000		
iv.	1,250	c/d	7,250
	7,250		7,250
b/d	7,250		

Trade Creditors A/c			
c/d		T.B.	22,500
	23,300	ii.	800
	23,300		23,300
		b/d	23,300

14.3b

Amended Trial Balance as at year end		
	Dr (£)	Cr (£)
Cash & Bank	66,000	
Capital		40,000
Drawings	7,000	
Motor Vehicles at Cost	29,000	
Provision for Depreciation of Motor Vehicles		8,250
Depreciation Expense	7,250	
Loans		35,000
Loan Interest	3,800	
Purchases	245,000	
Trade Creditors		23,300
Sales		357,500
Trade Debtors	47,500	
Wages	38,700	
Rates & Insurance	19,800	
	464,050	464,050

14.4a   *Angela's Business*

Cash & Bank A/c			
T.B.	30,470		
i.	630	c/d	31,100
	31,100		31,100
b/d	31,100		

Purchases A/c			
T.B.	125,000		
ii.	200	c/d	125,200
	125,200		125,200
b/d	125,200		

Suspense A/c			
T.B.	1,030	i.	630
		ii.	200
		ii.	200
		c/d	0
	1,030		1,030
b/d	0		

Sales A/c			
ii.	200	T.B.	183,750
c/d	183,550		
	183,750		183,750
		b/d	183,550

14.4b

Amended Trial Balance as at year end		
	Dr (£)	Cr (£)
Cash & Bank	31,100	
Capital		20,000
Drawings	500	
Fixtures & Fittings at Cost	13,500	
Provision for Depreciation of Fixtures & Fittings		3,500
Depreciation Expense	3,000	
Loans		12,500
Loan Interest	1,500	
Purchases	125,200	
Trade Creditors		11,250
Sales		183,550
Trade Debtors	23,750	
Wages	22,500	
Rates & Insurance	3,500	
Postage & Stationery	6,250	
	230,800	230,800

Tutorial 15

15.1

a. Motor expenses in the Profit & Loss Account: £6,000: + £50 = £6,050.

b. Accruals of £50 will be shown as Creditors payable within 1 year.

c. Debit Motor Expenses £50; Credit Trade Creditors £50.

15.2   The accruals concept dictates that profit should be calculated by matching income earned during an accounting period with expenses incurred during that period, irrespective of the timing of cash flows. If it is known that expenses have been incurred during a period, it is important that they are included in the profit calculation for that period to avoid distortions in the profit calculation. The Final Accounts should show a true and fair view of the activities of the organisation. The use of estimates does not invalidate the profit calculation, provided there are no material mis-statements. A material mis-statement is one which is likely to mislead the users of the accounts (**materiality concept**).

15.3
Anne's Business: Workings

Trade Creditors A/c				
			T.B.	11,250
			i.	600
			ii.	75
c/d	12,625		iii.	700
	12,625			12,625
			b/d	12,625

Postage & Stationery A/c				
T.B.	6,250			
ii.	75	P&L	6,325	
	6,325		6,325	

Loan Interest A/c				
T.B.	500			
iii.	700	P&L	1,200	
	1,200		1,200	

Wages A/c				
T.B.	22,500			
i.	600	P&L	23,100	
	23,100		23,100	

NOTE

Interest for year	£
£12,000 × 10% =	1,200
Per T.B.	500
Accrued interest	700

Anne's Business

Profit & Loss Account for year ended 31st December Year 6

	£	£
Sales		183,750
Less Cost of Sales		125,700
Gross Profit		58,050
Less Overhead Expenses		
Wages	23,100	
Postage & Stationery	6,325	
Rates & Insurance	3,500	
Depreciation	3,000	
Loan Interest	1,200	37,125
Net Profit		20,925

Capital Movements	£
Net Profit for the period	20,925
Less Drawings during the period	1,830
Retained Profit for the period	19,095
Add Opening Capital	20,000
Closing Capital	39,095

	Anne's Business		
Balance Sheet as at 31st December Year 6			
	Cost (£)	Acc. Dep. (£)	N.B.V. (£)
Fixed Assets			
Fixtures & Fittings	13,500	4,000	9,500
	13,500	4,000	9,500
Current Assets			
Stock		0	
Trade Debtors		23,750	
Cash & Bank		30,470	
		54,220	
Creditors payable within 1 year			
Trade Creditors		12,625	
Net current assets			41,595
			51,095
Representing			
Creditors payable after 1 year			
Loan			12,000
Equity			
Owner's Capital			39,095
			51,095

Tutorial 16

16.1

a. Rates in the Profit & Loss Account: £4,000 – £500 = £3,500.
b. Prepayment of £500 will be shown as Debtors.
c. Debit Debtors £500; Credit Rates £500.

16.2a   Rent in the Profit & Loss Account:

		£
Year 1	7 months × £300	2,100
Year 2	5 months × £300	1,500
	+ 7 months × £320	2,240
		3,740
Year 3	5 months × £320	1,600
	+ 7 months × £350	2,450
		4,050

16.2b   Prepayment as part of Debtors on Balance Sheet at end of:

	£
Year 1	1,500
Year 2	1,600
Year 3	1,750

16.2c

Rent Account					
	Ref	Debit (£)		Ref	Credit (£)
Cash & Bank		3,600			
			Debtors:		
			(closing prepayment)		1,500
			Year 1 P&L		2,100
			Balance c/d		0
		3,600			3,600
Balance b/d		0			
Debtors:			Debtors:		
(opening prepayment)		1,500	(closing prepayment)		1,600
Cash & Bank		3,840	Year 2 P&L		3,740
			Balance c/d		0
		5,340			5,340
Balance b/d		0			
Debtors:			Debtors:		
(opening prepayment)		1,600	(closing prepayment)		1,750
Cash & Bank		4,200	Year 3 P&L		4,050
			Balance c/d		0
		5,800			5,800
Balance b/d		0			
Debtors:					
(opening prepayment)		1,750			

16.3

Charlotte's Business: Workings

Trade Debtors A/c			
T.B.	47,500		
i.	400		
ii.	150	c/d	48,050
	48,050		48,050
b/d	48,050		

Rates A/c			
T.B.	3,200	i.	400
		P&L	2,800
	3,200		3,200

Insurance A/c			
T.B.	2,600	ii.	150
		P&L	2,450
	2,600		2,600

Charlotte's Business		
Profit & Loss Account for year ended 31st August Year 8		
	£	£
Sales		363,300
Less Cost of Sales		251,200
Gross Profit		112,100
Less Overhead Expenses		
Wages	45,000	
Postage & Stationery	12,500	
Rates	2,800	
Insurance	2,450	
Depreciation	6,000	71,150
Loan Interest	2,400	
Net Profit		40,950

Capital Movements	£
Net Profit for the period	40,950
Less Drawings during the period	3,660
Retained Profit for the period	37,290
Add Opening Capital	44,200
Closing Capital	81,490

Charlotte's Business

Balance Sheet as at 31st August Year 8

	Cost (£)	Acc. Dep. (£)	N.B.V. (£)
Fixed Assets			
Machinery	27,000	8,000	19,000
	27,000	8,000	19,000
Current Assets			
Stock		0	
Trade Debtors		48,050	
Cash & Bank		60,940	
		108,990	
Creditors payable within 1 year			
Trade Creditors		22,500	
Net current assets			86,490
			105,490
Representing			
Creditors payable after 1 year			
Loan			24,000
Equity			
Owner's Capital			81,490
			105,490

EXAMINATION QUESTIONS

1. The following Trial Balance was extracted from the books of Norma's business as at 31st October Year 9.

Trial Balance as at 31st October Year 9	Dr (£)	Cr (£)
Capital at 1st November Year 8		152,925
Drawings	15,670	
Trade Debtors	40,850	
Trade Creditors		3,580
Sales		180,500
Stock at 1st November Year 8	12,670	
Purchases	101,000	
Postage & Stationery	5,640	
Light & Heat	9,490	
Wages	37,000	
Bad Debts Expense	485	
Provision for Bad Debts at 31st October Year 8		580
Insurance	3,050	
Cash & Bank	12,530	
Fixtures & Fittings at cost	53,000	
Provision for Depreciation of Fixtures & Fittings to 31st October Year 8		31,800
Freehold Premises at Cost	100,000	
Provision for Depreciation of Freehold Premises to 31st October Year 8		22,000
	391,385	391,385

NOTES

i.   Stock at 31st October Year 9 is valued at £15,490.
ii. A balance of £600 is required on the Provision for Bad Debts Account at 31st October Year 9.

iii. The insurance on the Trial Balance includes a prepayment of £40.
iv. At 31st October Year 9, accrued wages of £375 and accrued electricity of £65 are to be accounted for.
v. New fixtures and fittings costing £5,000 have been debited to the Purchases Account in error.
vi. Depreciation is to be provided on the fixtures and fittings at the rate of 15% and on the freehold premises at the rate of 2% using the straight line method.

Required
Prepare the Final Accounts for the year ended 31st October Year 9.

2. The following Trial Balance was extracted from the books of Thelma's business as at 31st December Year 5.

Trial Balance as at 31st December Year 5	Dr (£)	Cr (£)
Capital at 1st January Year 5		148,350
Drawings	22,590	
Trade Debtors	107,850	
Trade Creditors		37,580
Sales		750,000
Stock at 1st January Year 5	45,840	
Purchases	456,000	
Postage & Stationery	37,010	
Wages	68,000	
Bad Debts Expense	1,460	
Provision for Bad Debts at 31st December Year 4		1,050
Rates & Insurance	7,700	
10% Loan		40,000
Loan Interest	3,000	
Cash & Bank	13,530	
Motor Vehicles at cost	60,000	
Provision for Depreciation of Motor Vehicles to 31st December Year 4		20,000
Proceeds of sale of Motor Vehicle		2,000
Freehold Premises at cost	220,000	
Provision for Depreciation of Freehold Premises to 31st December Year 4		44,000
	1,042,980	1,042,980

NOTES

i. Stock at 31st December Year 5 is valued at £47,000.
ii. The Provision for Bad Debts is to be increased by £200.
iii. Rates of £300 are prepaid at 31st December Year 5.

iv. At 31st December Year 5, accrued wages of £800 and the outstanding loan interest are to be accounted for.

v. A motor vehicle, which cost £12,000 in Year 3, was sold during Year 5 for £2,000. The proceeds of sale have been debited to the Cash & Bank Account and credited to the Proceeds of Sale of Motor Vehicle Account. No other entries have been made for this transaction.

vi. Thelma's depreciation policy is to provide 25% on vehicles owned at the year end and 4% on freehold premises using the straight line method.

vii. The following entries were made in the ledgers for the receipt of £4,000 from a trade debtor: Debit Cash & Bank; Credit Sales Account.

Required

Prepare the Final Accounts for the year ended 31st December Year 5.

3. The following Trial Balance has been extracted from the books of Dave's business as at 31st May Year 7.

Trial Balance as at 31st May Year 7	Dr (£)	Cr (£)
Capital at 1st June Year 6		126,230
Drawings	30,650	
Trade Debtors	135,800	
Trade Creditors		110,000
Sales		1,451,100
Discount Received		1,400
Stock at 1st June Year 6	112,000	
Purchases	981,000	
Postage & Stationery	15,600	
Light & Heat	18,240	
Discount Allowed	1,200	
Wages	187,000	
Bad Debts Expense	11,460	
Provision for Bad Debts at 31st May Year 6		7,800
Insurance	13,000	
Cash & Bank	39,080	
Machinery at Cost	108,000	
Provision for Depreciation of Machinery to 31st May Year 6		72,500
Freehold Premises at Cost	200,000	
Provision for Depreciation of Freehold Premises to 31st May Year 6		24,000
8% Loan		60,000
	1,853,030	1,853,030

NOTES

i.   Stock at 31st May Year 7 cost £115,490. This includes a batch of goods which have been damaged. The damaged goods cost £3,000 and can be sold for £1,800 provided repairs costing £400 are carried out.

ii.   A balance of £6,000 is required on the Provision for Bad Debts Account at 31st May Year 7.

iii.   The insurance on the Trial Balance includes a prepayment of £150.

iv.   At 31st May Year 7, accrued light & heat of £60 is to be accounted for.

v.   A machine, which cost £6,000 on 1st June Year 3, was sold during Year 7 for £2,500. The proceeds of sale have been debited to the Cash & Bank Account and credited to the Sales Account. No other entries have been made for this transaction.

vi.   Dave's depreciation policy is to provide 20% on machinery owned at the year end and 2% on freehold premises using the straight line method.

vii.   The 8% loan was taken out on 1st January Year 7. No interest has been paid on the loan.

Required

Prepare the Final Accounts for the year ended 31st May Year 7.

ANSWERS TO EXAMINATION QUESTIONS

1.

Norma's Business: Workings

Purchases A/c			
T.B.	101,000	v.	5,000
		COS	96,000
	101,000		101,000

Wages A/c			
T.B.	37,000		
iv.	375	P&L	37,375
	37,375		37,375

Cost of Sales A/c			
O St	12,670	C St	15,490
Pur.	96,000	P&L	93,180
	18,670		108,670

Light & Heat A/c			
T.B.	9,490		
iv.	65	P&L	9,555
	9,555		9,555

Bad Debts Expense A/c			
T.B.	485	P&L	505
ii.	20		
	505		505

Fixtures & Fittings at Cost A/c			
T.B.	53,000		
v.	5,000	c/d	58,000
	58,000		58,000
b/d	58,000		

Provision for Bad Debts A/c			
c/d	600	T.B.	580
		ii.	20
	600		600
		b/d	600

Provision for Depreciation of F&F A/c			
		T.B.	31,800
c/d	40,500	vi.	8,700
	40,500		40,500
		b/d	40,500

Trade Debtors A/c			
T.B.	40,850		
iii	40	c/d	40,890
	40,890		40,890
b/d	40,890		

Insurance A/c			
T.B.	3,050	iii.	40
		P&L	3,010
	3,050		3,050

Trade Creditors A/c			
		T.B.	3,580
		iv.	375
c/d	4,020	iv.	65
	4,020		4,020
		b/d	4,020

Note

£58,000 × 15% = £8,700

£100,000 × 2% = £2,000

Depreciation Expense A/c			
vi.	8,700		
vi.	2,000	P&L	10,700
	10,700		10,700

Prov'n for Dep'n of F'hold Prem. A/c			
		T.B.	22,000
c/d	24,000	vi.	2,000
	24,000		24,000
		b/d	24,000

Norma's Business: Answer

Norma's Business		
Profit & Loss Account for year ended 31st October Year 9		
	£	£
Sales		180,500
Less Cost of Sales		93,180
Gross Profit		87,320
		66,785
Less Overhead Expenses		
Wages	37,375	
Light & Heat	9,555	
Postage & Stationery	5,640	
Insurance	3,010	
Bad Debts	505	
Depreciation	10,700	
Net Profit		20,535

Capital Movements	£
Net Profit for the period	20,535
Less Drawings during the period	15,670
Retained Profit for the period	4,865
Add Opening Capital	152,925
Closing Capital	157,790

Norma's Business

Balance Sheet as at 31st October Year 9

	Cost (£)	Acc. Dep. (£)	N.B.V. (£)
Fixed Assets			
Freehold Premises	100,000	24,000	76,000
Fixtures & Fittings	58,000	40,500	17,500
	158,000	64,500	93,500
Current Assets			
Stock		15,490	
Trade Debtors	40,890		
Less Provision for Bad Debts	600	40,290	
Cash & Bank		12,530	
		68,310	
Creditors payable within 1 year			
Trade Creditors		4,020	
Net current assets			64,290
			157,790
Representing			
Equity			
Owner's Capital			157,790
			157,790

2.

Thelma's Business: Workings

Cost of Sales A/c

O St	45,840	C St	47,000
Pur.	456,000	P&L	454,840
	501,840		501,840

Bad Debts Expense A/c

T.B.	1,460	P&L	1,660
ii.	200		
	1,660		1,660

Provision for Bad Debts A/c

c/d		T.B.	1,050
	1,250	ii.	200
	1,250		1,250
		b/d	1,250

Trade Debtors A/c

T.B.	107,850	vii.	4,000
iii.	300	c/d	104,150
	108,150		108,150
b/d	104,150		

Rates & Insurance A/c

T.B.	7,700	iii.	300
		P&L	7,400
	7,700		7,700

Sales A/c

vii.	4,000	T.B.	750,000
P&L	746,000		
	750,000		750,000

Trade Creditors A/c

		T.B.	37,580
		iv.	800
c/d	39,380	iv.	1,000
	39,380		39,380
		b/d	39,380

Motor Vehicles at Cost A/c

T.B.	60,000	v.	12,000
		c/d	48,000
	60,000		60,000
b/d	48,000		

Provision for Depreciation of M. Vehicles. A/c

disp.	6,000	T.B.	20,000
c/d	26,000	Year 5	
		dep'n	12,000
	32,000		32,000
		b/d	26,000

Note

Accumulated depreciation of vehicle sold:
$12,000 \times 25\% \times 2$ years = £6,000
Year 5 depreciation of remaining vehicles:
£48,000 × 25% = £12,000

Proceeds A/c

Disp.		T.B.	2,000
	2,000		
	2,000		2,000

Disposals A/c

Cost	12,000	acc. dep.	6,000
		Proc.	2,000
		P&L	4,000
	12,000		12,000

Wages A/c				
T.B.	68,000			
iv.	800	P&L	68,800	
	68,800		68,800	

Depreciation Expense A/c				
vi.	12,000			
vi.	8,800	P&L	20,800	
	20,800		20,800	

Loan Interest A/c				
T.B.	3,000			
iv.	1,000	P&L	4,000	
	4,000		4,000	

Prov'n for Dep'n of F'hold Prem. A/c				
c/d		T.B.	44,000	
	52,800	vi.	8,800	
	52,800		52,800	
		b/d	52,800	

Note

Interest for year £40,000 × 10%	£4,000
Interest paid (per T.B.)	£3,000
Interest accrued	£1,000

Thelma's Business: Answer

Thelma's Business

Profit & Loss Account for year ended 31st December Year 5

	£	£
Sales		746,000
Less Cost of Sales		454,840
Gross Profit		291,160
Less Overhead Expenses		
Wages	68,800	
Postage & Stationery	37,010	
Rates & Insurance	7,400	
Bad Debts	1,660	
Depreciation	20,800	
Loss on Disposal	4,000	
Loan Interest	4,000	143,670
Net Profit		147,490

Capital Movements	£
Net Profit for the period	147,490
Less Drawings during the period	22,590
Retained Profit for the period	124,900
Add Opening Capital	148,350
Closing Capital	273,250

Thelma's Business

Balance Sheet as at 31st December Year 5

	Cost (£)	Acc. Dep. (£)	N.B.V. (£)
Fixed Assets			
Freehold Premises	220,000	52,800	167,200
Motor Vehicles	48,000	26,000	22,000
	268,000	78,800	189,200
Current Assets			
Stock		47,000	
Trade Debtors	104,150		
Less Provision for Bad Debts	1,250	102,900	
Cash & Bank		13,530	
		163,430	
Creditors payable within 1 year			
Trade Creditors		39,380	
Net current assets			124,050
			313,250
Representing			
Creditors payable after 1 year			
Loans			40,000
Equity			
Owner's Capital			273,250
			313,250

3.

Dave's Business: Workings

Valuation of Closing Stock
Undamaged at cost:
(£115,490 – £3,000)
Damaged at net realisable value: (£1,800 – £400)
At lower of cost and net realisable value

Cost of Sales A/c			
O St	112,000	C St	113,890
Pur.	981,000	P&L	979,110
	1,093,000		1,093,000

Bad Debts Expense A/c			
T.B.	11,460	ii.	1,800
		P&L	9,660
	11,460		11,460

Provision for Bad Debts A/c			
ii.	1,800	T.B.	7,800
c/d	6,000		
	7,800		7,800
		b/d	6,000

Trade Debtors A/c			
T.B.	135,800		
iii.	150	c/d	135,950
	135,950		135,950
b/d	135,950		

Insurance A/c			
T.B.	13,000	iii.	150
		P&L	12,850
	13,000		13,000

Trade Creditors A/c			
c/d		T.B.	110,000
		iv.	60
	112,060	vii.	2,000
	112,060		112,060
		b/d	112,060

Machinery at Cost A/c			
T.B.	108,000	v.	6,000
		c/d	102,000
	108,000		108,000
b/d	102,000		

Provision for Depreciation of Machinery A/c			
Disp.	3,600	T.B.	72,500
c/d		Year 7	
	89,300	dep'n	20,400
	92,900		92,900
		b/d	89,300

Note
Accumulated depreciation of machine sold:
£6,000 × 20% × 3 years = £3,600
Year 7 depreciation of remaining machines:
102,000 × 20% = £20,400

Disposals A/c			
Cost	6,000		
		acc. dep.	3,600
P&L	100	Sales.	2,500
	6,100		6,100

Depreciation Expense A/c			
vi.	20,400		
vi.	4,000	P&L	24,400
	24,400		24,400

Sales A/c			
Disp.	2,500	T.B.	1,451,100
P&L	1,448,600		
	1,451,100		1,451,100

Prov'n for Dep'n of F'hold Prem. A/c			
c/d		T.B.	24,000
	28,000	vi.	4,000
	28,000		28,000
		b/d	28,000

Light & Heat A/c			
T.B.	18,240		
iv.	60	P&L	18,300
	18,300		18,300

Loan Interest A/c			
T.B.	0		
vii.	2,000	P&L	2,000
	2,000		2,000

Note
Interest £60,000 × 8% × 5 months = £2,000

Dave's Business: Answer

Dave's Business

Profit & Loss Account for year ended 31st May Year 7

	£	£
Sales		1,448,600
Less Cost of Sales		979,110
Gross Profit		469,490
Other Income		
Discount Received		1,400
		470,890
Less Overheads		
Wages	187,000	
Postage & Stationery	15,600	
Insurance	12,850	
Light & Heat	18,300	
Discount Allowed	1,200	
Bad Debts	9,660	
Depreciation	24,400	
Less Gain on Disposal	100	24,300
Loan Interest		2,000	270,910
Net Profit		199,980

Capital Movements	£
Net Profit for the period	199,980
Less Drawings during the period	30,650
Retained Profit for the period	169,330
Add Opening Capital	126,230
Closing Capital	295,560

Dave's Business

Balance Sheet as at 31st May Year 7

	Cost (£)	Acc. Dep. (£)	N.B.V. (£)
Fixed Assets			
Freehold Premises	200,000	28,000	172,000
Machinery	102,000	89,300	12,700
	302,000	117,300	184,700
Current Assets			
Stock		113,890	
Trade Debtors	135,950		
Less Provision for Bad Debts	6,000	129,950	
Cash & Bank		39,080	
		282,920	
Creditors payable within 1 year			
Trade Creditors		112,060	
Net current assets			170,860
			355,560

ABSORPTION COSTING

Manual

CONTENTS

TUTORIAL 1

PRODUCT COST

Introduction

All organisations, new, existing or expanding, will need information about their costs. This costing information will be used for:

- Planning and Decision Making – detailed cost information is required for making decisions and planning future operations; costing information is essential to the budgeting process
- Controlling – cost control is vital to the survival of an organisation
- Reporting – sufficient costing information must be available to enable the published financial statements of an organisation to be produced

The term "product cost" is usually associated with the manufacture of a tangible product, such as a compact disc. The same costing principles may, however, be applied to organisations which provide a service, such as British Rail, where the "product" will be a passenger mile. All organisations will need to know the cost of each unit they produce. These units may be products or services.

EXAMPLE

Organisation	Units of Production
Honda (UK)	motor cars
Shell UK	litres of petrol
British Rail	passenger miles
Little Chef	portions of food

A business will incur many costs, for example:

- materials
- labour
- rent
- insurance

- light and heat
- canteen
- maintenance
- selling and distribution
- depreciation of fixed assets

Normally, for a business to survive, it must recover all its costs by selling its products at a high enough price. The selling price must also be sufficient to provide enough profit to justify the resources employed by the business.

It is not sensible to wait until the end of the accounting period (when actual overheads are known) to calculate the cost of making a product. Estimates must be made of product cost in order to assist decision making. For example, when asked to quote a price for servicing a vehicle, a garage will need an immediate estimate of the costs associated with that job. Budgeted data will generally be used to calculate product cost. Budgeted data will not be as accurate as actual data. There is, therefore, a trade-off between accuracy of information and speed of its availability.

Types of Cost

The costs of a business fall into three main areas.

MATERIALS

Most of the materials cost of a manufacturer will be in the form of raw materials.

LABOUR

Labour costs will be incurred in the following areas.

- production workers
- other factory workers, e.g. supervisors and cleaners
- office staff
- sales personnel

OTHER EXPENSES

Costs which cannot be classed as either materials or labour. These expenses will include:

- royalty payments
- rent
- light and heat
- depreciation of fixed assets
- insurance

Direct and Indirect Costs

When calculating product cost, it is important to differentiate between direct costs and indirect costs.

DIRECT COSTS

Direct costs are easily measurable. They can easily be pinned on an individual product. The direct costs of a product will be:

- direct (raw) materials, the materials from which the product is actually made, e.g. the steel used to make cars – these costs can be ascertained from stock records
- direct (production) labour, i.e. the wages of the people who actually make the product, e.g. assemble cars – details of these costs will be supplied by the payroll
- other direct expenses, which are relatively rare but an example would be a royalty paid by a radio station when it plays a rock star's record

The total of all direct costs is known as "prime cost".

INDIRECT COSTS (OVERHEADS)

Indirect costs are those costs which cannot easily be pinned on individual products. Examples of indirect costs include:

- indirect materials, e.g. lubricants for machinery
- indirect labour ,e.g. supervisors' salaries, salesmen's commission and salaries, office wages, directors' fees
- other indirect expense, e.g. rent, light and heat, power, depreciation of fixed assets, audit fee, advertising

As indirect costs cannot easily be traced to individual units of production, they are termed "overheads". The process of assigning indirect costs to individual units of production is known as "overhead absorption".

Solving the problem of how to pin a share of overheads to each unit of production is the main objective of this manual.

Total Cost

The total costs incurred by an organisation may be summarised as follows:

Direct Materials	+	Indirect Materials	=	Total Materials Cost
+		+		+
Direct Labour	+	Indirect Labour	=	Total Labour Cost
+		+		+
Other		Other		Total
Direct Expense	+	Indirect Expense	=	Other Expense
PRIME COST	+	OVERHEAD	=	TOTAL COST

Unit Cost

The cost of each unit produced will be built up as follows:

	£
Direct Materials per unit	X
Direct Labour per unit	X
Other Direct Expense (if any) per unit	X̲
PRIME COST	X
Add **Share** of OVERHEADS *	X̲
TOTAL COST per unit	X̲

* The main focus of this manual is how to arrive at this **share** of overheads.

Tutorial Questions

1.1 Are the following statements true or false?
a.   Detailed costing information is only required for reporting purposes.
b.   Costing information for planning and decision making will require an element of forecasting.
c.   A costing system is not necessary in a service industry.
d.   The total of all direct costs is termed "prime cost".
e.   Another term for indirect costs is "overheads".

1.2 Identify the cost units for which product cost will be calculated in the following organisations:
a.   A car manufacturer.
b.   A furniture manufacturer.
c.   A paint factory.
d.   An accountant's practice.

1.3 Identify whether the following costs, relating to a chemical factory, will be classified as direct costs or indirect costs (overheads).

a.   Raw materials.
b.   Office manager's salary.
c.   Advertising.
d.   Production workers' wages.
e.   Electricity.
f.   Depreciation of factory buildings.
g.   Canteen costs.

1.4 A company manufactures caravans. The following information relates to the production of the company's De-luxe model.

	£
Raw Materials	5,000
Share of Overheads:	
Machining Department	2,000
Assembly Department	1,500
Finishing Department	900

The production workers are paid £6.00 per hour
The De-luxe model takes 500 hours to produce.

Required
Produce a detailed costing statement to calculate the product cost of the De-luxe model.

DEPARTMENTAL OVERHEADS

Organisational Structure

Most businesses produce a diverse range of products. For management purposes, most organisations will be divided into a number of departments. Some of these departments will be involved in actual production, e.g. machining, assembly, finishing departments. Other departments will be service departments, e.g. stores, maintenance, canteen, administration departments. Management will need to know the total cost of running each department.

Departmental Overheads

It is easy to calculate the TOTAL amount spent on overheads, such as rent and electricity, for a business as a whole. However, to calculate the cost of running each department, the total overheads must be split between departments.

Some overheads may easily be ALLOCATED to a specific department, e.g. the wages of maintenance staff will be charged in total to the maintenance department.

Many overheads must be shared between two or more departments, e.g. rent and rates for the business as a whole will be APPORTIONED between all departments.

Overhead Analysis Schedule

An overhead analysis schedule will be used to calculate total departmental overhead.

Example

The following information relates to a company which manufactures furniture.

The factory has three production departments: a machining department, an assembly department and a finishing department. There are also two service departments: the stores and the canteen. The following overheads relate to the business as a whole.

	£
Indirect Labour	65,981
Food	62,019
Rent	250,000
Total	378,000

Overhead analysis schedule

	Service Departments		Production Departments			
	Canteen (£)	Stores (£)	Machining (£)	Assembly (£)	Finishing (£)	Total (£)
Indirect Labour						65,981
Food						62,019
Rent						250,000
Total						378,000

It will be easy to identify the departments to which certain overheads should be charged. The term for this is "overhead allocation". Other overheads will need to be shared between several departments. The term for this is "overhead apportionment".

INDIRECT LABOUR £65,981

According to the wages clerk, the indirect labour cost of each department is:

	£
Canteen	25,000
Stores	15,531
Machining Department	8,100
Assembly Department	12,000
Finishing Department	5,350
Total	65,981

Clearly, the indirect labour cost can be **allocated** to each department.

Overhead analysis schedule

	Service Departments		Production Departments			
	Canteen (£)	Stores (£)	Machining (£)	Assembly (£)	Finishing (£)	Total (£)
Indirect Labour	25,000	15,531	8,100	12,000	5,350	65,981
Food						62,019
Rent						250,000
Total						378,000

FOOD £62,019

The cost of the food obviously should be allocated to the canteen.

Overhead analysis schedule

	Service Departments		Production Departments			
	Canteen (£)	Stores (£)	Machining (£)	Assembly (£)	Finishing (£)	Total (£)
Indirect Labour	25,000	15,531	8,100	12,000	5,350	65,981
Food	62,019					62,019
Rent						250,000
Total						378,000

RENT £250,000

A basis must be chosen to **apportion** the rent to the departments in a fair manner. The most appropriate basis is the area occupied by each department. According to the site plan the area occupied by each department is as follows:

	Sq. Metres
Canteen	200
Stores	300
Machining Department	1,000
Assembly Department	400
Finishing Department	600
Total	2,500

The total rent is £250,000, the total floor area is 2,500 sq. metres, therefore the rent cost per sq. metre is:

$$\frac{\text{Overhead}}{\text{Basis}} = \frac{£250,000}{2,500\text{sq.m.}} = £100 \text{ per sq. metre}$$

The rent is therefore apportioned as follows:

		£
Canteen	(200 sq. m. × £100)	20,000
Stores	(300 sq. m. × £100)	30,000
Machining Dept	(1,000 sq. m. × £100)	100,000
Assembly Dept	(400 sq. m. × £100)	40,000
Finishing Dept	(600 sq. m. × £100)	60,000
Total		250,000

The overhead analysis schedule can now be completed.

Overhead analysis schedule

	Service Departments		Production Departments			
	Canteen (£)	Stores (£)	Machining (£)	Assembly (£)	Finishing (£)	Total (£)
Indirect Labour	25,000	15,531	8,100	12,000	5,350	65,981
Food	62,019					62,019
Rent	20,000	30,000	100,000	40,000	60,000	250,000
Total	107,019	45,531	108,100	52,000	65,350	378,000

Notes

- After the allocation and apportionment process all the overheads will have been assigned to departments.
- Normally there will be many overheads to be apportioned and a lot of information from which to choose the most appropriate base. E.g. depreciation of machinery may be apportioned according to the value of the machinery; power may be apportioned according to machine utilisation. There may well be two bases which are equally appropriate for the apportionment of an overhead. In such cases, one base will be selected and applied consistently for that overhead. The technique of overhead absorption is based, to some extent, on judgements.
- The overhead analysis schedule calculating departmental cost is only an intermediate stage in the process of pinning overheads on products. It does, however, produce information useful, to management, in its own right. E.g., in the above example, it has been calculated that the cost of running the canteen is £107,019. Management may decide that this cost is excessive and may consider various alternatives: close the canteen; charge higher prices; contract out the catering.

Tutorial Questions

2.1 Nelsons Plc is a boat builder. Each custom built boat passes through the three production departments: machining, assembly and finishing. In addition, the boat yard has two service departments: canteen and stores. The following information has been extracted from the budget of the company for the next financial year.

	Canteen	Stores	Mach	Assemb.	Finish.	Total
No. of Employees	0	5	28	28	35	96
Floor Space (sq. metres)	800	1,000	3,000	2,900	4,100	11,800
Direct Materials Issues (kgs)	0	0	18,300	16,200	27,300	61,800
Cubic Space (cubic metres)	8,000	12,000	34,000	33,000	56,000	143,000
Direct Labour Hrs			26,520	66,750	92,310	185,580
Machine Hrs			43,910	61,770	87,620	193,300

Required

Complete the following overhead analysis schedule and calculate the budgeted overhead cost of each department.

	Canteen (£)	Stores (£)	Mach. (£)	Assemb. (£)	Finish. (£)	Total (£)
Indirect Labour	0	4,350	24,380	24,190	29,760	
Indirect Material	130	410	32,870	25,650	35,240	
Space Heating						299,130
Rent & Rates						11,190
Motive Power						35,380
Canteen Contract	8,110	0	0	0	0	
Departmental Total						

2.2 Scrappit & Co. Ltd repair motor vehicles. The company has three workshops: the paint shop, the body shop and the mechanical department. These production departments are supported by two service departments: office services and stores. The following information has been extracted from the budget of the company for the next financial year.

	Office Services	Stores	Paint Shop	Body Shop	Mechanical Dept	Total
No. of Employees	2	3	10	14	25	54
Floor Space (sq. metres)	50	120	300	900	1,400	2,770
Direct Materials Issues (kgs)	0	0	2,300	6,200	7,300	15,800
Office Usage (%)	0	10	25	25	40	100
Direct Labour Hrs			18,520	26,200	45,380	90,100
Machine Hrs			3,910	61,770	17,620	83,300

Budgeted Overheads

	Office Services (£)	Stores (£)	Paint Shop (£)	Body Shop (£)	Mechanical Dept (£)	Total (£)
Indirect Labour	30,000	40,531	2,100	12,400	15,350	100,381
Stationery & Postage						5,000
Rent & Rates						45,260
Motive Power						29,750

Required

Calculate the budgeted overhead cost of each department.

2.3 Viper & Co. are a firm of accountants. The firm is structured into three main departments: audit, taxation and general practice. These departments are supported by two service departments: the secretariat and technical support services. The following information has been extracted from the budget of the firm for the next financial year.

	Sec.	Tech. Supp.	Audit	Tax.	General Practice	Total
No. of employees	10	5	60	4	35	114
Floor Space (sq. metres)	100	30	70	45	100	345
Technical Support Usage (%)	0	0	45	35	20	100
Secretariat Usage (%)	0	10	35	15	40	100
Direct Labour Hrs			94,520	6,200	55,125	155,845

Budgeted Overheads

	Sec. (£)	Tech. Supp. (£)	Audit (£)	Tax. (£)	General Practice (£)	Total (£)
Secretaries Salaries						100,000
Technical Support Salaries						120,000
Printing, Postage & Tel.	17,000	8,000	65,000	7,000	33,000	130,000
Rent & Rates						42,780
Personnel Services						30,000

Required

Calculate the budgeted overhead cost of each department.

RE-APPORTIONMENT OF SERVICE DEPARTMENT OVERHEADS

Introduction

Allocation and apportionment methods were used in Tutorial 2 to calculate total departmental overheads. At this stage all the overheads will have been assigned to departments. To calculate product cost, the departmental overheads must be pinned on (charged to) individual units of production. The service departments are not directly engaged in the production process, but the cost of making each unit must take into account the costs of these service departments. In order that the products can carry their full share of all the overheads incurred by the business, the overhead burden must be consolidated into the production departments. The normal way to achieve this is to re-apportion the service department costs to the production departments.

Re-apportionment of Service Department Overheads

A suitable basis must be chosen to re-apportion service department overheads to production departments, in proportion to the benefit received.

Example

Using the example from Tutorial 2, the following departmental overheads have been calculated.

Overhead Analysis

	Service Departments		Production Departments			
	Canteen (£)	Stores (£)	Machining (£)	Assembly (£)	Finishing (£)	Total (£)
Indirect Labour	25,000	15,531	8,100	12,000	5,350	65,981
Food	62,019					62,019
Rent	20,000	30,000	100,000	40,000	60,000	250,000
Sub Total	107,019	45,531	108,100	52,000	65,350	378,000

A suitable basis must be chosen to re-apportion the costs of the canteen and stores departments. The following information is available:

	Stores	Machining	Assembly	Finishing	Total
No. of Workers	3	70	100	80	253
Issues from Stores (kgs)	—	800	300	100	1,200

RE-APPORTIONMENT OF CANTEEN COSTS £107,019

From the information available, the most sensible basis to choose is the number of workers in each of the other departments. The total canteen cost is £107,019.

The total number of workers in the other departments is 253. The canteen costs per worker is therefore:

$$\text{Overhead (Canteen costs)} = \frac{£107,019}{253} = £423 \text{ per worker}$$
$$\text{Basis (workers)}$$

The canteen costs are, therefore, re-apportioned as follows:

		£
Stores	(3 workers × £423)	1,269
Machining Dept	(70 workers × £423)	29,610
Assembly Dept	(100 workers × £423)	42,300
Finishing Dept	(80 workers × £423)	33,840
		107,019

The overhead analysis table is now as follows:

Overhead Analysis

	Service Departments		Production Departments			
	Canteen (£)	Stores (£)	Machining (£)	Assembly (£)	Finishing (£)	Total (£)
Indirect Labour	25,000	15,531	8,100	12,000	5,350	65,981
Food	62,019					62,019
Rent	20,000	30,000	100,000	40,000	60,000	250,000
Sub Total	107,019	45,531	108,100	52,000	65,350	378,000
Canteen Costs	(107,019)	1,269	29,610	42,300	33,840	
		46,800				

RE-APPORTIONMENT OF STORES DEPARTMENT COSTS £46,800

After the canteen costs have been re-apportioned, the stores department overheads must be re-apportioned. The stores department overheads now include £1,269 of the canteen costs.

A suitable basis for re-apportioning the stores costs is the number of kilos of materials issued to each of the production departments. The total stores overhead is £46,800. The total kilos of materials issued is 1,200. The stores cost per kilo is therefore:

$$\frac{\text{Overhead (stores costs)}}{\text{Basis (issues – kilos)}} = \frac{£46,800}{1,200} = £39 \text{ per kilo}$$

The stores costs will be re-apportioned to the production departments as follows:

		£
Machining Dept	(800 kilos × £39)	31,200
Assembly Dept	(300 kilos × £39)	11,700
Finishing Dept	(100 kilos × £39)	3,900
		46,800

The overhead analysis table is now as follows:

Overhead Analysis

	Service Departments		Production Departments			
	Canteen (£)	Stores (£)	Machining (£)	Assembly (£)	Finishing (£)	Total (£)
Indirect Labour	25,000	15,531	8,100	12,000	5,350	65,981
Food	62,019					62,019
Rent	20,000	30,000	100,000	40,000	60,000	250,000
Sub Total	107,019	45,531	108,100	52,000	65,350	378,000
Canteen Costs	(107,019)	1,269	29,610	42,300	33,840	
Stores Costs		(46,800)	31,200	11,700	3,900	
Overhead Burden			168,910	106,000	103,090	378,000

After the re-apportionment process all the overheads will have been assigned to **production** departments only.

Problems in Assigning Overheads

It has already been stressed, in Tutorial 2, that there may be several bases which are equally appropriate for the apportionment of an overhead. In such cases, one base will be selected and applied consistently for that overhead. Similarly, this may apply to the re-apportionment of service department overheads.

Reciprocal services pose a further problem. This is where two or more non-production departments provide services for each other, as well as for production departments.

Example

A company has several production departments and two service departments, namely a canteen and a maintenance department. The maintenance department staff use the canteen and the canteen equipment is serviced by the maintenance department. Ideally, the canteen overheads to be re-apportioned should include a share of maintenance department overheads. Similarly, the maintenance department overheads to be re-apportioned, should include a share of the canteen overheads.

There are mathematical techniques which can be used to solve this problem. These techniques can be found in most costing text books. It must be stressed, however, that the whole process of assigning overheads to departments, and ultimately to individual products, is based on arbitrary judgements. There may, therefore, be little point in making lengthy calculations based on these arbitrary figures. In many cases, the end result will not be materially different, whether a simple or a complex method of re-apportioning service department overheads is used. For this reason, the reciprocal elements of service departmental overheads are often ignored.

Tutorial Questions

3.1 The following departmental overheads have been calculated for Nelsons Plc, a boat builder.

	Service Departments		Production Departments			
	Canteen (£)	Stores (£)	Mach. (£)	Assemb. (£)	Finish. (£)	Total (£)
Indirect Labour	0	4,350	24,380	24,190	29,760	82,680
Indirect Material	139	410	32,870	25,650	35,240	94,300
Space Heating	16,734	25,102	71,122	69,030	117,142	299,130
Rent & Rates	759	948	2,845	2,750	3,888	11,190
Motive Power	0	0	8,037	11,306	16,037	35,380
Canteen Contract	8,100	0	0	0	0	8,100
Departmental Total	25,733	30,810	139,254	132,926	202,067	530,790

Required
Using the following information, re-apportion the service department overheads and calculate the overhead burden of each of the production departments, for absorption purposes.

Budget Data	Canteen	Stores	Machining	Assembly	Finishing	Total
No. of Employees	0	5	28	28	35	96
Floor Space (sq. metres)	800	1,000	3,000	2,900	4,100	11,800
Direct Materials Issues (kgs)	0	0	18,300	16,200	27,300	61,800
Cubic Space (cubic metres)	8,000	12,000	34,000	33,000	56,000	143,000
Direct Labour Hrs			26,520	66,750	92,310	185,580
Machine Hrs			43,910	61,770	87,620	193,300

3.2 Scrappit & Co. Ltd repair motor vehicles. The following budgeted overheads have been calculated for each department.

	£
Service Departments	
Office Services	35,817
Stores	42,492
Production Departments	
Paint Shop	8,398
Body Shop	49,166
Mechanical Department	44,518

The following information is also available:

	Office Services	Stores	Paint Shop	Body Shop	Mechanic Dept	Total
No. of Employees	2	3	10	14	25	54
Floor Space (sq. metres)	50	120	300	900	1,400	2,770
Direct Materials Issues (kgs)	0	0	2,300	6,200	7,300	15,800
Office Usage (%)	0	10	25	25	40	100
Direct Labour Hrs			18,520	26,200	45,380	90,100
Machine Hrs			3,910	61,770	17,620	83,300

Required
Re-apportion the office services department, then the stores department, and calculate the overhead burden of each of the production departments, for absorption purposes.

3.3 Viper & Co. are accountants. The following budgeted overheads have been calculated for each department.

	£
Audit Department	89,469
Taxation Department	13,633
General Practice Department	54,610
Service Departments	
Secretariat	132,032
Technical Support Services	133,036

The following information is also available:

	Sec.	Tech. Supp.	Audit	Tax.	General Practice	Total
No. of Employees	10	5	60	4	35	114
Floor Space (sq. metres)	100	30	70	45	100	345
Technical Support Usage (%)	0	0	45	35	20	100
Secretariat Usage (%)	0	10	35	15	40	100
Direct Labour Hours			94,520	6,200	55,125	155,845

Required

Re-apportion the service departments and calculate the overhead burden of the audit, taxation and general practice departments, for absorption purposes.

ABSORBING OVERHEADS INTO PRODUCT COST

Introduction

The aim of overhead absorption is to recover overheads by charging them to individual products. In the previous tutorials, overheads were assigned to departments. After the re-apportionment process all the overheads will have been assigned to production departments.

The next step is to share the departmental overheads between the products made in each production department. The departmental overheads will be charged to units of production on the basis of productive capacity. For example, if a product utilises 10% of the productive capacity of the machining department, it will be charged with 10% of the machining department's overheads.

Productive Capacity

Productive capacity is normally defined as the time available to make a firm's products. A firm does not have unlimited productive capacity. In order to calculate the cost of making a product, it is, therefore, important to recognise the amount of productive capacity used up in making that product.

The most commonly used measures of productive capacity are direct labour hours and machine hours. The measure selected for a department will depend upon whether the department is labour intensive or machine intensive.

Overhead Absorption Rates (OARs)

In Tutorial 1, it was explained that, in principle, overheads (indirect costs) cannot be charged to products in the same way as direct costs, such as raw materials. However, it is possible to determine how much productive capacity (machine hours or direct labour hours) is utilised in making a product, if it is known how many hours in total are available for production, then productive capacity is an excellent basis for absorbing overheads.

The normal method is to calculate the overhead cost per hour of productive capacity. This is illustrated by the following simple example.

EXAMPLE

A department's total overhead is £5,000 and its productive capacity is 500 machine hours. The overhead absorption rate (OAR) for that department will be calculated as follows:

$$\frac{£5,000}{500 \text{ machine hours}} = £10 \text{ per machine hour}$$

Therefore, if a product uses 2 machine hours in that department, it will be charged with (absorb) £20 of that department's overheads (2 machine hours × OAR per machine hour of £10).

In the calculation of product cost, the overheads of £20 will be added to the product's direct costs, such as raw materials and direct labour costs:

	£
Direct Materials	X
Direct Labour	X
Other Direct Expense	X
PRIME COST	X
Add Share of OVERHEADS	20
TOTAL COST	X

Budgeted Overhead Absorption Rates

As it is not sensible to wait until the end of the accounting period to calculate product cost, overhead absorption rates will be calculated using budgeted data, i.e. budgeted overheads and budgeted productive capacity.

Departmental Overhead Absorption Rates

A separate overhead absorption rate must be calculated for each production department. Using the example from Tutorial 3, the total overheads have been assigned to the production departments as follows:

Overhead Analysis

	Service Departments		Production Departments			
	Canteen (£)	Stores (£)	Machining (£)	Assembly (£)	Finishing (£)	Total (£)
Indirect Labour	25,000	15,531	8,100	12,000	5,350	65,981
Food	62,019					62,019
Rent	20,000	30,000	100,000	40,000	60,000	250,000
Sub Total	107,019	45,531	108,100	52,000	65,350	378,000
Canteen Costs	(107,019)	1,269	29,610	42,300	33,840	
Stores Costs		(46,800)	31,200	11,700	3,900	
Overhead Burden			168,910	106,000	103,090	378,000

In order to calculate OARs, a business will need to decide which measure of productive capacity to use for each production department. In this example the following will be assumed.

MACHINING DEPARTMENT

A large amount of the overheads of this department relate to machine usage. As this department is machine intensive, machine hours will be used to calculate the overhead absorption rate.

It is ascertained that the total budgeted machine hours in the machining department are 12,500.

ASSEMBLY DEPARTMENT AND FINISHING DEPARTMENT

These departments are labour intensive, therefore direct labour hours will be used to calculate their overhead absorption rates.

It is ascertained that the total budgeted direct labour hours are as follows:

Assembly Department   20,000 direct labour hours
Finishing Department   16,000 direct labour hours

Calculation of Budgeted Overhead Absorption Rates

	Production Departments		
	Machining	Assembly	Finishing
Overhead Burden (a)	£168,910	£106,000	£103,090
Production Hours (b)	12,500	20,000	16,000
Type of Hours (c)	Machine	Direct Labour	Direct Labour
Budgeted Overhead Absorption Rate (OAR) (a/b)	£13.51	£5.30	£6.44

Use of Budgeted Overhead Absorption Rates

The budgeted overhead absorption rates calculated for each department are used to calculate the overhead cost of each unit produced. For instance, if a dining room table made in the furniture factory uses:

    20 machine hours in the machining department
    5 direct labour hours in the assembly department
    7 direct labour hours in the finishing department

the overhead cost of the table will be:

		£
Machining Department Overheads	20 × £13.51	270.20
Assembly Department Overheads	5 × £ 5.30	26.50
Finishing Department Overheads	7 × £ 6.44	45.08
Total Overhead Charged to Unit		341.78

NOTE

The total overhead to be charged to the dining room table is £341.78. This figure represents indirect costs only. To calculate the total cost of the table, the overheads must be added to prime cost (direct costs).

Alternative Methods of Absorbing Departmental Overheads

Alternative methods of calculating overhead absorption rates may be used, although generally overheads are pinned to products on the basis of the time taken to produce them, i.e. the proportion of productive capacity used.

Example

A department's total overhead is £5,000. Its productive capacity is 500 machine hours. The number of units produced is 200. And the total direct labour cost incurred in the department is £2,500. The alternative overhead absorption rates (OARs) for that department may be calculated as follows.

MACHINE HOUR RATE METHOD

$$\frac{£5,000}{500 \text{ machine hours}} = £10 \text{ per machine hour}$$

Therefore, if a product uses 2 machine hours in that department it will be charged with (absorb) £20 of that department's overheads (2 machine hours × OAR per machine hour of £10).

UNITS OF PRODUCTION METHOD

$$\frac{£5,000}{200 \text{ units}} = £25 \text{ per unit}$$

Therefore each unit will be charged with £25 for overheads. This method is only appropriate where all the units produced are identical.

DIRECT LABOUR COST METHOD

$$\frac{£5,000}{£2,500} = 200\% \text{ of direct labour cost of the product}$$

Therefore, if the direct labour cost of a product is £12, that product will be charged with overheads of £24 (200% × £12).

Note

Different methods of calculating overhead absorption rates will obviously result in different product costs. There is a need, therefore, to exercise caution when using absorption costing.

Tutorial Questions

4.1 Mammoth Appliances make all sorts of domestic appliances. The firm operates for 47 weeks of the year. There are three production departments: Metal cutting, enamelling, and final assembly. The metal cutting department is machine intensive and has 10 machines, each working 35 hours per week. The enamelling department employs

14 people, who hand spray the products. They each work 38 hours per week. There are 28 people employed in the final assembly department and they each work a 40 hour week.

Required

a.   Identify the most appropriate measure of productive capacity for each department.
b.   Calculate the productive capacity of each department for the year.

4.2   Using the answer to question 4.1, calculate the budgeted overhead absorption rate for each department, assuming the following overheads have been calculated for each department.

	£
Metal Cutting	340,000
Enamelling	210,000
Final Assembly	187,000
Total Overheads	737,000

4.3   Using the answer to question 4.2, calculate the overheads to be charged to a batch of fridges which take 40 hours of production time in the metal cutting department, 12 hours in the enamelling department, and 55 hours to assemble.

4.4   The following information has been extracted from the budget of Nelsons Plc, a

	Machining	Assembly	Finishing	Total
Overhead Burden (after re-apportionment of service departments)	£156,279	£148,860	£225,651	£530,790
Direct Labour Hours	26,520	66,750	92,310	185,580
Machine Hours	43,910	61,770	87,620	193,300

boat builder.

Required

Calculate the budgeted overhead absorption rate for each department. Assume the machining department to be machine intensive and the assembly and finishing departments to be labour intensive.

4.5   The following information has been extracted from the budget of Scrappit & Co. Ltd, motor vehicle repairers.

	Paint Shop	Body Shop	Mechanical Dept	Total
Overhead Burden (after reapportionment of service departments)	£24,059	£76,200	£80,132	£180,391
Direct Labour Hours	18,520	26,200	45,380	90,100
Machine Hours	3,910	61,770	17,620	83,300

Required

Calculate the budgeted overhead absorption rate for each department. Assume the body shop to be machine intensive and the other two departments to be labour intensive.

4.6   The following information has been extracted from the budget of Viper & Co., accountants.

	Audit	Taxation	General Practice	Total
Overhead Burden (after reapportionment of service departments)	£201,487	£84,622	£136,671	£422,780
Direct Labour Hours	94,520	6,200	55,125	155,845

Required

Calculate the budgeted overhead absorption rate for each department.

CALCULATION OF PRODUCT COST

Introduction

In Tutorial 4, departmental overhead absorption rates were calculated. These rates were calculated by dividing total overheads for a department by a measure of total productive capacity for that department. To recover the overheads, they must be charged to individual products. This is achieved by multiplying the OAR by the productive capacity utilised by the individual product.

Overheads are only part of the cost of a product. To find the total cost of a product, direct materials, direct labour and overheads must be added together. In other words, indirect costs (overheads) must be added to direct costs (prime cost).

Product Cost

This can be illustrated by the simple example of a garage business to which the following details relate.

Mechanics' wage rate: £7 per hour
Measure of productive capacity for absorbing overheads: direct labour hours
Overhead absorption rate (OAR): £35 per direct labour hour

The garage wishes to calculate the cost of carrying out a repair of a vehicle where direct materials cost £290 and which takes 15 direct labour hours.

Using absorption costing, the cost of the job is calculated as follows:

	£
Direct Materials	290
Direct Labour (15 hours × £7 per hour)	105
PRIME COST	395
Overhead Cost (15 hours × £35 OAR)	525
TOTAL COST OF REPAIR JOB	920

Note

In labour intensive departments, direct labour hours will be used for two separate purposes:

- to calculate how much the workers are to be paid (direct labour cost).
- to calculate the overhead absorption rates in order to pin overheads on products, because the direct labour hours also represent productive capacity.

Applications of Absorption Costing

Absorption costing is used widely by manufacturing and service industries. Various costing systems using absorption costing principles have evolved to cater for the specific needs of industry and commerce. One of these costing systems is job costing.

Job Costing

The essence of job costing is that an individual product, specific to customer requirements, is the focus of the costing system.

Job costing is used by service engineers (such as television repair firms), plumbers, painters and decorators and by firms of accountants and solicitors.

The key characteristics of job costing are:

- separately identifiable units
- individual units specific to customer requirements
- of short duration (generally less than one year)

All the examples of absorption costing used in this manual and the accompanying software relate to job costing. Other applications of absorption costing are explained at the end of this Tutorial.

Using the example of the furniture factory used in previous tutorials, the job cost of a dining room table which is started in the machining department, assembled in the assembly department and finished in the finishing department, will be calculated.

	Production Departments		
	Machining	Assembly	Finishing
Direct Labour Hrs	25	5	7
Machine Hours	20	2	4
Direct Labour Rate per hour	£4	£5	£5
Budgeted OAR	£13.51	£5.30	£6.44
OAR Basis	Machine Hrs	Direct Labour Hrs	Direct Labour Hrs

Job Cost of One Dining Room Table

	Production Departments			
	Machining (£)	Assembly (£)	Finishing (£)	Total (£)
Direct Material Cost	500.00	20.00	80.00	600.00
Direct Labour Cost (direct lab. hrs × direct lab. rate)	100.00	25.00	35.00	160.00
Overhead cost (OAR × recovery hours)	270.20	26.50	45.08	341.78
TOTAL JOB COST	870.20	71.50	160.08	1,101.78

Other Applications of Absorption Costing

Absorption costing is a method of determining product cost by adding a share of overheads to prime cost. Absorption costing is used widely by manufacturing and service industries. The examples used in this manual, and the accompanying software, relate to job costing. The same principles apply to other costing systems which have evolved to cater for the specific needs of industry and commerce.

Contract Costing

Many of the characteristics of contract costing are similar to those of job costing but contract costing is used where a job is of a relatively large cost and of a long duration (usually more than one year). It is generally used by the construction industry, e.g. ship building and motorway construction.

Contract costing has the following additional characteristics:

- site based – this, together with the size of the cost unit will enable many costs normally classified as overheads to be treated as direct costs, e.g. supervision salaries
- progress payments
- profit recognition before the completion of a contract

Process Costing

Process costing is widely used in industries involved in the production of chemicals and food. The key characteristics of process costing are:

- identical units of production
- costs of production are averaged over the number of units produced
- joint products and by-products
- process losses

Standard Costing

Standard costing is a system used in complex manufacturing plants to control the cost of production of mass produced items of relatively high value, e.g. motor cars.

Note

Although the above costing systems have been developed for individual industries, the costing method is basically the same, i.e. a share of overheads is added to prime cost.

Tutorial Questions

5.1   The following information relates to the cost of a yacht to be built by Nelsons Plc.

	Production Departments		
	Machining	Assembly	Finishing
Direct Labour Hrs	500	1,200	1,000
Machine Hours	800	690	560
Direct Labour Rate per hour	£5	£6	£4
Budgeted OAR	£3.56	£2.23	£2.44
OAR Basis	Machine Hrs	Direct Labour Hrs	Direct Labour Hrs

Job Cost of Yacht

	Machining (£)	Assembly (£)	Finishing (£)	Total (£)
Direct Material Cost	50,000	20,000	8,000	78,000
Direct Labour Cost				
Overhead Cost				
TOTAL JOB COST				

Required

Complete the above job cost card and calculate the total job cost of the yacht.

5.2 The following information relates to Scrappit & Co. Ltd, motor vehicle repairers.

	Production Departments		
	Paint Shop	Body Shop	Mechanical Department
Direct Labour Rate per hour	£4.50	£6.00	£7.50
Budgeted OAR	£1.30	£1.23	£1.77
OAR Basis	Direct Labour Hrs	Machine Hrs	Direct Labour Hrs

Required

a.   Calculate the job cost of servicing a vehicle in the mechanical department where direct materials used cost £25.00 and it takes a mechanic 4 hours to complete the job.

b.   Calculate the job cost of repairing accident damage to a vehicle to which the following details relate.

	£
Direct Materials	
Paint Shop	80
Body Shop	500
Mechanical Department	120

Hours Taken to Complete Job	*Direct Labour Hours*	*Machine Hours*
Paint Shop	4	2
Body Shop	10	15
Mechanical Department	3	1

5.3   The following information relates to Viper & Co. a firm of accountants.
Required
a.   Calculate the cost of preparing the accounts of a small business which takes 10 staff
hours in the general practice department.
b.   Calculate the cost of providing audit services and tax advice to a major client to
which the following details relate.

Hours Taken to Complete Job	*Direct Labour Hours*
Audit Department	6,500
Taxation Department	50

	£
Other Direct Costs (Audit Dept)	
Travel	2,000
Hotel Costs	5,000

CONTROL OF OVERHEADS

Budgeted Data

Overhead absorption rates are usually based on:

- budgeted overheads
- budgeted productive capacity based on normal levels of activity

The use of budgeted data enables the overhead absorption rates to be predetermined, i.e. calculated in advance.

It is essential that the cost of products can be calculated **during** an accounting period for the following reasons:

- periodic profit reporting
- stock valuations
- setting selling prices

It is recognised that budgeted data will not be as accurate as actual data. But timely information, provided it is approximately correct, will be of more use than information which is 100% accurate but is not available when required. There is, therefore, a trade-off between accuracy of information and the speed of its availability.

Actual Data

There are many variables which result in a budget not being 100% accurate. Budgets are based on estimates, so it is probable that:

- actual overheads incurred will be different from budgeted overheads
- actual productive capacity used will be different from budgeted activity

For example, if machines require less maintenance than anticipated, more machine hours will actually be available than budgeted hours; if the workforce is depleted due to illness, fewer labour hours will be worked than originally included in the budget; some products may be made faster or slower than anticipated.

Under and Over Recovery of Overheads

Management needs to know whether overheads actually incurred are being recovered, i.e. charged to units produced. Therefore, a key element in the control of overheads is to compare the overheads actually incurred with the overheads actually recovered. The overheads actually incurred will be recorded in the financial accounting system of the business. The overheads actually recovered will be:

budgeted OAR × actual hours (recovery hours)

The following example relates to the furniture factory introduced in previous tutorials.

	Departments			
	Machining	Assembly	Finishing	Total
Actual Direct Labour hrs	44,500	68,000	52,000	
Actual Machine Hrs	65,000	4,500	1,500	
Actual Overhead Incurred (a)				£1,581,900

	Departments			
	Machining	Assembly	Finishing	Total
Budgeted OAR (b)	£13.51	£5.30	£6.44	
OAR Basis (c)	Machine Hrs	Direct Labour Hrs	Direct Labour Hrs	
Recovery Hours (**actual** hours) (d)	65,000	68,000	52,000	
Overhead Recovered (e = b × d)	£878,150	£360,400	£334,880	£1,573,430

	Departments			
	Machining	Assembly	Finishing	Total
(Under)/Over Recovery (e minus a)				(£8,470)

Profit Implications of Under/Over Recovery of Overheads

Product costs, and sometimes selling prices, will be calculated using overhead absorption rates based on **budgeted** data. The calculation of overall profit, however, must be based on **actual** costs, which will not be known until the end of the accounting period.

The under or over recovery of overheads is thus a factor in explaining profit fluctuations. For instance, if overheads are under recovered by £8,470, this means that £8,470 more has been spent on overheads than is justified by production output. This under recovery, therefore, will have the effect of reducing profit. By contrast, an over recovery of overheads will have a profit increasing effect.

For control purposes, the amount of under/over recovered overhead may be analysed in greater detail. Further analysis is dealt with in most costing textbooks. Detailed analysis is not covered in this manual or the accompanying software.

Tutorial Questions

6.1 When reviewing their performance for the financial year which has just finished, Nelsons Plc, the boat builders, ascertain the following.

	Departments			
	Machining	Assembly	Finishing	Total
Actual Direct Labour Hrs	84,600	198,000	142,000	
Actual Machine Hrs	105,000	8,500	7,500	
Actual Overhead Incurred				£1,267,805

Overhead Recovery Table

	Departments			
	Machining	Assembly	Finishing	Total
Budgeted OAR	£3.56	£2.23	£2.44	
OAR Basis	Machine Hrs	Direct Labour Hrs	Direct Labour Hrs	
Recovery Hours				
Overhead Recovered				

Required
a. Complete the above overhead recovery table.
b. Calculate the total amount of overheads under or over recovered for the year.
c. State whether your answer to question b will have a profit increasing or profit decreasing effect.

6.2 When reviewing their performance for the financial year which has just finished, Scrappit & Co. Ltd, motor vehicle repairers, ascertain the following.

	Departments			
	Paint Shop	Body Shop	Mechanical Dept	Total
Actual Direct Labour Hrs	19,120	25,000	45,180	
Actual Machine Hrs	3,900	61,750	17,580	
Actual Overhead Incurred				£203,200

The company's budgeted overhead absorption rates are as follows:

Paint Shop	£1.30 per direct labour hour
Body Shop	£1.23 per machine hour
Mechanical Dept	£1.77 per direct labour hour

Required
Calculate the total amount of overheads under or over recovered for the year.

6.3   When reviewing their performance for the financial year which has just finished, Viper & Co., accountants, ascertain the following.

	Departments			
	Audit	Taxation	General Practice	Total
Actual Direct Labour Hrs	95,100	5,900	58,200	
Actual Overhead Incurred				£425,950

The company's budgeted overhead absorption rates are as follows:

Audit Department	£2.13 per direct labour hour
Taxation Department	£13.65 per direct labour hour
General Practice Department	£2.48 per direct labour hour

Required
Calculate the total amount of overheads under or over recovered for the year.

FLOW-CHART OF TRADITIONAL ABSORPTION COSTING

This manual uses the traditional method of absorption costing, based on departmental overhead absorption rates. The following flow-chart illustrates the build up of product cost using traditional absorption costing.

Traditional Absorption Costing

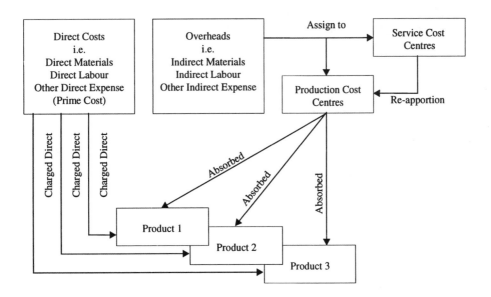

Note

Overheads are absorbed into product cost according to the % of productive capacity used in the product, e.g. direct labour hours or machine hours.

THE CALCULATION OF PRODUCT COST FOR DIFFERENT PURPOSES

Product cost can be calculated in different ways for a variety of purposes. The prime cost of a product will normally be the same regardless of the costing method used. The type of overhead to be included in product cost will depend upon the purpose for which the cost of the product is being calculated.

Production Cost for Stock Valuation for Reporting Purposes

Accounting Standards require that the product cost to be used in the valuation of stocks and work in progress, for inclusion in published financial statements, should be production cost.

	£
Prime Cost	X
Add Share of Variable and Fixed Production Overheads	X
Production Cost	X

In order to calculate the overhead absorption rates for the purpose of determining this share of overheads **production** overheads only would be included in the overhead analysis schedule. Distribution costs and administrative expenses would be excluded.

Total Product Cost for Decision Making

Total product cost may be used in some circumstances in decision making such as setting selling prices.

	£
Prime Cost	X
Add Share of all Variable and Fixed Overheads	X
Total Product Cost	X

In order to calculate the overhead absorption rates for the purpose of determining this share of **all** overheads would be included in the overhead analysis schedule, i.e. production, distribution and administrative overheads.

Note

Decision making frequently involves the evaluation of operating at different levels of activity. Product cost, calculated using absorption costing techniques, will include fixed costs. This cost will be distorted if activity levels fluctuate.

EXAMPLE

A company rents a factory for £200,000 per annum. The maximum number of units which could be produced in the factory is 120,000 per annum. Due to market constraints, normal output is 100,000 identical units per annum. Using absorption costing techniques, the rent per unit is:

$$\frac{£200,000}{100,000 \text{ units}} = £2.00 \text{ per unit}$$

If the company wishes to evaluate the implications of increasing output to 120,000 units, it must recognise that the cost per unit will change. Fixed costs, such as rent, will not change in total unless output exceeds 120,000 units; however, the unit cost will change, as the rent will be spread over more units.

Marginal Costing

Marginal costing is an alternative technique to absorption costing. Marginal costing is mainly used for short term decision making purposes. The main difference between absorption costing and marginal costing is in the treatment of fixed costs. Using absorption costing, product cost includes both variable and fixed costs. Using marginal costing no attempt is made to charge fixed costs to individual units of production.

ANSWERS TO TUTORIAL QUESTIONS

Tutorial 1

1.1
a. False.
b. True.
c. False.
d. True.
e. True.

1.2
a. Each model of car.
b. Each type of furniture, e.g. each type of chair, table, etc.
c. Each type of paint (probably measured in litres).
d. The work done for each client, i.e. each job will be costed separately.

1.3
a. Direct.
b. Indirect.
c. Indirect.
d. Direct.
e. Indirect.
f. Indirect.
g. Indirect.

1.4

Deluxe Model

	£	£
Direct Materials		5,000
Direct Labour (500 hours @ £6.00)		3,000
PRIME COST		8,000
Add Share of OVERHEADS		
Machining Department	2,000	
Assembly Department	1,500	
Finishing Department	900	4,400
TOTAL COST OF CARAVAN		12,400

Tutorial 2

2.1   Nelsons Plc

Overhead Analysis Schedule

	Service Departments		Production Departments			
	Canteen (£)	Stores (£)	Machining (£)	Assembly (£)	Finishing (£)	Total (£)
Indirect Labour	0	4,350	24,380	24,190	29,760	82,680
Indirect Material	130	410	32,870	25,650	35,240	94,300
Space Heating	16,734	25,102	71,122	69,030	117,142	299,130
Rent & Rates	759	948	2,845	2,750	3,888	11,190
Motive Power	0	0	8,037	11,306	16,037	35,380
Canteen Contract	8,110	0	0	0	0	8,110
Departmental Total	25,733	30,810	139,254	132,926	202,067	530,790

WORKINGS

Space Heating	$\dfrac{£299,130}{143,000}$ = £2.0918 per cubic metre
Rent & Rates	$\dfrac{£11,190}{11,800}$ = £0.9483 per square metre
Motive Power	$\dfrac{£35,380}{193,300}$ = £0.1830 per machine hour

2.2   Scrappit & Co. Ltd

Overhead Analysis Schedule

	Service Departments		Production Departments			
	Office Services (£)	Stores (£)	Paint Shop (£)	Body Shop (£)	Mechanical Dept (£)	Total (£)
Indirect Labour	30,000	40,531	2,100	12,400	15,350	100,381
Stationery & Postage	5,000					5,000
Rent & Rates	817	1,961	4,902	14,705	22,875	45,260
Motive Power	0	0	1,396	22,061	6,293	29,750
Departmental Total	35,817	42,492	8,398	49,166	44,518	180,391

WORKINGS

Rent & Rates $\frac{£45,260}{2,770}$ = £16.3393 per square metre

Motive Power $\frac{£29,750}{83,300}$ = £0.3571 per machine hour

2.3   Viper & Co.

Overhead Analysis Schedule

	Service Departments		Production Departments			
	Sec. (£)	Tech. Supp. (£)	Audit (£)	Tax. (£)	General Practice (£)	Total (£)
Secretaries Salaries	100,000					100,000
Technical Support Salaries		120,000				120,000
Printing, Postage & Tel.	17,000	8,000	65,000	7,000	33,000	130,000
Rent & Rates	12,400	3,720	8,680	5,580	12,400	42,780
Personnel Services	2,632	1,316	15,789	1,053	9,210	30,000
Departmental Total	132,032	133,036	89,469	13,633	54,610	422,780

WORKINGS

Rent & Rates	$\dfrac{£42,780}{345} = £124$ per square metre
Personnel Services	$\dfrac{£30,000}{114} = £263.158$ per employee

Tutorial 3

3.1   Nelsons Plc

Overhead Analysis

	Service Departments		Production Departments			
	Canteen (£)	Stores (£)	Machining (£)	Assembly (£)	Finishing (£)	Total (£)
Indirect Labour	0	4,350	24,380	24,190	29,760	82,680
Indirect Material	130	410	32,870	25,650	35,240	94,300
Space Heating	16,734	25,102	71,122	69,030	117,142	299,130
Rent & Rates	759	948	2,845	2,750	3,888	11,190
Motive Power	0	0	8,037	11,306	16,037	35,380
Canteen Contract	8,110	0	0	0	0	8,110
Sub Total	25,733	30,810	139,254	132,926	202,067	530,790
Canteen Costs	(25,733)	1,340	7,505	7,506	9,382	
Sub Total		32,150				
Stores Costs		(32,150)	9,520	8,428	14,202	
Overhead Burden			156,279	148,860	225,651	530,790

WORKINGS

Canteen costs	$\dfrac{£25,733}{96} = £268.05$ per employee
Stores costs	$\dfrac{£32,150}{61,800} = £0.5202$ per kilo

3.2   Scrappit & Co. Ltd

Overhead Analysis

	Service Departments		Production Departments			
	Office Services (£)	Stores (£)	Paint Shop (£)	Body Shop (£)	Mechanical Dept (£)	Total (£)
Dept Total	35,817	42,492	8,398	49,166	44,518	180,391
Office Services Costs	(35,817)	3,582	8,954	8,954	14,327	
Sub Total		46,074				
Stores Costs		(46,074)	6,707	18,080	21,287	
Overhead Burden			24,059	76,200	80,132	180,391

WORKINGS

Office Services costs
$$\frac{£35,817}{100} = £358.17 \text{ per \% of usage}$$

Stores costs
$$\frac{£46,074}{15,800} = £2.916 \text{ per kg}$$

3.3   Viper & Co.

Overhead Analysis

	Service Departments		Production Departments			
	Sec. (£)	Tech. Supp. (£)	Audit (£)	Tax. (£)	General Practice (£)	Total (£)
Dept Total	132,032	133,036	89,469	13,633	54,610	422,780
Secretariat Costs	(132,032)	13,203	46,211	19,805	52,813	
Sub Total		146,239				
Technical Support Costs		(146,239)	65,807	51,184	29,248	
Overhead Burden			201,487	84,622	136,671	422,780

WORKINGS

Secretariat costs	$\dfrac{£132,032}{100}$ = £1,320.32 per % of usage	
Technical Support costs	$\dfrac{£146,239}{100}$ = £1,462.39 per % of usage	

Tutorial 4

4.1a   Metal cutting department: machine intensive; use machine hours. Enamelling and final assembly departments: labour intensive; use direct labour hours for each of these departments.

4.1b

METAL CUTTING DEPARTMENT

47 weeks × 10 machines × 35 hours = 16,450 machine hours per annum.

ENAMELLING DEPARTMENT

47 weeks × 14 people × 38 hours = 25,004 direct labour hours per annum.

FINAL ASSEMBLY DEPARTMENT

47 weeks × 28 people × 40 hours = 52,640 direct labour hoursper annum.

4.2   Calculation of Budgeted Overhead Absorption Rates (OARS)

	Metal Cutting	Enamelling	Final Assembly
Overhead Burden	£340,000	£210,000	£187,000
Production Hours	16,450	25,004	52,640
Type of Hours	Machine Hrs	Direct Labour Hrs	Direct Labour Hrs
Budgeted Overhead Absorption Rate (OAR)	£20.67	£8.40	£3.55

4.3

	Metal Cutting	Enamelling	Final Assembly	Total
Overhead cost (OAR × recovery hours)	£826.80	£100.80	£195.25	£1,122.85

NOTES

- For the purposes of overhead absorption, the relevant production time for the metal cutting department will be machine hours. The relevant production time for the other departments will be labour hours.
- The total overhead to be charged to the batch of fridges is £1,122.85. This figure represents indirect costs only. To calculate the total cost of the fridges, overheads must be added to prime cost (direct costs).

4.4

	Machining	Assembly	Finishing
Overhead Burden	£156,279	£148,860	£225,651
Production Hours	43,910	66,750	92,310
Type of Hours	Machine Hrs	Direct Labour Hrs	Direct Labour Hrs
Budgeted Overhead Absorption Rate (OAR)	£3.56	£2.23	£2.44

4.5   Scrappit & Co. Ltd

	Paint Shop	Body Shop	Mechanic Dept
Overhead Burden	£24,059	£76,200	£80,132
Production Hours	18,520	61,770	45,380
Type of Hours	Direct Labour Hrs	Direct Machine Hrs	Direct Labour Hrs
Budgeted Overhead Absorption Rate (OAR)	£1.30	£1.23	£1.77

4.6   Viper & Co.

	Audit	Taxation	General Practice
Overhead Burden	£201,487	£84,622	£136,671
Direct Labour Hours	94,520	6,200	55,125
Budgeted Overhead Absorption Rate (OAR)	£2.13	£13.65	£2.48

Tutorial 5

5.1   Nelsons Plc

Job Cost of Yacht

	Machining (£)	Assembly (£)	Finishing (£)	Total (£)
Direct Material Cost	50,000	20,000	8,000	78,000
Direct Labour Cost	2,500	7,200	4,000	13,700
Overhead Cost	2,848	2,676	2,440	7,964
TOTAL JOB COST	55,348	29,876	14,440	99,664

5.2   Scrappit & Co. Ltd

a.   *Job Cost of Vehicle Service: Mechanical Department*

	£
Direct Materials	25.00
Direct Labour (4 hours × £7.50)	30.00
PRIME COST	55.00
Overhead Cost (4 hours × £1.77)	7.08
TOTAL JOB COST	62.08

b.   Job Cost of Accident Damage Repair

	Body Shop (£)	Mechanical Dept (£)	Paint Shop (£)	Total (£)
Direct Material Cost	500.00	120.00	80.00	700.00
Direct Labour Cost	60.00	22.50	18.00	100.50
Overhead Cost	18.45	5.31	5.20	28.96
TOTAL JOB COST	578.45	147.81	103.20	829.46

5.3   Viper & Co.

a.   *Cost of Accounts Preparation: General Practice Department*

	£
Direct Labour	180.00
Overhead Cost	24.80
TOTAL JOB COST	204.80

b.   Major Client – Audit Services and Tax Advice

	Audit (£)	Tax (£)	Total (£)
Direct Labour Cost	130,000.00	1,100.00	131,100.00
Other Direct Costs	7,000.00	0	7,000.00
Overhead Cost	13,845.00	682.50	14,527.50
TOTAL JOB COST	150,845.00	1,782.50	152,627.50

Tutorial 6

6.1   Nelsons Plc

a.   Overhead Recovery Table

	Departments			
	Machining	Assembly	Finishing	Total
Budgeted OAR	£3.56	£2.23	£2.44	
OAR Basis	Machine Hrs	Direct Labour Hrs	Direct Labour Hrs	
Recovery Hours	105,000	198,000	142,000	
Overhead Recovered	373,800	441,540	346,480	1,161,820

b.

	Departments			
	Machining	Assembly	Finishing	Total
(Under)/Over Recovery				(£105,985)

c.   The overheads have been under recovered. This will have a profit decreasing effect, i.e. the actual profit will be less than the budgeted profit.

6.2   Scrappit & Co. Ltd

| | Departments | | | |
	Paint Shop	Body Shop	Mechanical Dept	Total
Budgeted OAR	£1.30	£1.23	£1.77	
OAR Basis	Direct Labour Hrs	Direct Machine Hrs	Direct Labour Hrs	
Recovery Hours	19,120	61,750	45,180	
Overhead Recovered	£24,856	£75,953	£79,969	£180,778

| | Departments | | | |
	Paint Shop	Body Shop	Mechanical Dept	Total
(Under)/Over Recovery				(£22,422)

6.3   Viper & Co.

| | Departments | | | |
	Audit	Tax	General Practice	Total
Budgeted OAR	£2.13	£13.65	£2.48	
OAR Basis	Direct Labour Hrs	Direct Labour Hrs	Direct Labour Hrs	
Recovery Hours	95,100	5,900	58,200	
Overhead Recovered	£202,563	£80,535	£144,336	£427,434

| | Departments | | | |
	Audit	Tax	General Practice	Total
(Under)/Over Recovery				1,484

MARGINAL COSTING

Manual

CONTENTS

MARGINAL COSTING

What is a Marginal Cost?

The marginal cost of an item really means "the extra cost incurred by making one more". In more detail, we need to qualify this slightly by adding "In a given length of time (e.g. one week), the marginal cost of an item is the extra cost incurred by making one more."

Imagine that a business makes electric toasters and nothing else. Each week it budgets to make 400 of them. The workforce is paid by the week, not by the toaster, and direct labour costs (i.e. the wages of the people physically constructing the product, rather than managers', storekeepers' and supervisors' wages) for a week are £1,700. The direct material cost of 400 toasters (ie the cost of the toaster components) is £2,100. A week's overheads (chiefly rent, rates and office staff wages) total £1,900. A week's costs are therefore budgeted to be:

	£
Direct Labour	1,700
Direct Materials	2,100
Overheads	1,900
Total Costs	5,700

Fig. 1

If in reality 408 toasters are made (because there has been a particularly good production run for example), how much will the 8 extra toasters cost?

Direct labour costs will not go up, as the workforce is not paid by the item. Overheads will not go up – there won't be any more rent or rates or office costs because 8 extra toasters are made. Direct materials costs, however, will go up. If £2,100 is spent on components needed to make 400 toasters, the direct materials cost of 1 toaster is:

$$\frac{£2,100}{400} = £5.25$$

So the 8 extra toasters made that week will each cost an extra £5.25.

In this example the MARGINAL COST of a toaster is £5.25. Obviously you can't make extra toasters without using extra components!

Even though in this illustration the only marginal cost is direct materials, it is quite possible for elements of direct labour and overheads to be in it too. For example, if the workforce were paid a shared bonus of £1 for each toaster produced, the marginal cost per toaster would be £5.25 + £1 = £6.25.

The other costs in the illustration, the direct labour cost (£1,700) and overheads (£1,900), fall into another general category, called "fixed costs" (sometimes "period costs"). These costs are not normally sensitive to output changes; rather they are incurred for given lengths of time, regardless of output levels.

Nothing too difficult so far. To state in general terms what is illustrated above:

• Some costs will be volume of output sensitive. That is, the amount spent on them will go up when output goes up, and go down when output goes down. Most obviously, direct materials is one of these.
• Some costs will be incurred anyway, regardless of output volume (assuming there is a business in existence). Most obviously, rent, rates, office wages, are examples of these.

Marginal Costing Theory

Marginal costing theory assumes that every cost can be placed in one of these two categories. Output volume sensitive costs such as direct materials are called "variable costs". This means that the cost incurred will "vary in relation to output volume". (The terms "marginal cost" and "variable cost" are often interchangeable.)

Those costs incurred anyway, regardless of output volume (assuming the business is still functioning) are called "fixed costs". This is a slightly misleading term; for fixed costs can alter. In the marginal costing sense, "fixed" does not mean "unchanging": only "will not alter as a direct result of making one more item". Rent and rates can and do go up! But they don't go up because of making one more electric toaster, only as a result (in the case of rates) of the local authority spending more of our money for us than before.

The company's total costs for making 400 electric toasters in one week (see Fig. 1) can be split into the two categories: the volume sensitive costs, the variable costs; and the costs incurred regardless of how many are made, the fixed costs. In which case, Fig. 1 would look like this:

	£
Variable costs	2,100
Fixed Costs	3,600
Total Costs	5,700

Fig. 2

This is merely one of a number of ways used to classify costs. Fig. 1 showed the basic cost classification of direct labour, direct materials and overheads. Fig. 2 shows the same costs classified as marginal and fixed. The point of the marginal costing classification and its uses are the subject of the remainder of the manual.

Revenue Statements in Marginal Costing Format

If the business sells the electric toasters for £20 each, the profit on 400 will be:

	Quantity	×	Unit Price	= Revenue
				£
Revenue	400	×	£20	= 8,000
Less				
Total Costs				5,700
Profit				2,300

Fig. 3

If a marginal costing layout is used, it is normal to expand this statement into "contribution format" as follows:

	Quantity	×	Unit Price	= Revenue
				£
Revenue	400	×	£20	= 8,000
Less				
Variable Costs		×	£5.25	= 2,100
equals				
CONTRIBUTION		×	£14.75	= 5,900
Less				
Fixed Costs				3,600
Profit				2,300

Fig. 4

The costs are taken from the revenue in two stages. First the marginal (or variable) cost is subtracted. This leaves the amount of revenue left over after the variable costs are paid for. The amount left over is called "contribution".

Revenue less Variable Costs = Contribution

Then the fixed costs are taken away from contribution to give the profit (or loss).

Contribution less Fixed Costs = Profit

Marginal costing theory supposes that the revenue from the 400 electric toasters is first used to pay for the variable costs. Whatever is left after this determines the amount of contribution.

People get muddled by contribution; but it simply means what remains out of the revenue when the variable costs have been paid for. Consequently, contribution is all that is left to pay for the fixed costs.

The statement in Fig. 4 shows the position on a unit basis as well as in total, as far as the contribution line. There are important uses of the data on a unit basis, which are explained later in the manual.

The Role of Contribution

It is important to understand the central role that contribution plays in marginal costing theory and how it behaves. Going back to Fig. 4, we see that 400 electric toasters were sold for £20 each; total contribution was £5,900 (i.e. the amount of revenue left after the variable costs had been paid for, was £5,900); and after fixed costs of £3,600 had been paid for, a profit of £2,300 remained. If 408 toasters had been made and sold that week, then the revenue, variable costs and, most importantly, the contribution would change:

	Quantity	×	Unit Price	= Revenue
				£
Revenue	· 408	×	£20	= 8,160
Less				
Variable Costs		×	£5.25	= 2,142
equals				
CONTRIBUTION		×	£14.75	= 6,018
Less				
Fixed Costs				3,600
Profit				2,418

Fig. 5

But the fixed costs will not alter because 8 extra toasters have been made that week, so the profit increases by the same amount as the contribution:

	£
Profit on 400 (see Fig. 4)	2,300
Profit on 408 (see Fig. 5)	2,418
CHANGE	+ 118
Contribution on 400 (see Fig.4)	5,900
Contribution on 408 (see Fig.5)	6,018
CHANGE	+ 118

Fig. 6

Because the fixed element does not change as revenue alters, Contribution and Profit move up and down by equal amounts, i.e.

Extra Contribution = Extra Profit

On a unit basis, the profit and contribution relationship is useful for making quick calculations of the profit effects of output changes. We see from Figs. 4 and 5 that the unit contribution from one toaster is £14.75 (Unit Revenue – Unit Variable Costs = Unit Contribution: 20 – 5.25 = 14.75). The profit difference if 8 more items are sold will be the contribution gained by selling those 8 items. So if you know the contribution per unit, the extra profit can be calculated from this and the number of extra items sold:

Unit Contribution × Extra Sales = Extra Profit

£14.75 × 8 = £118

(as shown in Fig. 6)

Here is another example: what will the profit be if we only make and sell 368 electric toasters in the week? Full answer (a full "marginal costing statement"):

	Quantity	×	Unit Price	= Revenue
				£
Revenue	368	×	£20	7,360
Less				
Variable Costs		×	£5.25	1,932
equals				
CONTRIBUTION		×	£14.75	5,428
Less				
Fixed Costs				3,600
Profit				1,828

Fig. 7

Short answer (using contribution change only):

		£
Original profit on 400	=	2,300
Less		
Lost Output × Unit Contribution 32 × 14.75	=	(472)
Revised Profit		1,828

Fig. 8

Because we know profit and contribution will alter by equal amounts, once the contribution change is known, so is the profit change. Because Extra Contribution = Extra Profit, of course

Less Contribution = Less Profit too!

Contribution/Sales Ratios

Before going on to the uses of marginal costing, there is one more marginal costing term to learn. Students need to learn how all the bits of the theory work, before applying it to a business problem – however, this is the last piece.

The previous section dealt with the relationship between contribution and profits. (contribution and profit alter by equal amounts). This section deals with the relationship between contribution and sales. Take a simple example first:

	Quantity	Unit Price (£)	Revenue (£)	Percentage Relationship
Revenue	100	10	1,000	100
Less				
Variable Costs		6	600	60
equals				
Contribution		4	400	40

Fig. 9

If the business sells 20 more items, revenue goes up to £1,200 and the variable costs increase by the same proportion, i.e. by 1/5. (Remember that variable costs are output sensitive: when the number sold goes up so does the total variable cost.) If this happens the statement changes to:

	Quantity	Unit Price (£)	Revenue (£)	Percentage Relationship
Revenue	120	10	1,200	100
Less				
Variable Costs		6	720	60
equals				
Contribution		4	480	40

Fig. 10

Although the revenue has changed the proportion of that revenue that is left over as contribution remains the same, i.e. 40%.

This relationship is called the "contribution/sales ration". The contribution/sales (C/S) ratio means "the percentage of sales revenue that is left over as contribution". In Figs. 9 and 10 the C/S ratio is 40%.

WARNING: Some people call the C/S ratio the "profit/volume" ratio (P/V ratio). This is a misleading term but it means exactly the same thing. In this manual the term "C/S ratio" will be used throughout. If you see "P/V ratio" elsewhere, it means C/S ratio.

So what is the C/S ratio of the electric toaster firm?

	Quantity	Unit Price (£)	Revenue (£)	Percentage Relationship
Revenue	400	20	8,000	100
Less				
Variable Costs		5.25	2,100	26
equals				
Contribution		14.75	5,900	74

Fig. 11

The C/S ratio is 74%. The relationship holds good for any output level, providing unit prices and unit variable costs do not change.

One use of this ratio is to calculate the extra contribution from extra sales. For example, if 8 more toasters are sold, what is the extra contribution? Answer: C/S ratio is 74% (i.e. of ANY sales revenue, 74% will be left over as contribution when the variable costs have been paid for); extra revenue = 8 toasters at £20 each = £160; extra contribution = £160 × 74% = £118. Check with Figs 5 and 6, where this was calculated in full. Of course, the extra contribution is extra profit, so you know that profit will also increase by £118.

The Uses of Marginal Costing

To summarise: in a given period

- the extra cost of making one more item will be its marginal (variable) cost
- the profit made will rise and fall with the contribution
- certain costs do not change with output changes.

So what use is this information to businesses and managers? This manual introduces students to the following applications of marginal costing.

a.   Quick comparisons between alternative marketing strategies.
b.   Extra order profitability calculations.
c.   Break-even calculations.
d.   Cost structures and margins of safety.
e.   Make or buy decisions.

The following sections of the manual take each in turn.

a.   Quick comparisons between alternative marketing strategies

Consider a firm which makes compact disk players (CDs) with planned sales and revenues for the next six months of:

Output: 5,000 CDs
Sale price: £30 each
Total Costs: £135,000

There is enough spare capacity to make 6,000 CDs if necessary.

Although the total costs for six months at an output of 5,000 CDs are £135,000, some of these will be fixed and some variable. Below is a breakdown of the planned costs, analysed into the two marginal costing categories. The assumption in this illustration is that there is a 10% bonus element in wages which makes them partly variable.

	Total (£)	Fixed (£)	Variable (£)
Direct Labour	25,000	22,500	2,500
Direct Materials	45,000	0	45,000
Indirect Materials	10,000	9,000	1,000
Machinery Costs	8,000	8,000	
Building Establishment	15,000	15,000	
Sales & Distribution	16,000	16,000	
Administration	9,000	9,000	
Finance	6,000	6,000	
Sundry	1,000	1,000	
	135,000	86,500	48,500

Fig. 12

Note that the unit variable cost is found by dividing total variable costs by the output:

$$\text{Unit Variable Cost} = \frac{48,500}{5,000} = £9.70$$

The current sales and output plan can now be put into marginal costing format:

	Quantity	Unit Price (£)	Revenue (£)	Percentage Relationship
Revenue	5,000	30	150,000	100
Less				
Variable Costs		9.70	48, 500	32
equals				
CONTRIBUTION		20.30	101,500	68
Less				
Fixed Costs			86,500	
Profit			15,000	

Fig. 13

The basic marketing strategy, to make 5,000 CDs in six months and sell them for £30 each, gives a profit of £15,000 if all goes to plan. In business it often does not! However, there is enough capacity to make 6,000 CDs in the period.

The managers might want to consider alternative pricing policies, to make more profit, give competitors a hard time, or many other reasons. For instance, what if the business reduced the price per CD to £27 and aimed to sell all 6,000 CDs that could be made? The marginal cost per unit is known (9.70), so the marginal costing layout makes it very easy and quick to see if this alternative is viable from a profit angle:

	Quantity	Unit Price (£)	Revenue (£)	Percentage Relationship
Revenue	6,000	27	162,000	100
Less				
Variable Costs		9.70	58,200	36
equals				
CONTRIBUTION		17.30	103,800	64
Less				
Fixed Costs			86,500	
Profit			17,300	

Fig. 14

Figs. 13 and 14 show the alternatives in full; however, following the theory that "extra contribution = extra profit", there is a simpler method. Multiplying the new unit contribution by the new quantity gives the information needed to compare the alternatives:

	Original	Alternative 1
Unit Contribution	£20.30	£17.30
× Quantity	5,000	6,000
Total Contribution	£101,500	£103,800

Fig. 15

The option with the highest total contribution is the most profitable because fixed costs will not change.

Another manager might suggest that the product price could be pushed up to £35 and 4,000 CDs still be sold. This idea is quickly evaluated:

	Alternative 2
Unit Price	£35
Less	
Unit Variable Cost	£9.70
Unit Contribution	£25.30
× quantity	4,000
Total Contribution	£101,200

Fig. 16

You should realise that the second alternative is not a good idea, because the total contribution is lower than all the others.

This illustrates an important use of marginal costing: to enable a quick evaluation of alternative marketing strategies to be made. Also note how the C/S ratios change as selling prices change.

b.   Extra order profitability calculations

Firms are often approached by potential customers for special pricing deals, if extra large, or regular orders are placed. Often, the prices suggested are way below the average cost of the items. For example, the total cost of 5,000 CDs was £135,000 (see Fig. 12),. which gives an average (sometimes called "absorption" or "full") cost of:

$$\frac{£135,000}{5,000} = £27 \text{ each}$$

If a new customer says, "We like your CDs: we want 800 of them; but we will only pay £22 each", what should the business do? At first glance, to accept would seem a crazy thing to do, because the price being offered is below the £27 average cost. However, given that you have the spare capacity to make extra CDs and the cost of the extra CDs will only be their marginal cost, the order may be worth taking, if it increases the contribution. For here are no extra fixed costs involved with this extra order, any extra contribution will be extra profit. What will the extra contribution be?

	Extra Order
Unit Price	£22.00
Less	
Unit Variable Cost	£9.70
Unit Contribution	£12.30
× Quantity	800
Extra Contribution	£9,840

Fig. 17

The order is clearly worth taking. Contribution rises by £9,840, bringing a huge rise in profit. The full marginal costing layout shows the entire "before" and "after" position:

	Quantity	Unit Price (£)	Revenue (£)	Percentage Relationship (£)
Revenue	5,000	30	150,000	100
Extra Revenue	*800*	*22*	*17,600*	*100*
Less				
Variable costs		9.70	48,500	32
Extra variable Costs		*9.70*	*7,760*	*44*
equals				
CONTRIBUTION		20.30	101,500	68
Extra Contribution		*12.30*	*9,840*	*56*
Less				
Fixed Costs			86,500	
Extra Fixed Costs			*0*	
Profit			15,000	
Extra Profit			*9,840*	

Fig. 18

This illustrates the second use of marginal costing: to evaluate orders at special prices. This is one of the techniques most widely used by managers in making pricing marketing decisions.

c. Break-even calculations

This is the third use of marginal costing dealt with in this manual. All businesses try to make profits, and as far as the people working in them are concerned, the gloom which descends over a loss-making company has to be experienced to be believed. After a loss has been made, even a small profit does wonders for everyone's feelings. Therefore, the break-even point, the point at which a firm is no longer in danger of making a loss in the period under review, is an important point to reach. Alert managers need to know where it is, and when they have reached it.

To recapitulate, marginal costing theory works like this: the revenue is considered to pay first for the variable costs; this leaves an amount of revenue left over called "contribution"; next, the contribution pays for the fixed costs; if any is left over, it is profit. Now what if contribution only just covers the fixed costs? Under these circumstances, all the costs have been paid, because variable costs have been deducted before contribution is arrived at. The business has made neither a profit nor a loss, in fact it has "broken even", because its revenue has just met its costs. While it is true that at break even Total Revenue = Total Costs,

	£
Revenue	1,000
Less	
Variable Costs	600
equals	
CONTRIBUTION	400
Less Fixed Costs	400
Profit	0
Variable Costs	600
Add Fixed Costs	400
= Total Costs	1,000
Revenue	1,000

Fig. 19

it is also true that at break even:

$$\text{Contribution} = \text{Fixed Costs}$$

	£
Revenue	1,000
Less	
Variable Costs	600
equals	
CONTRIBUTION	400 = Fixed Costs
Less	
Fixed Costs	400 = Contribution
Profit	0

Fig. 20

Remember, the variable costs are paid for before arriving at the contribution, so the contribution only has to pay for the fixed costs (and provide profit). Therefore, a firm breaks even (makes neither a profit nor a loss) when Contribution = Fixed Costs. Grasping this point is important, because it enables break-even points to be easily calculated from marginal costing data.

The break-even point can be expressed as either:

1. the number of items needed to be sold to break even, or
2. the total sales revenue needed to break even. (Stable selling prices are assumed for any break-even calculation.)

It is quite easy to find the break-even point, provided you are clear about the concept of unit contribution. Revise the earlier parts of the manual if you are not clear on this point.

1.   TO FIND THE BREAK-EVEN POINT IN ITEMS NEEDED TO BE SOLD

Break even occurs when the contribution is just enough to pay for the fixed costs, with nothing left over for profit. So, provided that fixed costs are known, the amount of contribution needed to break even is known. If, at break even, contribution equals fixed costs, the contribution required to break even must equal fixed costs! For example, if a business has fixed costs per week of £400, it must generate a £400 contribution each week to break even.

Consider this example. A firm sells dresses for £25 each. The marginal (variable) cost per dress is £15. So the unit contribution is:

	£
Unit Price	25.00
Less	
Unit Variable Cost	15.00
Unit Contribution	10.00

Fig. 21

Assume that the fixed costs are £3,600 for one month. What is the break-even point in items needed to be sold?

Consider these steps:

i.   Fixed costs for one month are £3,600.
ii. Therefore, contribution of £3,600 is needed to break even.
iii. Therefore, when there are enough unit contributions to pay for £3,600 of fixed costs break even occurs.
iv. Unit contribution = £10.
v.   So 3,600/10 = Number of unit contributions needed to break even = 360.
vi. One unit contribution can only come from one unit being sold.
vii. Therefore, if 360 unit contributions are needed to break even, 360 unit sales are needed to break even, i.e. the break-even point is 360 units needed to be sold.

PROOF:

	Quantity	Unit Price (£)	Revenue (£)
Revenue	360	25	9,000
Less			
Variable Costs		15.00	5,400
equals			
CONTRIBUTION		10.00	3,600
Less			
Fixed Costs			3,600
Profit			0

Fig. 22

These steps can be summarised as a formula:

$$\text{Break-even Point in Units} = \frac{\text{Fixed Costs}}{\text{Unit Contribution}}$$

Another example. A firm makes an expensive range of furniture. Fixed costs are £54,750 per year, selling price per unit is £750, and variable costs per unit are £500. The unit contribution is therefore:

	£
Unit Price	750.00
Less	
Unit Variable Cost	500.00
Unit Contribution	250.00

Fig. 23

$$\text{Break Even} = \frac{\text{Fixed Costs}}{\text{Unit Contribution}} = \frac{£54,750}{£250} = 219 \text{ units}$$

PROOF:

	Quantity	Unit Price (£)	Revenue (£)
Revenue	219	750	164,250
Less			
Variable Costs		500	109,500
equals			
CONTRIBUTION		250	54,750
Less			
Fixed Costs			54,750
Profit			0

Fig. 24

2. TO FIND BREAK-EVEN POINTS IN REVENUE

Obviously, if the unit selling price is known, together with the number of units needed to be sold for break even, it is easy to find the break-even revenue. The proofs in Figs. 22 and 24 showed that break-even revenue was £9,000 per month, i.e. $360 \times £25$, for the dresses and £164,250 per year, i.e. $219 \times £750$, for the furniture, i.e.

Break-even revenue = Break-even Units × Unit Selling Price

In practical business you would always know what the unit prices were, but frequently in examinations they are not directly given. Consider the following information relating to a business selling bread. For the next six months projected costs and revenues are as follows:

	Revenue	Percentage Relationship
Revenue	100,000	100
Less		
Variable Costs	60,000	60
equals		
CONTRIBUTION	40,000	40
Less		
Fixed Costs	25,000	
Profit	15,000	

Fig. 25

With only the above data the break-even revenue can still be found. But, since the unit contribution cannot be found, because the number of loaves projected to be sold is not given, so finding the break-even point in units and multiplying it by the unit selling price (as in the proofs above) is not possible. What to do?

In the example above (Fig. 25), the C/S ratio is 40% (as shown). (Students not entirely clear what the contribution/sales ratio is, revise that section. Others read on.) This ratio is very important, because it reveals that for every £1 of revenue £0.40 will be contribution. Finding the break-even revenue is now possible, using essentially the same procedure as break even in units:

i.   Contribution from every £1 of revenue = £0.40
ii.   Therefore, we break even when there are enough £0.40's to pay for the £25,000 of fixed costs.
iii. 25,000/0.40 = 62,500. This shows the number of £0.40's needed to break even.
iv.   As £0.40 of contribution can only come from £1 of sales, and as we need 62,500 lots of £0.40 to break even, 62,500 individual £1's of revenue are needed to break even, i.e. the break even revenue is £62,500.

PROOF:

	Revenue (£)	Percentage Relationship
Revenue	62,500	100
Less		
Variable Costs	37,500	60
equals		
CONTRIBUTION	25,000	40
Less		
Fixed Costs	25,000	
Profit	0	

Fig. 26

These steps can be summarised. To find the break-even point in revenue (when units are not known):

i.   Find Contribution per £1 of Revenue (use the C/S ratio).
ii. Break-even Revenue = Fixed costs
     Contribution per £1 of Revenue

Another example. A fast food company sells hamburgers and has the following projected costs and revenues for the forthcoming 3 months:

	Revenue (£)	Percentage Relationship
Revenue	3,690,000	100
Less		
Variable Costs	1,660,500	45
equals		
CONTRIBUTION	2,029,500	55
Less		
Fixed Costs	1,650,000	
Profit	379,500	

Fig. 27

i.   The C/S ratio (i.e. contribution as a percentage of sales) = 55%. Therefore, Contribution per £1 of Sales = £0.55.

ii. Break-even Revenue = $\dfrac{\text{Fixed Costs}}{\text{Contribution per £1 of Sales}}$

$$= \dfrac{£1,650,000}{£0.55}$$

$$= £3,000,000.$$

PROOF:

	Revenue (£)	Percentage Relationship
Revenue	3,000,000	100
Less		
Variable Costs	1,350,000	45
equals		
CONTRIBUTION	1,650,000	55
Less		
Fixed Costs	1,650,000	
Profit	0	

Fig. 27A

This finishes the break-even point use of marginal costing.

d.   Cost structures and margins of safety

COST STRUCTURES

The balance, at normal output, between the levels of fixed and variable costs within total costs can have profound effects on the profitability of a business when trading conditions change.

By definition, variable costs automatically decrease as output falls – they are output volume sensitive. Equally, fixed costs are by definition insensitive to output volume changes, inasmuch as they will not automatically decrease when output drops. In fact, fixed costs can usually only be decreased by management action. If half of a factory or shop is unused because business is slack, the rent will not automatically reduce by half. To reduce fixed costs, the management will have to sub-let the unused half, or sub-let all of it and move to smaller premises.

The problem with reducing fixed costs is that they usually represent the productive capacity of the business, i.e. its capacity to make or sell. After any wasteful expenditure has been cut, further fixed costs reduction means a dismantling of the business to some extent. This is often a painful, lengthy and difficult process for everyone concerned. And from the cost point of view "lengthy" is the operative word. However, given the fact many managers are incapable of identifying their firm's wasteful expenditure, (hence the existence of management consultants), there is usually substantial scope for fixed costs reduction before the output capacity of a business is seriously affected.

It follows from all these points that if a business at normal output has a large proportion of fixed costs within total costs, and experiences a drop in sales and therefore output, it will have no automatic reduction in expenditure on its large proportion of fixed costs. Therefore, it will experience a drop in revenue – but a smaller drop in costs. Therefore, it will have its profits enormously affected by a drop in demand. For example:

	Normal Revenue (£)	15% Less Revenue (£)
Revenue	100,000	85,000
Less		
Variable costs	20,000	17,000
equals		
CONTRIBUTION	80,000	68,000
Less		
Fixed Costs	70,000	70,000
Profit	10,000	(2,000)

Fig. 28

When revenue falls 15%, the variable costs automatically reduce (£20,000 *less* 15% = £17,000) – but the fixed costs do not alter. Therefore, the business makes losses, unless management action is taken to reduce the fixed costs. This is usually a lengthy process, so a business with the cost structure of Fig. 28 would make losses for some considerable time before a fixed costs reduction programme was completed.

Contrast the structure shown in Fig. 28 above with that shown in Fig. 29 below:

	Normal Revenue (£)	15% Less Revenue (£)
Revenue	100,000	85,000
:Less		
Variable costs	70,000	59,500
equals		
CONTRIBUTION	30,000	25,500
Less		
Fixed Costs	20,000	20,000
Profit	10,000	5,500

Fig. 29

The cost structure in Fig. 29 has a high proportion of variable costs at normal output. Consequently, when revenue drops 15% the automatic reduction in costs is large. Therefore, profits do not disappear.

To summarise, the following general rules apply:

- Firms with mainly fixed costs will be highly vulnerable to downturns in trade.
- Firms with mainly variable costs will be far less vulnerable to downturns.

Equally, firms with mainly fixed costs, and spare capacity, will benefit from increases in revenue much more than firms with mainly variable costs:

	High Fixed Cost Proportion – revenue 10% above normal	Low Fixed Cost Proportion – revenue 10% above normal
Revenue	110,000	110,000
Less		
Variable Costs	22,000	77,000
equals		
CONTRIBUTION	88,000	33,000
Less		
Fixed Costs	70,000	20,000
Profit	18,000	13,000

Fig. 30

In this instance, the firm with the high proportion of fixed costs has recorded an 80% increase in profit for only a 10% increase in revenue.

To summarise, similar firms with different cost structures will be very differently affected by changes in demand for their products. A firm's cost structure will govern how its profits will react to changes in demand. Managers need to bear this in mind when deciding (for example) how to go about increasing output. The following section on make or buy decisions further expands this point.

In reality which businesses do have mainly fixed costs? Airlines, railways, hotels, and mines are all good examples. Once an airline's flying schedule is agreed, all its costs are fixed. An aircraft with two passengers costs just as much to fly the Atlantic as one with 300 people on board. If break-even seat loading for an airline is 100 passengers per transatlantic flight and it only gets 85, its profits will slump alarmingly quickly. That is why such businesses plunge out of profit so quickly. Of course, if the airline has 110 people on board each flight, its profits will increase sharply too.

MARGINS OF SAFETY

This aspect of cost structure can be quantified to some extent by calculating a firm's "margin of safety". Margin of safety is the distance between break even and target sales:

Target Revenue (or Units) *less* break-even Revenue (or Units) = Margin of Safety

The purpose of calculating the margin of safety is to quantify how vulnerable a company (or product) is to reductions in sales volume. If a product has a large margin of safety, then a slight sales under performance will not be disastrous. By contrast, a small margin of safety means that the firm will suffer losses even with small reductions in sales volume. Consider the following two new product plans between which management must choose:

	Product A (£)		Product B (£)	
Revenue	75,000	100%	75,000	100%
Less				
Variable Costs	25,000	33%	45,000	60%
equals				
CONTRIBUTION	50,000	67%	30,000	40%
Less				
Fixed Costs	40,000		20,000	
Profit	10,000		10,000	

Fig. 31

Because the two have different cost structures they will have different break-even points. The break-even points in revenue can be calculated (using the C/S ratios to identify the contributions per £1 of revenue) for both products:

$$\text{Break-even Revenue for Product A} = \frac{£40,000}{£0.67} = £59,700$$

$$\text{Break-even Revenue for Product B} = \frac{£20,000}{£0.40} = £50,000$$

The distance between target and break-even revenue, the margin of safety for each product, is now easily found:

	Product A (£)	Product B (£)
Target Revenue	75,000	75,000
Break-even Revenue	59,700	50,000
Margin of Safety	15,300	25,000

Fig. 32

Product B has a greater margin of safety, i.e. Product B's sales forecast can be more wrong before it makes losses.

It should be clear that (for similar budgeted profits) the product, or business, with the lower fixed costs will always have the higher margin of safety. Margins of safety and cost structures are linked.

It is usually impossible accurately to predict sales, especially of a new product. Consequently, the margin of safety is an important consideration when launching a new product. If there is a low margin of safety, then falling short on sales by a small amount will mean the product makes losses. Under which circumstances, the managers should come up with a better idea!

If Products A and B above were sold for £10 each, then their break-even points in units, target sales in units, and margins of safety in units would be:

	Product A	Product B
Target Sales *units*	7,500	7,500
Break-even *units*	5,970	5,000
Margin of Safety *units*	1,530	2,500

Fig. 33

This can be an important aspect: what if A's were sold for £10 each and B's for £500 each? Then the margins of safety in units would be:

	Product A (£)	Product B (£)
Target Sales *units*	7,500	150
Break Even *units*	5,970	100
Margin of Safety *units*	1,530	50

Fig. 34

This is valuable information. While B still has the greater margin of safety in revenue, its margin of safety in units is now lower. The question for managers then becomes, "Is it easier to sell 7,500 A's or 150 B's?" The figures help to concentrate the minds of the decision makers! If it were decided to make and sell B's, then a shortfall from target of (say) 10 units would be far more serious than a 10 unit shortfall of A's.

e.   Make or buy decisions

When a firm wants to expand output it must choose whether to expand its own production facilities, i.e. buy more machinery, employ more people, rent more factory space, in order to make more items, or to contract with other firms for the supply of certain components, sub-assemblies, and so forth, in order to increase output by buying in more items or part-items. In marginal-costing terms, this means that a firm can increase output by either incurring extra fixed costs (which are broadly the category of costs incurred when production facilities are increased), or incurring extra variable costs (buying in components or finished articles).

The decision matters (as explained above in the section on cost structures) because it affects the strategic ability of a business to withstand downturns in trade. Fixed costs are hard and painful to eliminate when demand drops. Factories have to be closed, people made redundant, machines disposed of. All this takes time, and is painful and expensive. By contrast variable costs are somewhat easier to reduce. It requires only a phone call to say, "Don't deliver any more items until next month please, and only half as many as usual then." It is noticeable that in the UK the main television channel operators (which used to have extensive production facilities of their own) are currently reducing these facilities and sub-contracting an increasing proportion of their programme making. Cost-structural reasons are not the only ones, but undoubtedly they are a very big component in the decision. (Refer to Figs. 28 and 29 above for illustrations of the effects of trade downturns on different cost structures.)

Therefore, when a firm is expanding, one of the considerations it should bear in mind when deciding whether to expand by making more items, or buying in more, is the effect on its cost structure. This apart, the cost per unit of making (compared with that of buying) will be the major influence on the management's decision.

There are two distinct situations managers face when considering whether to make extra items:

1.   When the firm has existing idle facilities that could be used to make extra output.
2.   When a "green field" site would be needed to make extra output (i.e. a wholly new factory, new labour force, and new machinery).

Taking each in turn:

1.   OUTPUT INCREASES WITH IDLE FACILITIES AVAILABLE

Under these circumstances, it is only the extra (marginal) costs incurred that are important. Remember, the costs of providing the idle facilities are being incurred anyway. For example, imagine that an engineering firm has two workshops, one of which is not being used, and existing fixed costs are allocated as follows:

	Workshop 1 (in use)	Workshop 2 (idle)	Total
1 Month's Fixed Costs	£30,000	£15,000	£45,000

Fig. 34A

The management are considering using Workshop 2 to make 5,000 extra saw-blades per month. Costs and sale price are: sale price £5 per blade; 3 extra workshop staff costing in total £1,200 per month; direct materials cost £1 per blade. The extra costs to the firm of making the 5,000 blades will thus be:

	£
Direct Labour:	1,200
Direct Materials:	5,000
Marginal Cost of Extra Items	6,200

The alternative is to sub-contract the work to another engineering firm at a cost of £3.20 per blade. Would it be better from a cost point of view to buy in the extra output, or to make it?

The true position is best illustrated by comparing the totals the business would spend if it either made, bought, or did nothing:

	Qty	Unit Price (£)	MAKE (£)	Qty	Unit Price (£)	BUY (£)
Revenue	5,000	5	25,000	5,000	5	25,000
Less						
Variable Costs		1.24	6,200		3.20	16,000
equals						
CONTRIBUTION		3.76	18,800		1.80	9,000
Less						
Fixed Costs			15,000			15,000
Profit			3,800			(6,000)

	Qty	Unit Price	DO NOTHING (£)
Revenue	0	0	0
Less			
Variable Costs		0	0
equals			
CONTRIBUTION		0	0
Less			
Fixed Costs			15,000
Profit			(15,000)

Fig. 35

Obviously, the firm is worst off if it does nothing, as it has to pay £15,000 per month for the idle workshop anyway. The second best option is to buy in the extra output, as this reduces the monthly loss to £6,000. Best of all is to make the extra output, as this produces a profit of £3,800. In marginal costing terms, the best option is the one with the highest contribution – providing the fixed costs are going to be incurred anyway.

The truth of this point relies upon the marginal costing premise that fixed costs do not disappear with output; and on the practical point that fixed costs are hard to reduce. Obviously, given time it is possible to eliminate "unused" fixed costs, so make or buy decisions, like all decisions, depend on the time factor.

To summarise, where there are existing idle facilities, the marginal costing contribution comparison is the key to the relative costs of making or buying the extra output.

2. OUTPUT INCREASES NEEDING WHOLLY NEW PRODUCTION FACILITIES

Under these circumstances, when extra fixed costs will be incurred, the extra costs incurred by making are ALL the costs of making. In other words, the total cost of the extra output produced by the totally new factory must be compared with the buying in costs. As far as marginal costing theory is concerned, this is the commonest occasion when marginal and variable costs differ. The marginal cost of the extra output is greater than its variable cost, because new fixed costs must also be incurred.

For instance, a firm might consider the following alternatives:

1. To build or rent a new factory, buy machinery and train staff, in order to make a new range of winter outdoor clothing.
2. To sub-contract this work to another garment-making company.

The demand is for 6,000 garments each year, selling to the retail trade at £25 each. Variable costs of making are £14 per garment and extra fixed costs of the new factory would be £52,500 per year. If the garments were sub-contracted to another manufacturer, they could be bought in for £16 each. Fig. 36 below shows the alternative results:

	Qty	Unit Price (£)	MAKE (£)	Qty	Unit Price (£)	BUY (£)
Revenue	6,000	25.00	150,000	6,000	25.00	150,000
Less						
Variable Costs		14.00	84,000		16.00	96,000
equals						
CONTRIBUTION		11.00	66,000		9.00	54,000
Less						
Extra Fixed Costs			52,500			0
Profit			13,500			54,000

Fig. 36

It is clearly more profitable to buy in the garments even though the make option has the higher contribution. This is because the fixed costs are not the same for each option. When extra fixed costs are incurred, the final profitability of each option must be considered – not just its contribution. This is because the true marginal cost of making (when new facilities are required) is ALL the costs of making.

SUMMARY

The key in both cases is to ensure that the comparison between the costs of making and buying in extra output compare ALL the costs incurred when making with ALL the costs incurred when buying in. This way there will be no possibility of error.

OTHER CONSIDERATIONS IN MAKE OR BUY DECISIONS

Before a real business decision were made, there would be a number of other points for the alert manager to consider, besides the cost differences and cost structures.

Available Capital.   It would probably require far more initial cash to make if wholly new production facilities are needed, than to buy in. All the costs of training, buying machinery, renting buildings and financing output until customers at last paid, would require a large amount of cash to be available from the start. Even using existing facilities to make extra output is liable to require more money, initially, than buying in. If a business buys in, it receives an invoice after the goods have been delivered, and it probably won't pay it for 2 months after that. Therefore, in terms of cash needed, buying in requires less to be available initially.

Possibility of Buying in.   Quite often it may not be possible to buy in what you are considering selling. A totally new product (e.g. the new type of high-definition television) which has just been designed by a firm's own research staff may be incapable of manufacture except by totally new facilities only the product developer has the know-how to build.

Security.   If there is anything confidential (from either a marketing or an industrial secret point of view), it is far less likely to be kept confidential if two companies know about it, i.e. the principal company and the sub-contractor.

Skilled Labour.   On the other hand, if the product is to be made, it probably requires extra skilled labour, which may not be available. If a factory is situated in an area where it is difficult to attract skilled (and therefore essential) labour, making may not be an option. In addition, quite frequently, specialised sub-contractors are capable of producing a better product than less specialised businesses.

Management Skills.   This is a specialised category of skilled labour of course. It needs to be realised that managing a factory is very much more difficult than buying from a supplier. If a firm has not got a suitable manager to run the expanded facilities among its existing staff, it may find it very difficult to recruit someone suitable.

Quality Control.   One of the problems with buying in items is that their quality can be unreliable. Therefore, businesses which regularly buy in large quantities of items need very strict quality control procedures. Of course, making items can still give poor quality; however, it is generally easier to build-in quality control checks while manufacturing the product than after it has been made. Quality control is also easier to make sure of if the entire operation is controlled by the principal firm's own management, rather than by a possibly less aware management at a sub-contractor. Evan so, many retail businesses, such as supermarkets and clothes stores, manage to deliver extremely high quality even though they make none of the items they sell.

Delivery Certainty.   Human nature being what it is, a sub-contractor having production problems is liable to hope against hope that the delivery date will be met, somehow. If it isn't, the first indication to the principal may be when the goods don't arrive as expected. By which time the principal company may be vastly inconvenienced by their non-appearance. If everything is made by the principal firm, then it is likely that earlier and better information on deliveries will be available.

The Type of Product.   Some products are very much easier than others to buy in, and yet control their quality and delivery. For instance, clothing is relatively easy to control in this way as (in the UK) Marks and Spencers and (worldwide) mail order catalogues prove. Electronic components are another example of items that it is relatively easy to buy in with confidence. Most radio, TV and PC manufacturers don't make their own transistor and chip components. By contrast, it would be very difficult to develop and market a new mass-production car if you did not also assemble it.

These are just some of the non-accounting considerations which are part of any "make or buy" decision managers may take. It is essential that all accountants realise that most business decisions have a non-accounting aspect to them. The purpose of this last section has been to introduce you to some of the commercial considerations. Any accountant who understands the broader view will be a vastly more useful person to have in a business.

Theoretical Assumptions of Marginal Costing

If marginal costing is to work in practice, then the conditions that the theory assumes to exist, must actually occur. So it is important to know what these theoretical assumptions are. If a real situation does not conform to the theoretical one, then marginal costing won't be much use to the management of that business. The main assumptions that marginal costing theory makes are:

1.   That variable costs can be identified in a business. In practice it may be quite hard to identify variable costs sufficiently precisely to make clear-cut decisions, especially in enormous factories, where there are complicated bonus systems and rules on attendance of various ancillary workers if the factory is open (e.g. firemen, nurses, security men). Under these circumstances, the variable cost of an extra Sunday shift may be completely different from the variable cost of producing extra items on a week-day evening's overtime. Allied to this is the assumption that fixed costs are predictable – of course,

they are not necessarily. A sudden breakdown can mean engineers working hours of overtime and a big bill for spare parts. These are all fixed costs, but hardly predictable ones. Fixed costs do change remember.

2.   That variable costs will go up and down exactly proportionately with output. In practice, if fewer items are made then raw materials prices may go up, because bulk-buying discounts are lost, for example. Equally, if electricity is a major item of variable cost (which in steel-making or aluminium-making it is), then if more of it is used there can be peak-loading penalties which greatly increase the price of the electricity.

3.   The assumption of price stability. In these examples we have assumed that prices remained stable throughout the period being examined. In practice, prices change quite quickly and this needs to be remembered. If petrol costs go up, then delivery costs go up, for instance. If direct material prices go up, so do the unit variable costs.

4.   The assumption that all elements within fixed costs provide the same amount of productive capacity. Fixed costs by and large represent the cost of the production facilities used, machines, buildings, sales force and so forth. In practice it is very unlikely indeed that all these separate facilities will have exactly the same amount of spare unused capacity. Take the works manager, whose salary will be a fixed cost. If a nightshift were to be added, then a night manager would be needed. The spare capacity of works management was, in fact, NIL. Similarly, the sales force might be fully stretched at normal output, and extra items to be sold might need more staff to be taken on. Also, extra output may mean that a particular machine becomes too busy, and another one needs to be purchased.

All these things happen in reality, and they all mean that fixed costs will not, in reality, remain unchanged over changes in output. Because some aspects of production have less spare capacity than others, extra fixed costs will in reality be incurred as output is increased.

The truth of this led to the rather oddly named concept of "step-variable costs". This is meant to describe elements of productive capacity, and therefore of fixed costs, which do not (in a particular case) have very much spare capacity, so that when output is increased past a certain limit, more fixed cost has to be incurred. The objection to this name is that they are not step-variable costs at all; but, rather, step-FIXED costs. In practice, therefore, the management accountant needs to be aware of the output levels at which these "fixed cost steps" occur.

5.   Finally, there is the assumption of a constant level of production efficiency. One of the most important factors in output efficiency is the speed with which items are made. In marginal costing theory it is assumed that this remains unchanged; but anyone in industry, or commerce, knows that this just is not the case. As output goes up or down, efficiency of output (i.e. speed of output and quality of it) changes.

Take variable costs for example. About 10% of most direct materials in the engineering industry are wasted for one reason or another, e.g. offcuts of sheet metal, quality control rejections of finished goods, metal swarf from boring holes, and so on. If production levels alter, so will material waste levels – they may go up or they may go down, but they won't remain the same. And if these things alter, so will the unit variable costs from one level of output to another.

These practical points do not invalidate the principles of marginal costing. However, the practical realities mean that care must be taken by the cost accountant to ensure that any marginal-cost-based information produced for managers as far as possible predicts what will really happen. To do this requires an understanding of where the theoretical assumptions of marginal costing may not completely co-incide with reality.

Marginal Costing and Selling Prices

There are two practical problems with setting selling prices based on the "can we take this extra order at a lower price" technique explained earlier.

1.   There can be timing problems. Businesses often take orders well in advance of delivery. For instance, the order to print a mail order catalogue or holiday brochure is often placed months ahead of delivery. Imagine that a customer offers a firm an order, based on a marginal-cost-based selling price, three months before delivery is required. Imagine also that the business has not yet achieved its sales targets based on normal full prices. What to do? Does the manager refuse the order, in which case the firm might lose valuable contribution and have machines standing idle? Or accept the order, in which case the firm may have to turn down full priced business offered later? A manager's job is not an easy one. Suffice it to emphasise here that in practical business, orders do not come along neatly timed: first the full-price-based business; then the marginal-cost-based work.

2.   If customers paying the full sales price find out that a firm is selling the same product for substantially less, then every customer will want the low price deal. Consequently, a firm can easily destroy its normal markets by selling at low marginal-cost-based prices. So businesses must be very careful how they go about such deals. "Own brand" goods in supermarkets are an example of how manufacturers protect their normal brands. The Giant Supermarket Co.'s Baked Beans will be made by a company that also makes its own (more expensive) beans. The perceived difference between a Giant Supermarket Co. can of baked beans and a branded one is enough to protect the manufacturer's core business from being eroded by a cheaper product.

Exporting is another way of that ensuring goods sold at lower prices do not ruin the full-price-based market. UK customers often have no idea of the prices paid for cars exported to India or Italy or the USA, so they don't pressurize the manufacturer to lower UK prices in line.

This is called "market segmentation" and it occasionally breaks down.

Marginal Costing and Shops

The most common application of marginal costing in day-to-day business life is in retail shops, whatever their size. Retail (i.e. ordinary) shops mainly use marginal-costing-based techniques.

Imagine a shop that opens up one day and nobody at all comes in to buy anything. That shop will incur all its fixed costs: the staff will all be there, the heating will be on, the rates will still be paid and the rent, the costs of the machinery and tills and signs and advertising will still be paid. Under these circumstances, the only costs that will not be incurred are the variable costs. For a shop the only significant variable cost is the cost of buying in whatever the shop sells. Although this cost will be saved, as no stock will have been used up, more importantly no sales revenue and no contribution will have been gained.

The following example illustrates this point for a shop which buys jackets for £30 each from its suppliers, sells them for £75 each to its customers, and incurs fixed costs of £1,600 each day:

	Day 1, zero customers			Day 2, fifty customers		
	Qty	Unit Price (£)	£	Qty	Unit Price (£)	£
Revenue	0	0	0	50	75	3,750
Less						
Variable Costs		0	0		30	1,500
equals						
CONTRIBUTION			0			2,250
Less						
Fixed Costs			1,600			1,600
Profit			(1,600)			650

Fig. 37

The only thing that matters to a shop is getting the maximum contribution every day. Shop managements are totally concerned with contribution per square metre per day. A shop has only so much space: if one item takes up a metre of shelf space, it means that another item cannot be sold there. Profitability is not simply a matter of mark-up (i.e. buy for £30 sell for £75, mark-up £45). It is a matter of how many mark-ups are gained in a day from a given product, in a given space, compared with how much would be earned from another product using it.

Consider this simplified example. A supermarket has 3 metres of shelf space available for canned beer. For marketing reasons it must sell both foreign and domestic brands; but the management are not certain which should predominate. The alternatives are to either:

i.   give 2 metres space to higher priced, higher unit contribution, imported beers, and only 1 metre to domestic beers, or
ii. give 2 metres space to lower priced, lower unit contribution, domestic beers, and only 1 metre to the foreign beers.

The estimated data are as given in Fig. 38.

	Imported Beer			Domestic Beer		
	Qty	Unit Price (£)	£	Qty	Unit Price (£)	£
Revenue	230	1.20	276	400	0.80	320
Less						
Variable Costs		0.60	138		0.40	160
equals						
Daily Contribution			138			160
No. of sq. metres			2			2
Daily Contribution per sq. metre			69			80

Fig. 38

As the cheaper, domestic beer will earn a bigger contribution per metre of shelf space, the supermarket will do better to devote two of the three metres of space to domestic beers. In the Fig. 38 example, the extra quantity of domestic beer sold per day more than makes up for the lower unit contribution per can. This illustrates why the speed with which things sell is so vital to shops, being at least as important to them as the mark-up on each individual sale. It further explains why shops are often keen to remain open as much as possible (e.g. on Sundays): extra opening gives a shop the chance to make extra contribution – with very little impact on the fixed costs.

Graphs of Marginal Costing Data

Marginal costing relationships lend themselves to graphical representation. Because of this, a special facility has been incorporated into the software that accompanies this manual to display automatically in graphical form the relationships entered into the screen.

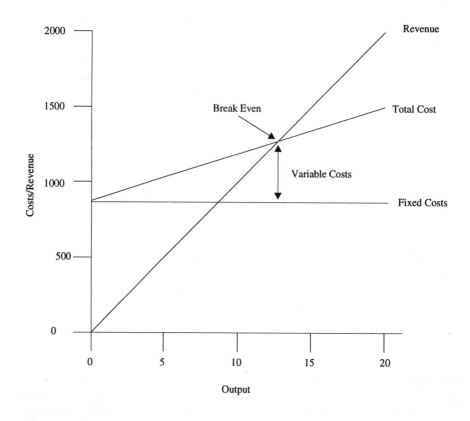

Practice Questions

The final section of this manual contains a number of questions to practise on. Also, the accompanying software will generate any number of random examples in Interactive or in Assignment modes. Therefore, students need have no concerns about lack of opportunities to practice and refine their understanding of marginal costing relationships.

1.   Tyres sell for £27 each. The variable cost per tyre is £9. 5,700 tyres are sold each month. Fixed costs for 1 month are £31,500. What will be the position if 10% fewer tyres are sold.

2.   A firm makes washing machines and sells them for £98 each to retail shops. The total variable costs for March were £23,200. Fixed costs for this period were £31,500. The firm made and sold 570 machines in this time. What would be the position if 10% more machines were sold but the price per machine was reduced by 10%?

3.   Total sales were £6,200 for one month and total variable costs were £2,790. Fixed costs were £3,150. What is (a) the total contribution, (b) the profit, (c) the contribution/sales ratio? (d) If sales increased by £2,000, what would the contribution be?

(e) What is the break-even point in revenue and the margin of safety in revenue for both options.

4. A machine sells for £900 and its unit variable cost is £254. The firm makes 610 each month, during which time fixed costs of £343,000 are incurred. If 510 machines are made and sold in September for £945 each, what will the firm's position be?

5. The following costs are estimated for 1 month's production of Alvispeed gear-boxes by the Simspeed Company:

	£
Labour Costs: 20% variable	4,000
Materials: £300 Fixed, £6,700 Variable	7,000
Rent	2,000
Machine Costs	4,000
Sales and Distribution: 10% Variable	1,000
Interest	2,000
Total Costs	20,000

A month's production is 50 gear boxes, which sell for £500 each. An alternative plan is under discussion to reduce the price to £450 and sell 65 gearboxes. Which is the more profitable?

6. Next year's budget for the Fashion Dress Co. is as follows:

	£
Revenue, Dress Sales (£10 each)	570,000
Costs	
Direct Materials: 100% Variable	150,000
Direct Labour: 20% Variable	83,000
Overheads	
Variable Overhead	70,000
Fixed Overhead	248,600
Total Cost	551,600
Profit	18,400

Would an extra order, at £4 per dress, for 20,000 dresses which incurred no extra fixed costs be profitable?

7. The following estimated costs relate to the production of racing bicycles for May:

	£
Labour: 45% Variable	3,000
Materials: 60% Variable	4,000
Machinery Costs	1,200
Establishment Costs: 5% Variable	400
Selling Expenses: 10% Variable	550
Finance Expenses	350
Administration Expenses	200
	9,700

These costs are based upon making 225 bikes and selling them to retailers for £45 each. Maximum capacity is 240 bikes per month. Is it worth taking an extra order of 10 bikes at £20 per bike if no further fixed costs are incurred? What is the C/S ratio of the extra order?

8. A company making cider has the following costs for each 6 monthly production cycle at the normal sales level of 150,000 gallons.

Fixed Costs   £320,000
Variable Costs £200,000

The cider sells for £4 per gallon. By spending a further £35,000 on fixed machinery costs per 6 months, the production level could be raised to 190,000 gallons, still at a selling price of £4 per gallon. Is it worth doing?

9. The L & P company produces a computer especially for use in schools and colleges. Their most recent model. It is hoped that sales will be £8,000,000 per year, representing 20,000 units. At this output, unit variable costs will be as follows:

Unit Variable Costs:	£
Direct Materials	100
Direct Labour	80
Overhead (Variable)	30.75
Total Unit Variable Cost	210.75

Fixed costs total £3,300,000 for the year. If the selling price per computer is raised by £50, only 80% of the intended sales quantity will be achieved. Is so raising the price a good idea?

10.   The Enginetune Company have a certain amount of spare capacity and are considering making their own bearings, instead of buying them as they do at present. You are asked to produce a statement showing, from a purely financial point of view, the advantage or otherwise of doing so. Your enquiries reveal the following data about making the 15,000 bearings needed each year:

	£
Allocation of rent for spare workshop	10,000
Cost per year of a new machine	26,000
Extra labour	40,000
Existing labour re-deployed	13,000
Materials for the bearings	39,000
Existing machinery costs re-allocated	12,000

To buy the same number of bearings would cost £126,500. The Enginetune company sell the bearings for £9.50 each.

11.   The type 19 ladies shoe costs £4.40 per pair in variable costs and output is 1,000 pairs each month. Fixed costs per month are £4,375. The shoes sell to the retail trade for £8.75 per pair. A sub-contractor has offered to make type 19's for £5 per pair, in which case management will have reduced the monthly fixed costs to £2,650. Should the firm continue making type 19's or buy them in from the sub- contractor?

12.   Charnwood Engineering Ltd expects its costs at a production level of 10,000 units per annum to be:

Direct Labour: 80% Fixed	120,000
Direct Materials	140,000
Factory Fixed Expenses	60,000
Selling Expenses: 70% Fixed	10,000
Fixed Administration Expenses	20,000
Total Costs	350,000

The selling price per unit is £40. Show the position if the selling price were reduced to £37 and sales rose to 14,000 units.

13.   A manufacturer of motor-cycle components has been operating at 80% of plant capacity. In order to utilise more capacity, the plant manager is considering making the handlebar and lever unit which is currently being purchased from outside suppliers for £6.10 per unit. The plant has the equipment necessary to manufacture this item, which the design engineer estimates would cost £1.10 per unit for raw materials and £3.20 per unit for direct labour. 380 units are needed each week, selling for £11.25 each. Fixed costs per week are £2,280, which will be incurred anyway, regardless of this decision. Should the company make the unit or continue to buy it from an outside supplier?

14.   Foley Speedway own a motor-cycle track. The entrance price per ticket is £4.75 and there is an average attendance of 3,600 at race meetings held 15 times per year. Variable costs are £0.60 per person and fixed costs are £190,000 per year. The company can increase seating capacity to 4,300 seats for an annual increase in fixed costs of £22,000. If variable costs per person and ticket prices remain the same, how many extra people would have to attend each year to break even on the extra fixed cost investment?

STANDARD COSTING

Manual

CONTENTS

INTRODUCTION

Business Management – Planning, Decision Making and Control

The management of a business organisation is a complex activity involving the three major processes of planning, decision making and control. The planning process involves setting corporate objectives, identifying appropriate strategies, making strategic plans and creating budgets.

A corporate, or business, objective is what the business aims to achieve in the long term. Management must develop a series of plans leading toward this goal, and the way management intend to achieve these aims is expressed in the strategic, or long-term, plan.

For example, a business may have as its corporate objective "to be the most successful business in the home computer market". A strategy to achieve this objective might be to bring one or more new products to the market, increase sales year by year or secure a greater share of the existing home computer market. Any one, or any combination of these strategies may achieve the desired goal and the strategic planning process helps the business identify the best strategy.

Having identified the best strategy, the next step in the planning, decision making and control processes is to identify the approach, or approaches to take. At this point, budgeting is used as a means of stating the approach to take in the short term in financial terms.

Thus, in order to secure a greater share of the home computer market, the business in the above example may decide to mount an aggressive advertising campaign, improve customer services and offer special discounts and incentive schemes to attract new customers away from competitors.

Budgets are produced to support the plans, but because the plans are based on estimates and predictions they may not be achieved. For example, a new competitor may appear offering a cheaper product or a more technically advanced product, or unexpected labour problems, such as strikes, may disrupt production, leading to lost customer orders.

Monitoring and control

In order to control the business effectively to achieve agreed objectives, managers must monitor performance regularly so that action can be taken whenever necessary.

Budgeting is essential to the management control process. Budgetary control systems seek to detect, as quickly as possible, those activities that fail to meet their budget target. Information is generated that indicates when an element of cost or revenue appears to be running out of control. This provides management information on which to base decisions.

In order to achieve their objectives, business managers therefore

- plan to make a profit
- monitor actual performance
- make decisions where budget and actual performance diverge
- exert control
- achieve the profit plan

Even when managers are aware of the need to plan and control there are practical difficulties that must be overcome. Most middle and top management operate at some distance from the factory floor, in administrative offices, sometimes sited remotely at headquarters. Add to this the growing complexity of modern manufacturing processes involving automation and advanced technology and it is not suprising that managers lose touch with activities on the factory floor. They are often too far away to detect when actual performance is failing to meet the target.

Global motor vehicle manufacturing organisations such as Toyota and Ford require sophisticated monitoring and control systems to assist management decision making. Even small organisations may suffer from the lack of direct control when they expand, for example, from an owner-managed sole trader or partnership to a limited company.

The information provided by accountants plays a significant role in the planning, decision making and control processes. Accountants use various management accounting techniques to show how actual performance differs from planned performance. Standard costing is one such technique.

What is Standard Costing?

Standard costing is a technique that estimates the costs of producing goods or providing services and then compares these estimates with the actual costs incurred. The estimated costs are called standards. The differences that arise between these standards and the actual costs are called variances.

If there is no variance, because the actual costs are the same as the planned standard costs, then no action need be taken. This approach embodies the principle of management by exception. This means that only where there is a difference need action be taken to investigate.

Standard costing is useful in a number of manufacturing approaches, such as batch and mass production and assembly processes.

A typical example is a large motor vehicle manufacturer, such as Ford, where high volumes of output (cars) are assembled from many hundreds of manufactured or bought components. In order to plan and control, management need answers to questions such as:

- Why have we overspent on materials?
- Are we wasting materials?
- Is the labour force working efficiently?
- Do the actual results show a continuing trend that needs investigation?

Mass production on such a scale means that the answers to questions like these cannot be obtained easily without a system such as standard costing.

Because standard costing in practice is a very detailed process, it is best suited to high volume, high value mass production businesses, but it can even be applied to repetitive clerical procedures.

The Elements of Standard Costing

- identifying standard unit costs
- setting a master budget
- collecting actual data
- flexing the master budget
- comparing actual data with the flexed budget
- identifying variances
- applying variance analysis techniques.

What is a standard?

In the context of management accounting, a standard is a target cost and usage of resource relating to one unit of output. It is a planned cost and usage similar to a budget. However, the budget is a financial plan for the total production over a period of time, whereas a standard identifies a target for one unit of output only.

The uses of standard costing

Standard costing is commonly used in manufacturing industries to:

- identify and record cost data
- aid in the budgeting process
- deduce product costs
- assist in stock control
- provide information for performance evaluation

Providing information for performance evaluation is achieved by analysing variances and applying responsibility targets to managers.

Assumptions

Throughout this manual, we shall refer to units of output. Standard costing is equally useful when applied to units of service, individual operations or processes. For the sake of simplicity, however, the assumption is made that standard costing is being used in a business to control the costs of producing units of goods or services.

CALCULATING STANDARD COSTS AND PREPARING THE BUDGET

Types of Costs

The costs of a business fall into three main areas.

MATERIALS

Most of the materials cost of a manufacturer will be in the form of raw materials.

LABOUR

Labour costs will be incurred in the following areas:

- production workers
- other factory workers, e.g. supervisors and cleaners
- office staff
- sales personnel

OTHER EXPENSES (OVERHEADS)

Costs which cannot be classed as either materials or labour. These expenses will include:

- rent
- light and heat
- insurance
- depreciation of fixed assets

Classification of Costs

When calculating product cost, it is important to differentiate between direct costs and indirect costs.

DIRECT COSTS

Direct costs are easily measurable. They can easily be pinned on an individual product. The direct costs of a product will be:

- direct (raw) materials, the materials from which the product is actually made, e.g. the steel used to make cars – this cost can be ascertained from stock records
- direct (production) labour, i.e. the wages of the people who actually make the product, e.g. assemble cars –details of this cost will be supplied by the payroll
- direct expenses, which are relatively rare but an example would be a royalty paid by a radio station when it plays a rock star's record

INDIRECT COSTS (OVERHEADS)

Indirect costs are those costs which cannot easily be pinned on individual products. For example:

- indirect materials, e.g. lubricants for machinery
- indirect labour, e.g. supervisors' salaries, salesmen's commission and salaries, office wages, directors' fees
- other indirect expense, e.g. rent, light and heat, power, depreciation of fixed assets, audit fees, advertising

As indirect costs cannot easily be traced to individual units of output, they are termed "overheads".

Behaviour of Costs

In order to calculate the standard cost for a unit of output it is also necessary to identify how costs behave. Costs can be:

- variable
- fixed
- a combination of variable and fixed

Variable costs are linked to the units of output. Examples are

- direct materials
- direct labour

Clearly, as units are produced the amount of direct material costs and direct labour costs increases in proportion to the number of units produced.

Fixed costs do not vary with the level of output. Even if there is no activity, fixed costs will still be incurred. Examples of fixed costs are

- factory rent
- insurance

For example, there may be no production of units during a holiday week when the factory is closed down, but the rent is still charged by the landlord and insurance is still needed.

Certain costs may be partly variable and partly fixed. Where these costs are overheads, (that is, indirect costs, for example lubricants for machinery, supervisors' salaries), they are called:

- variable overheads, and
- fixed costs

Standard Cost

The standard cost of each unit produced may be built up as follows:

	Direct Materials per unit
plus	Direct Labour per unit
plus	Share of Variable Overheads per unit
plus	Allocation of Fixed Cost per unit
equals	Total Cost per unit

How overheads are shared

The direct materials per unit and the direct labour per unit are relatively easy to measure. In principle, overheads are indirect costs that cannot be identified with individual units of output in the same way as direct materials for example. The amount of variable overhead cost per unit depends on how the total variable overheads used in producing the units of output are shared.

A reasonable method of sharing variable overheads is to calculate how much overhead is used or absorbed in relation to a known measurable direct cost, such as labour hours. This method, called overhead absorption, aims to charge overheads to units of output in proportion to the amount of time available to make those units.

For example, if the standard time taken to produce one unit is 1% of the direct labour hours available, then it will be charged with 1% of the variable overhead. This is a logical approach, because the variable overheads arise through the manufacturing process and labour time is often the most significant element in that process. The variable overhead cost per unit is expressed as the overhead absorption rate (OAR) per direct labour hour (DLH).

If the manufacturing process is highly machine intensive, machine hours may be used instead.

For more information about overhead absorption rates, refer to the Absorption Costing manual.

Standard Cost Card

The standard cost card for a particular product shows all the costs associated with the manufacture of that product.

DIRECT MATERIALS COST

This is calculated by specifying the quantity of material, in for example kilograms, needed to make one unit of output and multiplying by the price paid for the material per kilogram.

standard quantity of material per unit × standard material cost per unit

DIRECT LABOUR COST

This is calculated by assessing the labour hours needed to produce the unit of output and multiplying by the hourly wage rate.

standard labour time per unit × standard rate of labour payment

VARIABLE OVERHEAD COST

Variable overhead cost is calculated by taking the standard labour hours needed to produce one unit of output and multiplying by the standard overhead absorption rate per hour.

standard rate of variable overhead absorption × standard labour time per unit

FIXED OVERHEAD COST

Fixed overhead cost is taken as the standard fixed cost allocated to one unit.

standard fixed cost per unit

Standard cost cards may take the form of paper records or computer files. In this manual the layout of the standard cost card is:

Standard Cost Card						
	Quantity	Price	Time	Rate	Cost per unit output	
Type					£	£
Std. Direct materials						
Std. Direct labour						
Std. Var OAR/DLH						Total
Std. Fixed cost per unit						

Fig. 1

The standard cost for one unit of output is built up by multiplying the standard quantities of each resource used by the standard price per unit of that resource.

Example

The standards associated with one unit of a particular product are:

Direct Materials	10 kgs at £5 per kg
Direct Labour	3 hours at £7.50 per hour
Variable Overhead	3 hours at £4 per direct labour hour
Fixed Cost	£7 per unit

The completed standard cost card shows the standard cost of producing one unit of output:

Standard Cost Card						
	Quantity	Price	Time	Rate	Cost per unit output	
Type	Kgs	£	Hours	£	£	£
Std. Direct materials	10.00	5.00			50.00	
Std. Direct labour			3.00	7.50	22.50	
Std. Var OAR/DLH			3.00	4.00	12.00	Total
Std. Fixed cost per unit					7.00	91.50

Fig. 2

Different Types of Standards

There are different types of standards used in management accounting and described in textbooks, for example

- basic
- ideal
- attainable

Basic standards

Basic standards tend to remain unchanged over long periods, possibly years. For this reason they are useful for identifying trends over time. They are not normally used in short-term decision making.

Ideal v. attainable standards

An ideal standard reflects perfect efficiency. It is based on the assumption that operating conditions are ideal, e.g. no wastage of materials, no machine breakdowns or labour stoppages.

Whilst ideal standards may be useful for theoretical production design purposes, they are not normally appropriate for management planning and control. This is because they are clearly unattainable in practice and are considered to have a strong de-motivating effect.

Attainable standards, by comparison, are based on assumptions of efficient operating conditions. Allowances are made for natural wastage of materials, for realistic expectations of machine breakdowns, and so on.

This does not mean that attainable standards are easy to achieve – quite the contrary. Such standards are set in order to provide a realistic target, one that it is possible to reach, but also one whose achievement requires a high degree of performance. As a result, attainable standards need to be revised regularly to ensure that they reflect changes in operating conditions. Otherwise, they may cease to be attainable.

Attainable standards, like all other types of standard, rely on good forecasting techniques and the application of management skill and judgement to ensure that they are as accurate as possible.

From now on in this manual, when we refer to standards, we mean attainable standards.

Setting Standards

In order to be useful, standards must be meaningful. It is no use trying to set a standard cost for a product until the production methods and standards for each resource contributing to the product have been established.

Management face a number of problems in the standard setting process. Business organisations operate in a dynamic environment in which many variables cannot be controlled. The impact of technology, and political and economic pressures, contribute to the difficulty in establishing future resource, production and cost standards. The introduction of new standards or the revision of existing standards represents a change that may be resisted by employees. Time and motion studies and performance evaluation procedures necessary to collect information for standard setting may be feared and resented. If standards are perceived to be unreasonable the labour force will be reluctant to adopt a positive attitude to the process. Establishing standards for the sharing of indirect costs between different products, processes and departments can cause friction between managers who are judged on cost efficiency. Also, the information needed about production methods and standards for each resource may be time consuming and costly to collect in practical terms.

The Budget

As we explained in Tutorial 1, budgeting is a means of expressing, in financial terms, the approach the business needs to take in the short term in order to achieve its long term goals. It is essential to the processes of planning decision making and control. However, budgeting does have other roles.

COMMUNICATION

Regular monitoring of performance helps managers keep in touch with developments, so that they can be pro-active rather than reactive in approach.

RESPONSIBILITY AND MOTIVATION

Where individual managers have clear plans indicating areas of responsibility, a system of devolved decision making can operate efficiently. As long as they operate within budget limits, managers have a clear sense of direction.

CO-ORDINATION

Budgets can be used to co-ordinate the activities of different departments or sections of the organisation, helping them function more smoothly.

GOAL CONGRUENCE

The budget planning and control process allows the business, as a group of individuals acting together, to focus on the corporate objectives, so that personal aims and ambitions can be integrated into the overall goals of the organisation.

The practical steps taken to draw up budgets need not concern us here. However, it is important to know that budgets within an organisation are logically related. This means, for example, that the sales budget is linked to the production budget, which is in turn linked to the finished stock budget, and so on.

In this manual we are concerned with budgets related to the costs of producing goods and services, production cost budgets.

Standards and Budgets Compared

As you have just learned, the standard cost is the predetermined or target cost for one unit of output and the budget is the financial plan for the total production over a period of time. Where standard cost records are kept, the detailed information on resources and costs that they contain is used as a basis for generating the total output cost budget.

Although budgets may be revised regularly standards are not generally changed, unless they prove to be inappropriate for some reason.

Once the planned output level has been agreed, the production cost budget figures are built up using the information from the standard cost card.

Example

The standard costs associated with one unit of output in Figure 2 were:

Standard Cost Card						
	Quantity	Price	Time	Rate	Cost per unit output	
Type	Kgs	£	Hours	£	£	£
Std. Direct materials	10.00	5.00			50.00	
Std. Direct labour			3.00	7.50	22.50	
Std. Var OAR/DLH			3.00	4.00	12.00	Total
Std. Fixed cost per unit					7.00	91.50

If the planned output level for a week is 1,000 units, then the output budget for the period becomes:

	Master Budget
Output (units)	1000
Costs	£
Direct materials	50000
Direct labour	22500
Variable overheads	12000
Fixed overheads	7000
Total costs	91500

Fig. 3

The budget provides the financial plan for the period, in this case one week, and is known as the master production cost budget, or "master budget" for short. This budget statement forms part of the overall budget and planning process for the business and will link in with other budgets.

Tutorial Questions

2.1 Calculate the missing information to complete the following standard cost card and master budget.

	Quantity	Price	Time	Rate	Standard Cost Card	
					Cost per unit output	
Type	Kgs	£	Hours	£	£	£
Std. Direct materials	10.00	5.00				
Std. Direct labour			3.00	7.50		
Std. Var OAR/DLH			3.00	4.00		Total
Std. Fixed cost per unit				7.00		

	Master Budget
Output (units)	1000

Costs	£
Direct materials	
Direct labour	
Variable overheads	
Fixed overheads	
Total costs	

2.2 Calculate the missing information to complete the following standard cost card and master budget.

Standard Cost Card

Type	Quantity Tonnes	Price £	Time Hours	Rate £	Cost per unit output £	£
Std. Direct materials	2.00	350.00				
Std. Direct labour			16.00	6.00		
Std. Var OAR/DLH			16.00	8.00		Total
Std. Fixed cost per unit					76.00	

	Master Budget
Output (units)	300

Costs	£
Direct materials	
Direct labour	
Variable overheads	
Fixed overheads	
Total costs	

2.3   Calculate the missing information to complete the following standard cost card and master budget.

Standard Cost Card						
	Quantity	Price	Time	Rate	Cost per unit output	
Type	Litres	£	Hrs	£	£	£
Std. Direct materials	100.00	0.60				
Std. Direct labour			0.50	10.00		
Std. Var OAR/DLH			0.50	3.50		Total
Std. Fixed cost per unit					2.00	

	Master Budget
Output (units)	2000

Costs	£
Direct materials	
Direct labour	
Variable overheads	
Fixed overheads	
Total costs	

2.4   Calculate the missing information to complete the following standard cost card and master budget.

					Standard Cost Card	
	Quantity	Price	Time	Rate	Cost per unit output	
Type	Kilos	£	Hrs	£	£	£
Std. Direct materials	7.00	35.00				
Std. Direct labour			8.00	7.25		
Std. Var OAR/DLH			8.00	6.75		Total
Std. Fixed cost per unit					5.00	

	Master Budget
Output (units)	1000

Costs	£
Direct materials	
Direct labour	
Variable overheads	
Fixed overheads	_____
Total costs	========

2.5 Motorparts UK Ltd is a major manufacturer and supplier of motor vehicle spares and accessories to the motor trade. The company has decided to install a standard costing at the Coventry factory in the department devoted to the manufacture of air conditioning units. Motorparts produce just one model that can be fitted to most saloon cars produced for the UK market. The factory manager has collected the following relevant data about the various processes and costs involved in the manufacture of each unit.

- The amount of materials used to manufacture one unit is 2 kilograms.
- Management believe that the operation should take no more than 90 minutes to complete.
- The current materials supplier charges £35 per kilogram, including delivery charges.
- Pay rates are now £7.50 per labour hour.
- For the time being, an estimate of £4.00 of variable overhead cost per direct labour hour is being used in order to establish the costing system. A fixed cost figure of £2.75 per air conditioning unit produced is to be used initially.

Required
Design a standard cost card for the manufacture of one air conditioning unit and draw up a master budget for a 10 day production run of 4,000 units.

FLEXING THE BUDGET

Using the Budgets

In order to achieve their profit objectives business managers must monitor actual performance. This means that they need to compare budget plans with actual performance in some meaningful way.

Example

Following on from the last example, suppose that production went ahead for one week and the data were collected on actual performance for that week. The direct comparison of actual output with budgeted output reveals the following information

	Master Budget		Actual
Output (units)	1000		1200
Direct materials	Kgs		12500
Direct labour	Hours		3400
Costs	£		£
Direct materials	50000		62000
Direct labour	22500		26000
Variable overheads	12000		14000
Fixed overheads	7000		7700
Total costs	91500		109700

Fig. 4

It is clear that the budgeted material cost was £50,000 but the actual cost turned out to be £62,000. Why might this be?

- The production manager allowed too much material to be wasted in the manufacturing process?
- The purchasing manager paid much more than the standard price for the materials?

Either explanation might be true, but both managers would be quick to point out that the comparison is not particularly useful for finding out what has gone wrong, for the budgeted and actual output levels are different.

In order to produce a realistic basis for comparison the budgeted output level must be "flexed" to the level of the actual output, which means adjusting the budget to show how it would look if it had been prepared for an output level of 1,200 units, the actual output level.

	Master Budget	Flexed Budget	Actual
Output (units)	1000	1200	1200
Direct materials	Kgs	12000	12500
Direct labour	Hours	3600	3400
Costs	£	£	£
Direct materials	50000	60000	62000
Direct labour	22500	27000	26000
Variable overheads	12000	14400	14000
Fixed overheads	7000	7000	7700
Total costs	91500	108400	109700

Fig. 5

The budgeted direct materials, direct labour and variable overheads costs have been re-calculated to the new flexed budgeted output level. Notice that the budgeted fixed overheads cost remains the same as in the original budget, because this cost does not vary with the level of output.

Now a direct comparison can be made between budget and actual performance.

Tutorial Questions

3.1   Given the following master budget and actual performance information prepare the flexed budget.

	Master Budget	Flexed Budget	Actual
Output (units)	1000		1200
Direct materials	Kgs		12500
Direct labour	Hours		3400
Costs	£		£
Direct materials	50000		62000
Direct labour	22500		26000
Variable overheads	12000		14000
Fixed overheads	7000		7700
Total costs	91500		109700

3.2   Given the following master budget and actual performance information prepare the flexed budget.

	Master Budget	Flexed Budget	Actual
Output (units)	300		288
Direct materials	Tonnes		598
Direct labour	Hours		4579
Costs	£		£
Direct materials	210000		217500
Direct labour	28800		26600
Variable overheads	38400		37750
Fixed overheads	22800		22000
Total costs	300000		303850

3.3   Given the following master budget and actual performance information prepare the flexed budget.

	Master Budget	Flexed Budget	Actual
Output (units)	2000		2120
Direct materials	Litres		230000
Direct labour	Hrs		1200
Costs	£		£
Direct materials	120000		135250
Direct labour	10000		11875
Variable overheads	3500		3800
Fixed overheads	4000		4200
Total costs	137500		155125

3.4   Given the following master budget and actual performance information prepare the flexed budget.

	Master Budget	Flexed Budget	Actual
Output (units)	1000		987
Direct materials	Kilos		6891
Direct labour	Hrs		8037
Costs	£		£
Direct materials	245000		242010
Direct labour	58000		55463
Variable overheads	54000		53257
Fixed overheads	5000		4200
Total costs	362000		354930

3.5   Motorparts UK Ltd is a major manufacturer and supplier of motor vehicle spares and accessories to the motor trade. The company has decided to install a standard costing at the Coventry factory in the department devoted to the manufacture of air conditioning units. Motorparts produce just one model that can be fitted to most saloon cars produced for the UK market. The factory manager has collected the following relevant data about the various processes and costs involved in the manufacture of each unit.

- The amount of materials used to manufacture one unit is 2 kilograms.
- Management believe that the operation should take no more than 90 minutes to complete.
- The current materials supplier charges £35 per kilogram, including delivery charges.
- Pay rates are now £7.50 per labour hour.
- For the time being, an estimate of £4.00 of variable overhead cost per direct labour hour is being used in order to establish the costing system. A fixed cost figure of £2.75 per air conditioning unit produced is to be used initially.

The standard costs of producing one air conditioning unit have now been calculated as follows:

Standard Cost Card	Item: Air conditioning unit						
	Quantity	Price	Time	Rate	Cost per unit output	
Type	Kilos	£	Hrs	£	£	£
Std. Direct materials	2.00	35.00			70.00	
Std. Direct labour			1.50	7.50	11.25	
Std. Var OAR/DLH			1.50	4.00	6.00	Total
Std. Fixed cost per unit					2.75	90.00

From this information, a master budget for a 10 day production run of 4,000 units was prepared:

Air conditioning units	Master Budget
Output (units)	4000
	Kilos
	Hrs
Costs	£
Direct materials	280000
Direct labour	45000
Variable overheads	24000
Fixed overheads	11000
Total costs	360000

After the first production run under the new standard costing system, actual output and cost information was collected. This revealed that only 3,812 units had been produced during the 10 day period. 7,943 kilograms of material had been used up and the workers' time sheets indicated that 5,565 hours had been clocked against this production run. Costs associated with the 3812 units were £271549 for materials, £43906 for wages and a total of £33774 for overheads, of which £10675 related to fixed costs.

Required
Produce a flexed budget based on the information given above and compare your answer with the actual performance figures.

ANALYSING THE VARIANCES

Introduction

We explained in Tutorial 1 that the difference between the budgeted total cost of producing one unit of output and the actual total cost of producing that unit is known as the production cost variance. The process of identifying where the variances arise is known as variance analysis.

Variance analysis can be applied to other types of variances, e.g. sales variances, but this manual concentrates on the analysis of production cost variances.

Calculating the Variances

The total cost variance for each resource is simple to calculate by subtracting the actual cost from the flexed budgeted cost for each item:

	Flexed Budget	Actual	Total Variance	
Output (units)	1200	1200		
Direct materials	12000	12500		
Direct labour	3600	3400		
Costs	£	£	£	F/A
Direct materials	60000	62000	2000	A
Direct labour	27000	26000	1000	F
Variable overheads	14400	14000	400	F
Fixed overheads	7000	7700	700	A
Total costs	108400	109700	1300	A

Fig. 6

When the actual cost is greater than the budgeted cost we say there is an ADVERSE variance (A). When the actual cost is less than the budgeted cost we say there is a FAVOURABLE variance (F).

Types of Cost Variances

Cost variances fall into two groups:

- variances arising because the quantity actually used differed from the budget
- variances arising because the price actually paid differed from the budget

QUANTITY VARIANCES

Quantity variances are described as "usage variances" when related to direct materials, and "efficiency variances" when related to direct labour and variable overheads. When the quantity actually used is greater than budgeted we say there is an ADVERSE variance. When the quantity actually used is less than budgeted we say there is a FAVOURABLE variance.

PRICE VARIANCES

Price variances are described as "price variances" when related to direct materials, "rate variances" when related to direct labour and variable overheads, and "expenditure variances" when related to fixed overheads. When the price actually paid is greater than budgeted we say there is an ADVERSE variance. When the price actually paid is less than budgeted we say there is a FAVOURABLE variance.

In practice, price variances are normally calculated when materials are bought, not when they are used. This is because price variances arise when materials are purchased for more, or less, per unit, than the standard price estimated. Once purchased, the variance remains, regardless of when the materials are used in production.

The individual cost, variances descriptions and names are summarised in the following table:

Cost	Description of quantity variances		Description of price variances	
Direct materials	Usage	Direct materials usage variance (DMUV)	Price	Direct materials price variance (DMPV)
Direct labour	Efficiency	Direct labour efficiency variance (DLEV)	Rate	Direct labour rate variance (DLRV)
Variable overheads	Efficiency	Variable overhead efficiency variance (VOEV)	Rate	Variable overhead rate variance (VORV)
Fixed overheads			Expenditure	Fixed overhead expenditure variance (FOEV)

Each of these variances will now be explained in detail and calculated in the example we have been using so far.

Direct Materials Variances

Direct materials cost has two variances attributable to it, a quantity variance and a price variance

Quantity (usage) variance

The difference between the standard quantity for the actual output and the actual quantity used, at standard price, is the direct materials usage variance (DMUV).

DMUV = (flexed budget usage – actual usage) × standard price per unit of material

The standard price per unit of material purchased is, for example, per kilo or per metre.

Example

The standard price of the material is £5 per kilo.

$$DMUV = (12,000 - 12,500) \times £5 = -£2,500$$

The actual usage was greater than the standard usage for the actual output, so the variance is ADVERSE.

	Flexed Budget	Actual Usage	Total Variance			Usage or Efficiency		Price or Rate	
Output (units)	1200	1200						Analysed variances	
Direct materials	12000	12500							
Direct labour	3600	3400							
Costs	£	£	£	F/A		£	F/A	£	F/A
Direct materials	60000	62000	2000	A		2500	A		
Direct labour	27000	26000	1000	F					
Variable overheads	14400	14000	400	F					
Fixed overheads	7000	7700	700	A					
Total costs	108400	109700	1300	A					

Fig. 7

Price variance

The difference between the actual price per unit and the standard price per unit for the actual quantity of material used is the direct materials price variance (DMPV).

DMPV = (standard price per unit – actual price per unit) × actual quantity of materials used

Example

The actual direct materials cost is given as a single figure for the whole quantity used, so the first stage of the calculation must be to find the actual price per unit:

Actual price per unit = actual direct materials costs = £62000 = £4.96 actual quantity used 12500

The second stage of the calculation is to complete the formula

$$DMPV = (£5 - £4.96) \times 12500 = £500$$

In this example, the standard price of the actual usage was less than the actual price of materials used, so the variance is FAVOURABLE.

	Flexed Budget	Actual Usage	Total Variance		Analysed variances			
					Usage or Efficiency		Price or Rate	
Output (units)	1200	1200						
Direct materials	12000	12500						
Direct labour	3600	3400						
Costs	£	£	£	F/A	£	F/A	£	F/A
Direct materials	60000	62000	2000	A	2500	A	500	F
Direct labour	27000	26000	1000	F				
Variable overheads	14400	14000	400	F				
Fixed overheads	7000	7700	700	A				
Total costs	108400	109700	1300	A				

Actual:	£
Mat. price	4.96

Fig. 8

The two variances, when added together, give the total direct materials variance (TDMV). This is the difference between the standard direct materials cost of the actual output volume and the actual cost of the direct materials used.

$$\text{TDMV} = \text{direct materials usage variance (DMUV)} +$$
$$\text{direct material price variance (DMPV)}$$

In the current example:

$$\text{TDMV} = £2,500 \text{ A} + £500 \text{ F} = £2,000 \text{ A}$$

Direct Labour Variances

Direct labour cost has two variances attributable to it, a quantity variance and a price variance

Quantity (efficiency) variance

The difference between the standard time allowed for the actual output and the actual time taken, at standard rate, is the direct labour efficiency variance (DLEV).

$$\text{DLEV} = (\text{flexed budget time} - \text{actual time}) \times \text{standard rate}$$

The standard rate is usually given as a rate per hour.

EXAMPLE

The standard rate is £7.50 per hour.

$$\text{DLEV} = (3,600 - 3,400) \times £7.50 = £1,500$$

The actual time taken was less than the standard time allowed for the actual output, so the variance is FAVOURABLE.

	Flexed Budget	Actual Usage	Total Variance					
Output (units)	1200	1200						
Direct materials	12000	12500				Analysed variances		
Direct labour	3600	3400			Usage or Efficiency		Price or Rate	
Costs	£	£	£	F/A	£	F/A	£	F/A
Direct materials	60000	62000	2000	A	2500	A	500	F
Direct labour	27000	26000	1000	F	1500	F		
Variable overheads	14400	14000	400	F				
Fixed overheads	7000	7700	700	A				
Total costs	108400	109700	1300	A				

Actual:	£
Mat. price	4.96

Fig. 9

Price (rate) variance

Because labour is usually paid by the hour, day, week or month we call this variance a rate variance.

The direct labour rate variance (DLRV) is the difference between the actual rate and the standard rate for the total time actually worked.

DLRV = (standard direct labour rate – actual direct labour rate) × actual time worked

EXAMPLE

The actual direct labour cost is given as a single figure for the total time taken, so the first stage of the calculation must be to find the actual labour rate per hour:

$$\text{Actual labour rate} = \frac{\text{actual direct labour costs}}{\text{actual time taken}} = \frac{£26,000}{3,400} = £7.65$$

The second stage of the calculation is to complete the formula:

$$\text{DLRV} = (£7.50 - £7.65) \times 3,400 = -£500$$

The actual cost of direct labour used was greater than the standard cost for the actual time taken, so the variance is ADVERSE.

	Flexed Budget	Actual Usage	Total Variance			Usage or Efficiency		Price or Rate	
Output (units)	1200	1200							
Direct materials	12000	12500					Analysed variances		
Direct labour	3600	3400							
Costs	£	£	£	F/A		£	F/A	£	F/A
Direct materials	60000	62000	2000	A		2500	A	500	F
Direct labour	27000	26000	1000	F		1500	F	500	A
Variable overheads	14400	14000	400	F					
Fixed overheads	7000	7700	700	A					
Total costs	108400	109700	1300	A					
Actual:	£		£						
Mat. price	4.96	Lab. rate	7.65						

Fig. 10

The two variances when added together give the total direct labour variance (TDLV). This is the difference between the standard direct labour cost and the direct labour cost incurred.

TDLV = direct labour efficiency variance (DLEV) + direct labour rate variance (DLRV)

In the current example:

$$\text{TDLV} = £1,500 \text{ F} + £500 \text{ A} = £1,000 \text{ F}$$

Variable Overhead Variances

Quantity (efficiency) variance

The difference between the standard time allowed for the actual production and the actual time taken, at standard rate, is the variable overhead efficiency variance (VDEV).

$$\text{VOEV} = (\text{flexed budget time} - \text{actual time}) \times \text{standard rate}$$

The standard rate in this example is given as an overhead absorption rate per labour hour. Remember that the absorption basis is related to the activity generating the variable overhead cost.

EXAMPLE

The standard rate is given as £4 per hour.

$$\text{VOEV} = (3,600 - 3,400) \times £4.00 = £800$$

The actual time taken for the actual output was less than the standard time allowed for the actual output, so the variance is FAVOURABLE.

	Flexed Budget	Actual Usage	Total Variance			Analysed variances			
						Usage or Efficiency		Price or Rate	
Output (units)	1200	1200							
Direct materials	12000	12500							
Direct labour	3600	3400							
Costs	£	£	£	F/A		£	F/A	£	F/A
Direct materials	60000	62000	2000	A		2500	A	500	F
Direct labour	27000	26000	1000	F		1500	F	500	A
Variable overheads	14400	14000	400	F		800	F		
Fixed overheads	7000	7700	700	A					
Total costs	108400	109700	1300	A					

Actual:	£		£
Mat. price	4.96	Lab. rate	7.65

Fig. 11

Price (rate) variance

The difference between the standard rate for the total time actually worked and the actual variable overhead rate is the variable overhead rate variance (VORV).

$$VORV = (\text{standard variable overhead rate} - \text{actual variable overhead rate}) \times \text{actual time worked}$$

EXAMPLE

The actual variable overhead cost is given as a single figure for the total time taken so the first stage of the calculation must be to find the actual overhead rate per hour:

$$\text{Actual overhead rate} = \frac{\text{actual direct overhead costs}}{\text{actual time taken}} = \frac{\pounds14,000}{3,400} = \pounds4.1$$

The second stage of the calculation is to complete the formula:

$$VORV = (\pounds4 - \pounds4.12) \times 3,400 = -\pounds400$$

The actual cost of variable overhead expenditure was greater than the standard variable overhead cost for the actual time taken, so the variance is ADVERSE.

	Flexed Budget	Actual Usage	Total Variance						Analysed variances		
						Usage or Efficiency			Price or Rate		
Output (units)	1200	1200									
Direct materials	12000	12500									
Direct labour	3600	3400									
Costs	£	£	£	F/A		£	F/A		£	F/A	
Direct materials	60000	62000	2000	A		2500	A		500	F	
Direct labour	27000	26000	1000	F		1500	F		500	A	
Variable overheads	14400	14000	400	F		800	F		400	A	
Fixed overheads	7000	7700	700	A							
Total costs	108400	109700	1300	A							
Actual:	£		£						£		
Mat. price	4.96	Lab. rate	7.65				V. O/H rate		4.12		

Fig. 12

The sum of these two variances is the total variable overhead variance (TVOV). This is the difference between the standard variable overhead cost and the actual variable overheads incurred.

$$\text{TVOV} = \text{variable overhead efficiency variance (VOEV)} +$$
$$\text{variable overhead rate variance(VORV)}$$

In the current example:

$$\text{TVOV} = £800 \text{ F} + £400 \text{ A} = £400 \text{ F}$$

Fixed Overhead Variance

The difference between the budgeted fixed overhead cost and the actual fixed overhead expenditure incurred is the fixed overhead expenditure variance (FOEV). Remember that the budgeted fixed overheads cost remains the same as the original budget, because this cost does not vary with the level of output.

FOEV = budgeted fixed overhead cost − actual fixed overhead expenditure incurred

EXAMPLE

$$\text{FOEV} = £7,000 − £7,700 = -£700$$

The actual fixed overhead expenditure was greater than the budgeted fixed overhead cost, so the variance is ADVERSE.

	Flexed Budget	Actual Usage	Total Variance			Analysed variances			
						Usage or Efficiency		Price or Rate	
Output (units)	1200	1200							
Direct materials	12000	12500							
Direct labour	3600	3400							
Costs	£	£	£	F/A		£	F/A	£	F/A
Direct materials	60000	62000	2000	A		2500	A	500	F
Direct labour	27000	26000	1000	F		1500	F	500	A
Variable overheads	14400	14000	400	F		800	F	400	A
Fixed overheads	7000	7700	700	A				700	A
Total costs	108400	109700	1300	A					
Actual:	£		£					£	
Mat. price	4.96	Lab. rate	7.65			V. O/H rate	4.12		

Fig. 13

Reconciling the Variances

When all the individual variances have been calculated, it becomes clear that their sum must be equal to the difference between the total flexed budgeted cost and the total actual cost.

EXAMPLE

	Flexed Budget	Actual Usage	Total Variance			Usage or Efficiency		Price or Rate	
							Analysed variances		
Output (units)	1200	1200							
Direct materials	12000	12500							
Direct labour	3600	3400				Usage or Efficiency		Price or Rate	
Costs	£	£	£	F/A		£	F/A	£	F/A
Direct materials	60000	62000	2000	A		2500	A	500	F
Direct labour	27000	26000	1000	F		1500	F	500	A
Variable overheads	14400	14000	400	F		800	F	400	A
Fixed overheads	7000	7700	700	A				700	A
Total costs	108400	109700	1300	A		200	A	1100	A
Actual:	£		£					£	
Mat. price	4.96	Lab. rate	7.65			V. O/H rate	4.12		

Fig. 14

Once the variances have been analysed, management must identify the reasons for those variances that are unacceptable to them.

Interpreting the Variances

It is very important to understand that variance analysis can only answer the "where" and "how" questions relating to the differences between budgeted total cost and actual total cost. The reasons for the differences must be investigated and established by management.

Usually, specific variances are not sufficiently detailed to assign responsibility to any one employee. On investigation it is often the case that several managers may share responsibility for a variance or group of related variances. In reality many variances are dependent on each other. These interdependent variances make the process of investigation more complex.

The variances shown in Fig. 14 are very useful because they provide a basis for decision making. However, the information provided by the analysis must be interpreted. For example, the £2,500 adverse material usage variance does not, of itself, tell management anything about the reason for the variance. There may be several reasons and each must be investigated in order to find out where management responsibility for the variance lies.

Possible Reasons for Variances

MATERIALS USAGE VARIANCES

- gains or losses resulting from the use of material of a higher or lower grade or quality than standard
- smaller or larger amounts of wastage or scrap than estimated in the standard

MATERIALS PRICE VARIANCES

- suppliers increased or reduced prices from planned levels
- costs or savings arising from bulk quantity discounts
- obtaining materials of a higher or lower quality than originally planned

LABOUR EFFICIENCY VARIANCES

- workers insufficiently trained or experienced for the job
- poor supervision of workers
- incorrect use of materials leading to inefficient working

LABOUR RATE VARIANCES

- higher wage rates paid than originally planned
- labour of a higher and more costly, or lower and cheaper, grade used than planned
- unplanned bonuses

VARIABLE AND FIXED OVERHEAD VARIANCES

The causes of variable overhead variances can be difficult to identify but labour efficiency greater or less than planned is an obvious factor where the overhead is absorbed on the basis of labour hours.

Fixed overhead variances can only arise through spending more or less than planned on fixed overheads.

INAPPROPRIATE STANDARDS

In this case, the standard setting process has failed to achieve an attainable standard. Unlike the budgeting process, which involves regular review and possible revision of targets, standards are not normally changed in the short term.

Summary

Standard costing provides management with information about the differences between actual and planned performance by analysing the variances and providing possible answers to questions such as:

*   why have we overspent?
*   are we wasting materials?
*   is the labour force working efficiently?

For standard costing to operate effectively within the budgetary control system management must ensure that there is:

*   the support and commitment of senior management to the standard costing approach
*   a clear understanding of the purpose of standard costing and its role in the budgetary control process
*   education and training for managers in the use of standard costing and the interpretation of variances
*   the setting of standards that are reasonable and achievable
*   participation and commitment of the workforce at all stages in the process
*   an accounting information system that provides timely and accurate information
*   a clearly defined management structure with the responsibilities of individual managers identified

Tutorial Questions

4.1   Using the information about standard cost, flexed budget and actual performance shown below, complete the table by calculating the total variances and analysing each one in as much detail as possible.

Standard Cost Card

Type	Quantity Kgs	Price £	Time Hours	Rate £	Cost per unit output £	£
Std. Direct materials	10.00	5.00			50.00	
Std. Direct labour			3.00	7.50	22.50	
Std. Var OAR/DLH			3.00	4.00	12.00	Total
Std. Fixed cost per unit					7.00	91.50

	Flexed Budget	Actual Usage	Total Variance		Analysed variances				
					Usage or Efficiency			Price or Rate	
Output (units)	1200	1200							
Direct materials	12000	12500							
Direct labour	3600	3400							
Costs	£	£	£	F/A	£	F/A		£	F/A
Direct materials	60000	62000							
Direct labour	27000	26000							
Variable overheads	14400	14000							
Fixed overheads	7000	7700							
Total costs	108400	109700							
Actual:	£		£					£	
Mat. price		Lab. rate			V. O/H rate				

4.2   Using the information about standard cost, flexed budget and actual performance shown below, complete the table by calculating the total variances and analysing each one in as much detail as possible.

Standard Cost Card

Type	Quantity Tonnes	Price £	Time Hours	Rate £	Cost per unit output £	£
Std. Direct materials	2.00	350.00			700.00	
Std. Direct labour			16.00	6.00	96.00	
Std. Var OAR/DLH			16.00	8.00	128.00	Total
Std. Fixed cost per unit					76.00	1000.00

	Flexed Budget	Actual Usage	Total Variance			Analysed variances				
Output (units)	288	288								
Direct materials	576	598				Analysed variances				
Direct labour	4608	4579				Usage or Efficiency		Price or Rate		
Costs	£	£	£	F/A		£	F/A	£	F/A	
Direct materials	201600	217500								
Direct labour	27648	26600								
Variable overheads	36864	37750								
Fixed overheads	22800	22000								
Total costs	288912	303850								
Actual:	£		£					£		
Mat. price		Lab. rate				V. O/H rate				

4.3   Using the information about standard cost, flexed budget and actual performance shown below, complete the table by calculating the total variances and analysing each one in as much detail as possible.

Standard Cost Card							
		Quantity	Price	Time	Rate	Cost per unit output	
	Type	Litres	£	Hrs	£	£	£
Std. Direct materials		100.00	0.60			60.00	
Std. Direct labour				0.50	10.00	5.00	
Std. Var OAR/DLH				0.50	3.50	1.75	Total
Std. Fixed cost per unit						2.00	68.75

	Flexed Budget	Actual Usage	Total Variance						
Output (units)	2120	2120							
Direct materials	212000	230000			Analysed variances				
Direct labour	1060	1200			Usage or Efficiency			Price or Rate	
Costs	£	£	£	F/A	£	F/A		£	F/A
Direct materials	127200	135250							
Direct labour	10600	11875							
Variable overheads	3710	3800							
Fixed overheads	4000	4200							
Total costs	145510	155125							
Actual:	£		£					£	
Mat. price		Lab. rate				V. O/H rate			

4.4 Using the information about standard cost, flexed budget and actual performance shown below, complete the table by calculating the total variances and analysing each one in as much detail as possible.

Standard Cost Card						
	Quantity	Price	Time	Rate	Cost per unit output	
Type	Kilos	£	Hrs	£	£	£
Std. Direct materials	7.00	35.00			245.00	
Std. Direct labour			8.00	7.25	58.00	
Std. Var OAR/DLH			8.00	6.75	54.00	Total
Std. Fixed cost per unit					5.00	362.00

	Flexed Budget	Actual Usage	Total Variance		Analysed variances				
						Usage or Efficiency		Price or Rate	
Output (units)	987	987							
Direct materials	6906	6891							
Direct labour	7896	8037							
Costs	£	£	£	F/A		£	F/A	£	F/A
Direct materials	241815	242010							
Direct labour	57246	55463							
Variable overheads	53298	53257							
Fixed overheads	5000	4200							
Total costs	357359	354930							
Actual:	£		£					£	
Mat. price		Lab. rate				V. O/H rate			

4.5   Motorparts UK Ltd is a major manufacturer and supplier of motor vehicle spares and accessories to the motor trade. The company has decided to install a standard costing at the Coventry factory in the department devoted to the manufacture of air conditioning units. Motorparts produce just one model that can be fitted to most salon cars produced for the UK market. The factory manager has collected the following relevant data about the various processes and costs involved in the manufacture of each unit.

- The amount of materials used to manufacture one unit is on average 2 kilograms. However, sometimes as much as 0.25 kg can be saved on each unit if the workers take time and care when operating the machinery. On the other hand, when one of the older forming machines was breaking down every day as much as 2.5 kgs was needed for each unit. The old machine has since been replaced.
- The current materials supplier charges £35 per kilogram, including delivery charges.
- It has usually taken about 100 minutes for a worker to operate the forming machine and assemble the air conditioning unit. However, after carrying out detailed time and motion studies, management have introduced new incentive schemes for workers and believe that the operation should now take no more than 90 minutes to complete. The incentive scheme involves a new pay rate of £7.50 per labour hour.
- It has proven difficult to establish the relevant variable overhead costs associated with the manufacturing process. This is mainly because the factory produces several different lines besides air conditioning units. The department managers cannot agree on an equitable basis to share these costs. For the time being, an estimate of £4.00 per direct labour hour is being used in order to establish the costing system. The fixed overheads are also difficult to identify and allocate precisely. A figure of £2.75 per air conditioning unit produced is to be used initially.

The standard costs of producing one air conditioning unit have now been calculated as follows:

Standard Cost Card	Item: Air conditioning unit					
	Quantity	Price	Time	Rate	Cost per unit output	
Type	Kilos	£	Hrs	£	£	£
Std. Direct materials	2.00	35.00			70.00	
Std. Direct labour			1.50	7.50	11.25	
Std. Var OAR/DLH			1.50	4.00	6.00	Total
Std. Fixed cost per unit					2.75	90.00

From this information, a master budget for a production run of 4,000 units was prepared.

After the first production run under the new standard costing system, actual output and cost information was collected. This revealed that only 3,812 units had been produced during the 10 day period. 7,943 kilograms of material had been used up and the workers' time sheets indicated that 5,565 hours had been clocked against this production run. Costs associated with the 3,812 units were £271,549 for materials, £43,906 for wages and a total of £34,774 for overheads, of which £10,675 related to fixed costs.

A flexed budget was produced and a comparison made with the actual performance figures of the 10 day period of the production run:

Air conditioning units	Master Budget	Flexed Budget	Actual
Output (units)	4000	3812	3812
Direct materials	Kilos	7624	7943
Direct labour	Hrs	5718	5565
Costs	£	£	£
Direct materials	280000	266840	271549
Direct labour	45000	42885	43906
Variable overheads	24000	22872	23099
Fixed overheads	11000	11000	10675
Total costs	360000	343597	349229

Required

Draft a report to Motorparts UK Ltd that analyses the variances and offers reasons for the variances you have calculated.

ANSWERS TO TUTORIAL QUESTIONS

Tutorial 2

2.1

Standard Cost Card						
	Quantity	Price	Time	Rate	Cost per unit output	
Type	Kgs	£	Hours	£	£	£
Std. Direct materials	10.00	5.00			50.00	
Std. Direct labour			3.00	7.50	22.50	
Std. Var OAR/DLH			3.00	4.00	12.00	Total
Std. Fixed cost per unit					7.00	91.50

	Master Budget
Output (units)	1000

Costs	£
Direct materials	50000
Direct labour	22500
Variable overheads	12000
Fixed overheads	7000
Total costs	91500

2.2

Standard Cost Card

	Type	Quantity Tonnes	Price £	Time Hours	Rate £	Cost per unit output £	£
Std. Direct materials		2.00	350.00			700.00	
Std. Direct labour				16.00	6.00	96.00	
Std. Var OAR/DLH				16.00	8.00	128.00	Total
Std. Fixed cost per unit						76.00	1000.00

	Master Budget
Output (units)	300

Costs	£
Direct materials	210000
Direct labour	28800
Variable overheads	38400
Fixed overheads	22800
Total costs	300000

2.3

Standard Cost Card

	Type	Quantity Litres	Price £	Time Hrs	Rate £	Cost per unit output £	£
Std. Direct materials		100.00	0.60			60.00	
Std. Direct labour				0.50	10.00	5.00	
Std. Var OAR/DLH				0.50	3.50	1.75	Total
Std. Fixed cost per unit						2.00	68.75

	Master Budget
Output (units)	2000

Costs	£
Direct materials	120000
Direct labour	10000
Variable overheads	3500
Fixed overheads	4000
Total costs	137500

2.4

Standard Cost Card						
	Quantity	Price	Time	Rate	Cost per unit output	
Type	Kilos	£	Hrs	£	£	£
Std. Direct materials	7.00	35.00			245.00	
Std. Direct labour			8.00	7.25	58.00	
Std. Var OAR/DLH			8.00	6.75	54.00	Total
Std. Fixed cost per unit					5.00	362.00

	Master Budget
Output (units)	1000

Costs	£
Direct materials	245000
Direct labour	58000
Variable overheads	54000
Fixed overheads	5000
Total costs	362000

2.5

Standard Cost Card						
	Quantity	Price	Time	Rate	Cost per unit output	
Type	Kilos	£	Hrs	£	£	£
Std. Direct materials	2.00	35.00			70.00	
Std. Direct labour			1.50	7.50	11.25	
Std. Var OAR/DLH			1.50	4.00	6.00	Total
Std. Fixed cost per unit					2.75	90.00

	Master Budget
Output (units)	4000
	Kilos
	Hrs
Costs	£
Direct materials	280000
Direct labour	45000
Variable overheads	24000
Fixed overheads	11000
Total costs	360000

Tutorial 3

3.1

	Master Budget	Flexed Budget	Actual
Output (units)	1000	1200	1200
Direct materials	Kgs	12000	12500
Direct labour	Hours	3600	3400
Costs	£	£	£
Direct materials	50000	60000	62000
Direct labour	22500	27000	26000
Variable overheads	12000	14400	14000
Fixed overheads	7000	7000	7700
Total costs	91500	108400	109700

3.2

	Master Budget	Flexed Budget	Actual
Output (units)	300	288	288
Direct materials	Tonnes	576	598
Direct labour	Hours	4608	4579
Costs	£	£	£
Direct materials	210000	201600	217500
Direct labour	28800	27648	26600
Variable overheads	38400	36864	37750
Fixed overheads	22800	22800	22000
Total costs	300000	288912	303850

3.3

	Master Budget	Flexed Budget	Actual
Output (units)	2000	2120	2120
Direct materials	Litres	212000	230000
Direct labour	Hrs	1060	1200
Costs	£	£	£
Direct materials	120000	127200	135250
Direct labour	10000	10600	11875
Variable overheads	3500	3710	3800
Fixed overheads	4000	4000	4200
Total costs	137500	145510	155125

3.4

	Master Budget	Flexed Budget	Actual
Output (units)	1000	987	987
Direct materials	Kilos	6909	6891
Direct labour	Hrs	7896	8037
Costs	£	£	£
Direct materials	245000	241815	242010
Direct labour	58000	57246	55463
Variable overheads	54000	53298	53257
Fixed overheads	5000	5000	4200
Total costs	362000	357359	354930

3.5

	Master Budget	Flexed Budget	Actual
Output (units)	4000	3812	3812
Direct materials	Kilos	7624	7943
Direct labour	Hrs	5718	5565
Costs	£	£	£
Direct materials	280000	266840	271549
Direct labour	45000	42885	43906
Variable overheads	24000	22872	23099
Fixed overheads	11000	11000	10675
Total costs	360000	343597	349229

Tutorial 4

4.1

	Flexed Budget	Actual Usage	Total Variance	F/A	Usage or Efficiency	F/A	Price or Rate	F/A
Output (units)	1200	1200						
Direct materials	12000	12500				Analysed variances		
Direct labour	3600	3400			Usage or Efficiency		Price or Rate	
Costs	£	£	£	F/A	£	F/A	£	F/A
Direct materials	60000	62000	2000	A	2500	A	500	F
Direct labour	27000	26000	1000	F	1500	F	500	A
Variable overheads	14400	14000	400	F	800	F	400	A
Fixed overheads	7000	7700	700	A			700	A
Total costs	108400	109700	1300	A	200	A	1100	A
Actual:	£		£				£	
Mat. price	4.96 Lab. rate	7.65			V. O/H rate	4.12		

4.2

	Flexed Budget	Actual Usage	Total Variance						
Output (units)	288	288							
Direct materials	576	598					Analysed variances		
Direct labour	4608	4579				Usage or Efficiency		Price or Rate	
Costs	£	£	£	F/A	£	F/A	£	F/A
Direct materials	201600	217500	15900	A	7700	A	8200	A
Direct labour	27648	26600	1048	F	174	F	874	F
Variable overheads	36864	37750	886	A	232	F	1118	A
Fixed overheads	22800	22000	800	F			800	F
Total costs	288912	303850	14938	A	7294	A	7644	A
Actual:	£		£				£	
Mat. price	363.71	Lab. rate	5.81		V. O/H rate		8.24	

4.3

	Flexed Budget	Actual Usage	Total Variance						
Output (units)	2120	2120							
Direct materials	212000	230000					Analysed variances		
Direct labour	1060	1200				Usage or Efficiency		Price or Rate	
Costs	£	£	£	F/A	£	F/A	£	F/A
Direct materials	127200	135250	8050	A	10800	A	2750	F
Direct labour	10600	11875	1275	A	1400	A	125	F
Variable overheads	3710	3800	90	A	490	A	400	F
Fixed overheads	4000	4200	200	A			200	A
Total costs	145510	155125	9615	A	12690	A	3075	F
Actual:	£		£				£	
Mat. price	0.59	Lab. rate	9.90		V. O/H rate		3.17	

4.4

	Flexed Budget	Actual Usage	Total Variance	F/A	Usage or Efficiency £	F/A	Price or Rate £	F/A
Output (units)	987	987						
Direct materials	6909	6891					Analysed variances	
Direct labour	7896	8037						
Costs	£	£	£	F/A	£	F/A	£	F/A
Direct materials	241815	242010	195	A	630	F	825	A
Direct labour	57246	55463	1783	F	1022	A	2805	F
Variable overheads	53298	53257	41	F	952	A	993	F
Fixed overheads	5000	4200	800	F			800	F
Total costs	357359	354930	2429	F	1344	A	3773	F
Actual:	£		£				£	
Mat. price	35.12	Lab. rate	6.90		V. O/H rate		6.63	

4.5 Your report should include an analysis of the variances as follows:

	Flexed Budget	Actual Usage	Total Variance	F/A	Usage or Efficiency £	F/A	Price or Rate £	F/A
Output (units)	3812	3812						
Direct materials	7624	7943					Analysed variances	
Direct labour	5718	5565						
Costs	£	£	£	F/A	£	F/A	£	F/A
Direct materials	266840	271549	4709	A	11165	A	6456	F
Direct labour	42885	43906	1021	A	1148	F	2169	A
Variable overheads	22872	23099	227	A	612	F	839	A
Fixed overheads	11000	10675	325	F			325	F
Total costs	343597	349229	5632	A	9406	A	3774	F
Actual:	£		£				£	
Mat. price	34.19	Lab. rate	7.89		V. O/H rate		4.15	

Suggested reasons for the variances include:

- Material may be being wasted; investigation of the reason for this could indicate material quality problems. However, the favourable labour efficiency variance indicates that workers might be wasting material in their efforts to keep within the standard time allowed of 1.5 hours for the forming and assembly of each unit.
- The favourable materials price variance could have arisen from quantity discounts that were not allowed for when the standard price was set. A different supplier may have been used however.
- The adverse labour rate variance could possibly be traced to overtime payments, unplanned bonuses or the use of more highly paid workers. If these workers were more highly skilled, then this may help to explain the favourable labour efficiency variance (and the favourable variable overhead efficiency variance), but presumably not the adverse materials usage variance.
- The adverse variable overhead rate variance may have been caused by increases in overhead costs, though this is by no means certain. The reason for the favourable fixed overhead expenditure variance, on the other hand, should be simple to trace through the accounting records.

Management must investigate the reason for each variance thoroughly and carefully before taking any action.

CAPITAL INVESTMENT APPRAISAL

Manual

CONTENTS

Introduction to Capital Investment Appraisal

Business Goals

The main aims of most businesses are:

- to maximise profits (profitability)
- to have sufficient cash resources to meet commitments as they fall due (liquidity)

In order for a business to survive, it must reconcile these twin goals.

Capital Expenditure

Before a business can earn profits, it will usually need to invest in fixed assets. This is known as capital expenditure.

A retailing business, for example, will need to acquire fixed assets, such as premises, shop fixtures and delivery vans before it can commence trading. Similarly, a manufacturing business will need to finance the research and development of its products and the acquisition of factory premises, machinery and other assets before production can commence.

There may be a considerable time lag between initial cash outlays and the subsequent inflows of cash from sales.

Working Capital

In addition to the finance required to purchase fixed assets, a business will need working capital. This working capital must be sufficient to enable the business to acquire stock and to offer credit facilities to its customers. Capital investment decisions will be concerned with the total investment requirements of a project.

Capital Rationing

The funds available for investing in the assets required for business activities will be limited, for a variety of reasons. Not only may external sources of finance, such as debt capital, be difficult and expensive to acquire, but when a business acquires cash resources there will usually be a number of alternative projects competing for these limited funds.

Capital Investment Appraisal

Capital projects may tie up large amounts of money for long time periods. Capital investment (project) appraisal is, therefore, a very important type of long term decision making.

Capital investment appraisal involves a comparison of the cost of a project now (the investment) with the expected net benefits (returns) in the future.

Capital investment appraisal decisions may concern:

- The acquisition of fixed assets, where there may be a choice between the outright purchase of the asset, with a single cash outflow at the start of the asset's life, and the leasing of the asset, with a number of rental payments to be made over several years.
- Project evaluation, where there may be a number of cash inflows and outflows occurring over several years and there may be a number of competing projects. For example, a business may be considering two projects, one involving investment in the development of product A, the other the acquisition of a machine which will enable it to produce product B. Where capital is rationed, the business may have to make a choice between these two projects.

Aims of Capital Investment Appraisal

The aims of capital investment appraisal are:

- to test the viability of a project or projects
- to compare different or competing projects for achieving the same goal
- to rank projects competing for a limited amount of finance, maybe to achieve different goals

Non-Financial Considerations

This manual will concentrate on the financial aspects of capital investment appraisal. Non-financial considerations, however, also play an important part in the decision making process, e.g. a hospital trust may be faced with a choice between the purchase of a new scanner and the expansion of its intensive care unit. In such a situation, social and political factors may over-ride the financial considerations.

Predicted Data

Capital investment appraisal decisions involve the use of predicted data. In making capital investment decisions there is always a risk that the predicted data may prove to be unreliable. Capital investment appraisal techniques do not assist managers to predict the future.

Alternative Methods of Capital Investment Appraisal

Various methods may be employed in the evaluation of alternative strategies – even though, basically, all methods compare the investment required with the expected returns. The main appraisal methods focus on the timing of cash inflows and outflows. These methods are:

- Payback
- Discounted Cash Flow (NPV and IRR)

Another appraisal method, which focuses on the profitability of a project, is:

- Accounting Rate of Return (ARR).

Cash flows, however, are more objective than profit and are, therefore, preferred for decision making. It should be noted that all the above methods may provide conflicting answers.

Project Data

The following predicted information for a project will be required before any of the techniques can be used:

- investment required
- project life (years)
- cash inflows from trading, i.e. cash received from project sales
- cash outflows from trading, i.e. payments for project costs
- residual value, i.e. receipts from the sale of project assets

The project information is generally set out in the following format.

	Inflows (£)	Outflows (£)	Net Cashflows (£)
Investment		50,000	(50,000)
Year 1	35,000	10,000	25,000
Year 2	35,000	10,000	25,000
Year 3	25,000	12,000	13,000
Year 4	40,000	14,000	26,000
Year 5	40,000	19,000	21,000
Residual Value	0		0
Project Lifetime Surplus			60,000

The above data could, for example, relate to the projected costs of opening a new restaurant where £50,000 is spent on a 5 year lease and fittings. The cash inflows would then represent revenue from customers, and the cash outflows the costs of food, wages, laundry, insurance, etc.

Assumptions

For the sake of simplicity the following assumptions will be made in this manual:

- all investments occur on Day 1 of the project
- All trading inflows/outflows occur on the last day of each year
- Taxation and inflation are to be ignored

Tutorial Questions

1.1   Calculate the missing information to complete the following project data table.

	Inflows (£)	Outflows (£)	Net Cashflows (£)
Investment		80,000	(80,000)
Year 1	25,000	15,000	
Year 2	30,000	12,000	
Year 3	35,000	14,000	
Year 4	40,000	18,000	
Year 5	50,000	25,000	
Residual Value	0		
Project Lifetime Surplus			

1.2   Calculate the missing information to complete the following project data table.

	Inflows (£)	Outflows (£)	Net Cashflows (£)
Investment		60,000	
Year 1	35,000	15,000	
Year 2	40,000		22,000
Year 3		12,000	25,000
Year 4	40,000		(5,000)
Year 5	50,000	25,000	
Residual Value	7,500		
Project Lifetime Surplus			

1.3 Calculate the missing information to complete the following project data table.

	Inflows (£)	Outflows (£)	Net Cashflows (£)
Investment			(70,000)
Year 1	45,000	12,000	
Year 2	50,000		22,000
Year 3		27,000	30,000
Year 4		33,000	15,000
Year 5	80,000		
Residual Value	2,500		
Project Lifetime Surplus	40,000		

1.4 Challenge Ltd is considering commencing manufacturing operations on 1 January Year 1. The company has an option to acquire a 5 year lease on a factory at a cost of £15,000 payable on 1 January Year 1, when the lease is signed. Machinery costing £23,000 will be bought and paid for on 1 January Year 1. It is estimated that this machinery will be in use for five years, at the end of which time it will have a residual value of £3,000. The company expects cash inflows from trading of £15,000 for each of the first two years and £18,000 for each of the remaining three years of the project. Cash outflows from trading are budgeted to be £7,000 in Year 1, £6,000 in Year 2 and £8,000 in each of the next three years.

Required
Using the above information, calculate the project lifetime surplus.

THE PAYBACK METHOD OF CAPITAL INVESTMENT APPRAISAL

Payback

Payback is a measure of how quickly a project will repay its initial capital investment. The Payback method is the most widely used method of capital investment appraisal. Business risk involves making investments with no certainty of a return: the speed with which a project repays its capital investment is thus an important consideration.

Using the data shown in Tutorial 1, the payback period may be calculated for the project, which will now be called Project A. An additional column is required to show the predicted cumulative net cashflow (cumulative netflow):

Project A

	Inflows	Outflows (£)	Net Cashflows (£)	Cumulative Netflow (£)
Investment		50,000	(50,000)	(50,000)
Year 1	35,000	10,000	25,000	(25,000)
Year 2	35,000	10,000	25,000	0*
Year 3	25,000	12,000	13,000	13,000
Year 4	40,000	14,000	26,000	39,000
Year 5	40,000	19,000	21,000	60,000
Residual Value	0		0	60,000
Project Lifetime Surplus			60,000	
Pays back by end of Year			2	

*The payback period will be 2 years, i.e. it will take 2 years for the initial investment of £50,000 to be recovered

Alternative Projects

Given alternative projects to choose between, the one projected to pay back its capital investment the quickest would have at least one reason to be preferred, although the Payback method of capital investment appraisal is not on its own a sufficient test of the financial viability of a project.

Project A, above, may be compared with a competing project, Project B, to which the following data relate.

Project B

	Inflows (£)	Outflows (£)	Net Cashflows (£)	Cumulative Netflow (£)
Investment		50,000	(50,000)	(50,000)
Year 1	35,000	10,000	25,000	(25,000)
Year 2	35,000	10,000	25,000	0
Year 3	0	0	0	0
Year 4	0	0	0	0
Year 5	0	0	0	0
Residual Value	0		0	0
Project Lifetime Surplus			0	
Pays back by end of Year			2	

NOTES

- Projects A and B have the same payback period of 2 years.
- Project B, which finishes in Year 2, has no lifetime surplus.
- If Payback on its own is used to assess the viability of the projects, Project B would have the same ranking as Project A.

Advantages of the Payback Method

- Many people involved in the decision making process may have had little or no financial training. The Payback method is simple to use and understand.
- Many firms suffer from liquidity (cash) constraints and rely on a rapid repayment of investment. Payback highlights the speed at which a project repays the initial capital outlay.
- Where the investment involves a high degree of risk, the Payback method may be the most appropriate. It is probable that forecasting of cash flows in the earlier years will be more accurate than the forecasts for later years. By focusing on the shorter term,

the Payback method helps to reduce the risks of forecasting. Early obsolescence of a project is, therefore, not so damaging to a business.

Limitations of the Payback Method

- The Payback method does not recognise the overall return on the investment. Under its sole guidance the decision will be taken to accept the project with the shortest payback period, regardless of cash flows after the payback period.
- Payback normally ignores the time value of money. An important aspect of capital investment appraisal is the recognition that cash flows received in later years have less value than those received in earlier years.

Payback in Practice

Despite its limitations, Payback is, as we have seen, the most widely used method of capital investment appraisal. Most organisations will set a maximum payback period for project assessment. Payback is thus used as a filter for projects. Projects which fail to meet the organisation's established "speed" criterion will be rejected without further consideration.

Tutorial Questions

2.1 From the following information calculate the cumulative netflow for each year and ascertain the payback period.

	Inflows (£)	Outflows (£)	Net Cashflows (£)	Cumulative Netflow (£)
Investment		80,000	(80,000)	
Year 1	25,000	15,000	10,000	
Year 2	30,000	12,000	18,000	
Year 3	35,000	14,000	21,000	
Year 4	40,000	18,000	22,000	
Year 5	50,000	25,000	25,000	
Residual Value	0		0	
Project Lifetime Surplus			16,000	
Pays back by end of Year				

2.2 From the following information calculate the cumulative netflow for each year and ascertain the payback period.

	Inflows (£)	Outflows (£)	Net Cashflows (£)	Cumulative Netflow (£)
Investment		60,000	(60,000)	
Year 1	35,000	15,000	20,000	
Year 2	40,000	18,000	22,000	
Year 3	37,000	12,000	25,000	
Year 4	40,000	45,000	(5,000)	
Year 5	50,000	25,000	25,000	
Residual Value	7,500		7,500	
Project Lifetime Surplus			34,500	
Pays back by end of Year				

2.3 From the following information calculate the cumulative netflows for each year and ascertain the payback period.

	Inflows (£)	Outflows (£)	Net Cashflows (£)	Cumulative Netflow (£)
Investment		70,000	(70,000)	
Year 1	45,000	12,000	33,000	
Year 2	50,000	28,000	22,000	
Year 3	57,000	27,000	30,000	
Year 4	48,000	33,000	15,000	
Year 5	80,000	72,500	7,500	
Residual Value	2,500		2,500	
Project Lifetime Surplus			40,000	
Pays back by end of Year				

2.4 Challenge Ltd is considering commencing manufacturing operations on 1 January Year 1. The company has an option to acquire a five year lease on a factory at a cost of £15,000 payable on 1 January Year 1, when the lease is signed. Machinery costing £23,000 will be bought and paid for on 1 January Year 1. It is estimated that this machinery will be in use for five years, at the end of which time it will have a residual value of £3,000. The company expects cash inflows from trading of £15,000 for each of the first two years and £18,000 for each of the remaining three years of the project. Cash outflows from trading are budgeted to be £7,000 in Year 1, £6,000 in Year 2 and £8,000 in each of the next three years.

Required

Using the above information, calculate the project's payback period.

NET PRESENT VALUE (NPV): A DISCOUNTING METHOD OF CAPITAL INVESTMENT APPRAISAL

The Time Value of Money

Capital investment decisions involve the commitment of resources for many years. The traditional Payback method of capital investment appraisal uses actual cash flows without regard to the time value of money. Yet the recognition of the time value of money is crucial in decision making. This can be demonstrated by asking an individual to choose between receiving £100 now, or £100 in one year's time. Even ignoring risk and inflation, £100 now has more value because it can be used productively. It can, for example, be invested to earn interest, which is the compensation paid to lenders for providing finance which will not be repaid until a future date. This preference for payment now, rather than at some time in the future, is known as time (liquidity) preference.

In making decisions which involve future cash flows, it is thus necessary to take interest rates into account. These are usually expressed as a percentage (%):

Interest rate = interest for a period × 100 amount borrowed or invested

Decisions which will result in future cash flows will be affected by the relationship between:

- **P** the ca**P**ital invested
- **N** the **N**umber of years of investment
- **I** The **I**nterest rate

Discounting and compounding are two mathematical techniques which examine the relationship between **P**, **N** and **I**. Although it is discounting which is used in capital investment appraisal, an understanding of compounding often makes discounting calculations more comprehensible. Therefore compounding will be explained first. Those who are already familiar with these techniques may omit the following section on compounding.

Compounding

Compounding is the calculation of the future value of a sum of money invested today at a certain rate of interest. The interest is added periodically to the capital sum invested, so that interest in future periods is earned on the "compounded" sum, i.e. the interest earned also earns interest in subsequent periods.

In compounding and discounting calculations, the % interest rate should be expressed as a decimal, e.g.:

$$5\% \text{ which is } \frac{5}{100} \text{ should be expressed as } 0.05$$

EXAMPLE

A saver invests £1,000 at an annual rate of interest of 5% (0.05) for four years.

	£
Capital invested (**P**) at start of year 1	1,000
Add Interest (**I**) for Year 1 (£1,000 × 0.05)	50
Value of investment at end of Year 1	1,050
Add Interest for Year 2 (£1,050 × 0.05)	53
Value of investment at end of Year 2	1,103
Add Interest for Year 3 (£1,103 × 0.5)	55
Value of investment at end of Year 3	1,158
Add Interest for Year 4 (£1,158 × 0.05)	58
Value of investment at end of Year 4	1,216

The future value, in four years' time, of £1,000 invested at a compound interest rate of 5% per annum will thus be £1,216.

Compounding "Factors"

Tables of factors are available to save time in "future value" calculations. This section should only be studied by those who need to understand the derivation of the factors.

The compounding factors, i.e. the "multipliers", which can be used to calculate the future value of any ca**P**ital sum invested at an **I**nterest rate of 5% (0.05) per annum can be calculated from the above example.

$$\frac{£1,050}{£1,000} = 1.05 \text{ for Year}$$

This factor of 1.05 is the multiplier to be used to calculate the at the end of one year value of any capital sum invested at 5% per annum.

$$\frac{£1,103}{£1,000} = 1.103 \text{ for Year 2}$$

This factor of 1.103 is the multiplier to be used to calculate the value at the end of two years of any capital sum invested at 5% per annum.

$$\frac{£1,158}{£1,000} = 1.158 \text{ for Year 3}$$

This factor of 1.158 is the multiplier to be used to calculate the value at the end of three years of any capital sum invested at 5% per annum.

$$\frac{£1,216}{£1,000} = 1.216 \text{ for Year 4}$$

This factor of 1.216 is the multiplier to be used to calculate the value at the end of your years of any capital sum invested at 5% per annum.

Compounding Tables

Future value (compounding) tables may be used to calculate the future value of an investment. These tables provide the compounding factors at various rates of interest and for various time periods. Refer to a future value table and you will see, for example, that the compounding factor to use to calculate the future value of £1 invested at 5% per annum for four years is 1.216. If this factor is applied to the investment in the previous example of £1,000, it is simple to calculate the value of the investment after four years:

$$£1,000 \times 1.216 = £1,216$$

It should be noted that the compounding always increases the value of an investment. The compounding factors, therefore, will always be greater than 1.

Mathematical Formula for Calculating Compounding Factors

Where compounding tables are not available, the following mathematical formula must be used to calculate the compounding factors.

$$\text{Compounding Factor} = (1 + \text{Interest rate})^{\text{Number of years}}$$

This formula will now be applied to the previous example. The compounding factor to be used to calculate the value of an investment of £1,000 at the end of Year 4 at an interest rate of 5% (0.05) per annum will be:

$$\text{Compounding Factor} = (1 + 0.05)^4$$

$$= 1.05 \times 1.05 \times 1.05 \times 1.05$$

$$= 1.216$$

Discounting

When making capital investment decisions, cash flows for different years must be converted into a common value, i.e. converted into their respective values at the same point in time. The point in time chosen in capital investment appraisal is the "present" – the time at which the decision is taken. That is, all cash flows are converted to their "present values". This will involve discounting future values to present values. Discounting is, therefore, a technique which allows a fair comparison of competing projects which have different life spans.

Discounting is based on the same mathematical principle as compounding, but while compounding increases present value to future value, i.e. calculates the future value of £1 invested today, discounting decreases future value to present value, i.e. calculates the present value of £1 received in the future. Discounting is, therefore, the mathematical opposite of compounding.

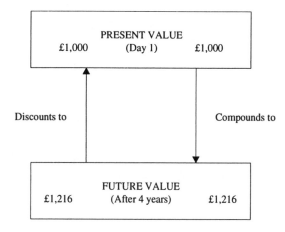

Using the example of an investment of £1,000 at a rate of interest of 5% (0.05) per annum (employed above in the section on compounding), the present values of future sums can be calculated as follows:

Future Value		Present Value
£1,050	received in 1 year's time	= £1,000
£1,103	2	= £1,000
£1,158	3	= £1,000
£1,216	4	= £1,000

The present value of £1,216 to be received in four years' time is £1,000 when the interest rate is 5% per annum.

Discounting Factors

The discounting factors, i.e. the "multipliers" which can be used to calculate the present value of ANY future cash flows at an interest rate of 5% per annum can be calculated from the above figures.

$$\frac{£1{,}000}{£1{,}050} = 0.9524 \text{ for Year 1}$$

This factor of 0.9524 is the multiplier to be used to calculate the present value of any future cash flows to be received at the end of one year when the interest rate is 5% per annum.

$$\frac{£1{,}000}{£1{,}103} = 0.9070 \text{ for Year 2}$$

This factor of 0.9070 is the multiplier to be used to calculate the present value of any future cash flows to be received at the end of two years when the interest rate is 5% per annum.

$$\frac{£1{,}000}{£1{,}158} = 0.8638 \text{ for Year 3}$$

This factor of 0.8638 is the multiplier to be used to calculate the present value of any future cash flows to be received at the end of three years when the interest rate is 5% per annum.

$$\frac{£1{,}000}{£1{,}216} = 0.8227 \text{ for Year 4}$$

This factor of 0.8227 is the multiplier to be used to calculate the present value of any future cash flows to be received at the end of four years when the interest rate is 5% per annum.

Discounting Tables

Discounting tables may be used to calculate the present value of future cash flows. These tables provide the discounting factors at various rates of interest and for various time periods. They will show, for example, that the discounting factor to be used to calculate the present value of £1 received or paid in 4 years' time where the interest rate is 5% per annum is 0.8227. If this factor is applied to £1,216 to be received in four years' time, it is a simple matter to calculate the present value of the cash flow:

$$£1{,}216 \times 0.8227 = £1{,}000$$

It should be noted that discounting always decreases the value of cash flows. The discounting factors, therefore, will always be less than 1.

Mathematical Formula for Calculating Discounting Factors

Where discounting tables are not available, the following mathematical formula must be used to calculate the discounting factors.

$$\text{Discounting Factor} = \frac{1}{(1 + \text{Interest rate})^{\text{Number of years}}}$$

This formula will now be applied to the previous example. The discounting factor to be used to calculate the present value of a cash flow of £1,216 at the end of Year 4 at an annual interest rate of 5% (0.05) will be:

$$\begin{aligned}
\text{Discounting Factor} &= 1\ (1 + 0.05)^4 \\
&= 1\ 1.05 \times 1.05 \times 1.05 \times 1.05 \\
&= 1\ 1.216 \\
&= 0.8227
\end{aligned}$$

The Use of Discounting in Capital Investment Appraisal

The Net Present Value (NPV) and Internal Rate of Return (IRR) methods are two methods of capital investment appraisal which discount cash flows to make allowance for the time value of money. (See Tutorial 4 for the IRR method.)

Appraising Projects Using Net Present Values (NPVs)

Using this method, projects are evaluated as follows:

i.   An interest rate is chosen. Firms will usually choose an interest rate which represents their cost of capital or the cost of borrowing to finance the project.
ii. The net cash flows of the project, on a year by year basis, are discounted to present values.
iii. The present values are totalled to give the net present value of the project.

The project details are normally set out as follows (assume that an interest rate of 10% per annum is chosen)

Project A

	Inflows (£)	Outflows (£)	Net Cashflows (£)	10% Discount Factors	Present Value (£)
Investment		50,000	(50,000)	1.0000	(50,000)
Year 1	35,000	10,000	25,000	0.9091	22,727
Year 2	35,000	10,000	25,000	0.8264	20,660
Year 3	25,000	12,000	13,000	0.7513	9,767
Year 4	40,000	14,000	26,000	0.6830	17,758
Year 5	40,000	19,000	21,000	0.6209	13,039
Residual Value	0		0	0.6209	0
Project Lifetime Surplus			60,000	**NPV**	33,951

NOTES

- It is assumed that the capital investment is made on Day 1 of the project. There is, therefore, no need to discount the initial investment as the outflow is already at present value i.e. it occurs immediately not in the future – there is no timing difference. Discounting tables will show this as Year 0, and a factor of 1.0000 is applied to the initial investment. For simplicity it will be assumed that all other cash flows occur at the end of the year.
- Any residual value of the project assets will normally be realised on the last day of the final year of the project.
- A project which yields a positive net present value is viable, subject to the reliability of the predicted data. This means that the present value of the future cash flows is greater than the initial investment.

The Use of the NPV Method to Evaluate Two or More Projects

The NPV method may be used to compare the viability of several projects which may be competing for limited capital resources.

Project A, which yielded a net present value of £33,951, will now be compared with Project C. The two projects have the same lifetime surplus, but the timing of the cash flows differs.

Project C

	Inflows (£)	Outflows (£)	Net Cashflows (£)	10% Discount Factors (£)	Present Value (£)
Investment		50,000	(50,000)	1.0000	(50,000)
Year 1	25,000	10,000	15,000	0.9091	13,636
Year 2	25,000	10,000	15,000	0.8264	12,396
Year 3	25,000	12,000	13,000	0.7513	9,767
Year 4	50,000	14,000	36,000	0.6830	24,588
Year 5	50,000	19,000	31,000	0.6209	19,248
Residual Value	0		0	0.6209	0
Project Lifetime Surplus			60,000	**NPV**	29,635

COMPARISON OF THE TWO PROJECTS

	NPV £
Project A	33,951
Project C	29,635

- Both projects would appear to be viable, as each has a positive NPV.
- Project A has a substantially higher NPV. If the two projects were competing for limited funding, Project A would be preferred from a financial return point of view.
- With the exception of that for the initial investment, all the figures in the tables will be based on estimates. Any variations in the actual cash inflows, cash outflows or interest rate will result in a different outcome.

Tutorial Questions

3.1 From the following information calculate the present value for each year, and ascertain the net present value of the project, using an annual interest rate of 5%.

	Inflows (£)	Outflows (£)	Net Cashflows (£)	Discount Factors	Present Value (£)
Investment		80,000	(80,000)		
Year 1	25,000	15,000	10,000		
Year 2	30,000	12,000	18,000		
Year 3	35,000	14,000	21,000		
Year 4	40,000	18,000	22,000		
Year 5	50,000	25,000	25,000		
Residual Value	0		0		
Project Lifetime Surplus			16,000	**NPV**	

3.2 From the following information calculate the present value for each year, and ascertain the net present value of the project, using an annual interest rate of 7%.

	Inflows (£)	Outflows (£)	Net Cashflows (£)	Discount Factors	Present Value (£)
Investment		60,000	(60,000)		
Year 1	35,000	15,000	20,000		
Year 2	40,000	18,000	22,000		
Year 3	37,000	12,000	25,000		
Year 4	40,000	45,000	(5,000)		
Year 5	50,000	25,000	25,000		
Residual Value	7,500		7,500		
Project Lifetime Surplus			34,500	**NPV**	

3.3   From the following information calculate the present value for each year and ascertain the Net Present Value of the project using an interest rate of 15%.

	Inflows (£)	Outflows (£)	Net Cashflows (£)	Discount Factors	Present Value (£)
Investment		70,000	(70,000)		
Year 1	45,000	12,000	33,000		
Year 2	50,000	28,000	22,000		
Year 3	57,000	27,000	30,000		
Year 4	48,000	33,000	15,000		
Year 5	80,000	72,500	7,500		
Residual Value	2,500		2,500		
Project Lifetime Surplus			40,000	**NPV**	

3.4   Challenge Ltd is considering commencing manufacturing operations on 1 January Year 1. The company has an option to acquire a 5 year lease on a factory at a cost of £15,000 payable on 1 January Year 1, when the lease is signed. Machinery costing £23,000 will be bought and paid for on 1 January Year 1. It is estimated that this machinery will be in use for 5 years, at the end of which time it will have a residual value of £3,000. The company expects cash inflows from trading of £15,000 for each of the first two years and £18,000 for each of the remaining three years of the project. Cash outflows from trading are budgeted to be £7,000 in Year 1, £6,000 in Year 2 and £8,000 in each of the next three years. To finance the project Challenge Ltd would need to take out a loan at an interest rate of 10% per annum.

Required
Using the above information advise, Challenge Ltd on the viability of the project.

DISCOUNTING TO FIND THE INTERNAL RATE OF RETURN (IRR)

The Internal Rate of Return (IRR) method uses discounted cash flows to calculate the percentage rate of return a project is capable of providing, this being equivalent to the maximum cost of capital (% interest rate) the project can remunerate. This rate, the IRR of a project. is thus defined as the % interest rate which will discount net cash flows to a net present value (NPV) of zero. Any project, then, with an IRR greater than the cost of its finance will be worth undertaking.

The Calculation of IRR by the Trial and Error Method

The IRR (the % interest rate which will discount net cash flows to a zero NPV) may be found by trial and error:

i.   An interest rate, chosen at random, is used to calculate the NPV of a project.
ii. If the NPV using this interest rate is positive, the NPV is recalculated using a higher interest rate, as this will result in a lower NPV.
iii. Where this second calculation results in a negative NPV, it follows that the % IRR will lie somewhere between the two randomly chosen rates.
iv. Several calculations (iterations) may be necessary to hit the target interest rate which represents the % IRR of a project, i.e. the % interest rate which will discount net cash flows to a zero NPV.

The following example shows a project which yields a positive net present value of £29,635 at an interest rate of 10%.

Project C

	Inflows (£)	Outflows (£)	Net Cashflows (£)	10% Discount Factors	Present Value (£)
Investment		50,000	(50,000)	1.0000	(50,000)
Year 1	25,000	10,000	15,000	0.9091	13,636
Year 2	25,000	10,000	15,000	0.8264	12,396
Year 3	25,000	12,000	13,000	0.7513	9,767
Year 4	50,000	14,000	36,000	0.6830	24,588
Year 5	50,000	19,000	31,000	0.6209	19,248
Residual Value	0		0	0.6209	0
Project Lifetime Surplus			60,000	**NPV**	29,635

NOTES

- The net present value of Project C is positive at an interest rate of 10%. It follows, therefore, that the internal rate of return yielded by Project C must be higher than 10%.
- In order to find the IRR of Project C (the interest rate which will yield a zero net present value), a higher interest rate must be chosen for the next iteration.

The following table shows the NPV of Project C using a rate of 30% per annum.

	Inflows (£)	Outflows (£)	Net Cashflows (£)	30% Discount Factors	Present Value (£)
Investment		50,000	(50,000)	1.0000	(50,000)
Year 1	25,000	10,000	15,000	0.7692	11,538
Year 2	25,000	10,000	15,000	0.5917	8,875
Year 3	25,000	12,000	13,000	0.4552	5,918
Year 4	50,000	14,000	36,000	0.3501	12,604
Year 5	50,000	19,000	31,000	0.2693	8,348
Residual Value	0		0	0.2693	0
Project Lifetime Surplus			60,000	**NPV**	(2,717)

At a 30% interest rate Project C shows a negative NPV. It follows, therefore, that the IRR yielded by the project is lower than 30%. By trial and error it has now been ascertained that the IRR lies somewhere between 10% and 30%.

The following table shows the NPV of Project C using a rate of 27.5% per annum.

	Inflows (£)	Outflows (£)	Net Cashflows (£)	27.5% Discount Factors	Present Value (£)
Investment		50,000	(50,000)	1.0000	(50,000)
Year 1	25,000	10,000	15,000	0.7843	11,764
Year 2	25,000	10,000	15,000	0.6151	9,227
Year 3	25,000	12,000	13,000	0.4824	6,271
Year 4	50,000	14,000	36,000	0.3784	13,622
Year 5	50,000	19,000	31,000	0.2967	9,198
Residual Value	0		0	0.2967	0
Project Lifetime Surplus			60,000	**NPV**	82

At an interest rate of 27.5% the NPV is practically zero. The IRR may be taken as 27.5% without further calculation.

The Use of the IRR method to Compare Alternative Projects

The IRR method may be used where several projects are competing for limited funds. The project with the highest % IRR will normally be chosen, as this is the project which will generate the highest return on the cash outlay.

Comparison of the NPV and IRR Methods

Both the NPV method and the IRR method use discounted cash flows. Where the cost of capital (% interest rate) is known with a high degree of certainty, the NPV method will probably be used.

The IRR method is useful where "what if?" questions arise such as "What if the interest rate changes?" or "Will the project meet certain performance targets expressed in terms of a given interest rate?". There is a high degree of risk that the data used to make capital investment decisions may not be accurate, as they involve the prediction of future events. IRR may be used to assess the risk of undertaking a project. If the % IRR is only marginally above the required rate of return, it may not be prudent to undertake the project.

The IRR, unlike the NPV, is a percentage rate and not a cash figure. The IRR takes no account of the size of a project, neither the initial investment nor the absolute cash flows. Consider Projects X and Y, to which the following data relate:

	IRR	NPV
	%	£
Project X	28	+3,825
Project Y	15	+569,000

It would clearly be unwise to prefer Project X to the exclusion of Project Y on the grounds of a higher IRR; Project Y will provide a much greater contribution towards the total profits of the organisation.

Limitations of Discounting

Discounting is a fair way of comparing projects as it takes into consideration overall profitability and the timing of cash flows. There are, however, several limitations of discounting methods of capital investment appraisal:

- Discounting may be too complex a method for managers who have little financial training.
- The selection of an appropriate discount rate is crucial. As discounting is exponential in its effect on future cash flows, a small increase in the discount rate is a more than proportionate increase in the severity of the test of the viability of a project. For example, an increase in the discount rate from 12% to 15% represents more than a one quarter increase in the severity of the test of a project. The selection of too high a rate, therefore, may result in the rejection of worthwhile projects.

Tutorial Questions

4.1 From the following information calculate the internal rate of return (IRR) of the project.

	Net Cashflows (£)	5% Discount Factors (£)	Present Value (£)	Iterative Rate (%) Discount Factors	Present Value (£)
Investment	(80,000)	1.0000	(80,000)		
Year 1	10,000	0.9524	9,524		
Year 2	18,000	0.9070	16,326		
Year 3	21,000	0.8638	18,140		
Year 4	22,000	0.8227	18,099		
Year 5	25,000	0.7835	19,588		
Residual Value	0	0.7835	0		
NPV			1,677		

4.2 From the following information calculate the internal rate of return (IRR) of the project.

	Net Cashflows (£)	7% Discount Factors (£)	Present Value (£)	Iterative Rate (%) Discount Factors	Present Value (£)
Investment	(60,000)	1.0000	(60,000)		
Year 1	20,000	0.9346	18,692		
Year 2	22,000	0.8734	19,215		
Year 3	25,000	0.8163	20,407		
Year 4	(5,000)	0.7629	(3,814)		
Year 5	25,000	0.7130	17,825		
Residual Value	7,500	0.7130	5,347		
NPV			17,672		

4.3   From the following information calculate the internal rate of return (IRR) of the project:

	15% Net Cashflows (£)	Discount Factors (£)	Present Value (£)	Iterative Rate (%) Discount Factors	Present Value (£)
Investment	(70,000)	1.0000	(70,000)		
Year 1	33,000	0.8696	28,697		
Year 2	22,000	0.7561	16,634		
Year 3	30,000	0.6575	19,725		
Year 4	15,000	0.5718	8,577		
Year 5	7,500	0.4972	3,729		
Residual Value	2,500	0.4972	1,243		
NPV			8,605		

4.4   Challenge Ltd is considering commencing manufacturing operations on 1 January Year 1. The company has an option to acquire a 5 year lease on a factory at a cost of £15,000 payable on 1 January Year 1, when the lease is signed. Machinery costing £23,000 will be bought and paid for on 1 January Year 1. It is estimated that this machinery will be in use for 5 years, at the end of which time it will have a residual value of £3,000. The company expects cash inflows from trading of £15,000 for each of the first two years and £18,000 for each of the remaining three years of the project. Cash outflows from trading are budgeted to be £7,000 in Year 1, £6,000 in Year 2 and £8,000 in each of the next three years.

Required
Using the above information, calculate the maximum cost of capital which the project is capable of remunerating.

ACCOUNTING RATE OF RETURN (ARR)

The Accounting Rate of Return (ARR) method of capital investment appraisal focuses on the overall profitability of a project (its lifetime surplus). It relates the average yearly surplus to the average investment. ARR is stated as a percentage. The higher the rate of return, the more profitable the project is deemed to be.

Calculating ARR

ARR may be calculated in a variety of ways. Care must, therefore, be exercised when using this method. For the purposes of this manual, ARR will be calculated as follows:

i. Calculate the average yearly surplus of the project:

$$= \frac{\text{Project lifetime surplus}}{\text{number of years of project}}$$

ii. Calculate the net investment:

$$\text{initial investment} - \text{residual value}$$

iii. Calculate the average investment:

$$\frac{\text{net investment} + \text{residual value}}{2}$$

This calculation attempts to identify the average capital invested during the project's duration. The initial capital outlay will not be "tied up" for the whole of the project's life. A simple average of the investment "tied up" in the project may be calculated by the division of the net investment by 2. The residual value has been added back to the simple average as this amount will be invested for the entire life of the project.

iv. Calculate the accounting rate of return (ARR):

$$\frac{\text{average yearly surplus} \quad \text{(see i above)}}{\text{average investment} \quad \text{(see iii above)}}$$

Express the answer as a percentage.

For example, take the following project:

Project D

	Inflows (£)	Outflows (£)	Net Cashflows (£)
Investment		50,000	(50,000)
Year 1	25,000	19,000	6,000
Year 2	25,000	15,000	10,000
Year 3	25,000	12,000	13,000
Year 4	50,000	19,000	31,000
Year 5	50,000	34,000	16,000
Residual Value	4,000		4,000
Project Lifetime Surplus			30,000

ARR may be calculated as follows:

i. Average yearly surplus = $\dfrac{£30,000}{5 \text{ years}}$ = £6,000

ii. Net investment = £50,000 – £4,000 = £46,000

iii. Average investment = $\dfrac{£46,000 + £4,000}{2}$ = £27,000

iv. Accounting rate of return (ARR) = $\dfrac{£6,000}{£27,000} \times 100$ = 22%

Limitations of the ARR Method

The main limitation of the ARR method of capital investment appraisal is that it ignores the time value of money. But the variety of methods of calculation also severely limits the usefulness of ARR as a method of capital investment appraisal.

Tutorial Questions

5.1   From the following information calculate the accounting rate of return (ARR).

	Inflows (£)	Outflows (£)	Net Cashflows (£)
Investment		80,000	(80,000)
Year 1	25,000	15,000	10,000
Year 2	30,000	12,000	18,000
Year 3	35,000	14,000	21,000
Year 4	40,000	18,000	22,000
Year 5	50,000	25,000	25,000
Residual Value	0		0
Project Lifetime Surplus			16,000

5.2   From the following information calculate the accounting rate of return (ARR).

	Inflows (£)	Outflows (£)	Net Cashflows (£)
Investment		60,000	(60,000)
Year 1	35,000	15,000	20,000
Year 2	40,000	18,000	22,000
Year 3	37,000	12,000	25,000
Year 4	40,000	45,000	(5,000)
Year 5	50,000	25,000	25,000
Residual Value	7,500		7,500
Project Lifetime Surplus			34,500

5.3 From the following information calculate the accounting rate of return (ARR).

	Inflows (£)	Outflows (£)	Net Cashflows (£)
Investment		70,000	(70,000)
Year 1	45,000	12,000	33,000
Year 2	50,000	28,000	22,000
Year 3	57,000	27,000	30,000
Year 4	48,000	33,000	15,000
Year 5	80,000	72,500	7,500
Residual Value	2,500		2,500
Project Lifetime Surplus			40,000

5.4 Challenge Ltd is considering commencing manufacturing operations on 1 January Year 1. The company has an option to acquire a 5 year lease on a factory at a cost of £15,000 payable on 1 January Year 1, when the lease is signed. Machinery costing £23,000 will be bought and paid for on 1 January Year 1. It is estimated that this machinery will be in use for 5 years, at the end of which time it will have a residual value of £3,000. The company expects cash inflows from trading of £15,000 for each of the first two years and £18,000 for each of the remaining three years of the project. Cash outflows from trading are budgeted to be £7,000 in Year 1, £6,000 in Year 2, and £8,000 in each of the next three years.

Required
Using the above information, calculate the project's accounting rate of return (ARR).

ANSWERS TO TUTORIAL QUESTIONS

Tutorial 1

1.1

	Inflows (£)	Outflows (£)	Net Cashflows (£)
Investment		80,000	(80,000)
Year 1	25,000	15,000	10,000
Year 2	30,000	12,000	18,000
Year 3	35,000	14,000	21,000
Year 4	40,000	18,000	22,000
Year 5	50,000	25,000	25,000
Residual Value	0		0
Project Lifetime Surplus			16,000

1.2

	Inflows (£)	Outflows (£)	Net Cashflows (£)
Investment		60,000	(60,000)
Year 1	35,000	15,000	20,000
Year 2	40,000	18,000	22,000
Year 3	37,000	12,000	25,000
Year 4	40,000	45,000	(5,000)
Year 5	50,000	25,000	25,000
Residual Value	7,500		7,500
Project Lifetime Surplus			34,500

1.3

	Inflows (£)	Outflows (£)	Net Cashflows (£)
Investment		70,000	(70,000)
Year 1	45,000	12,000	33,000
Year 2	50,000	28,000	22,000
Year 3	57,000	27,000	30,000
Year 4	48,000	33,000	15,000
Year 5	80,000	72,500	7,500
Residual Value	2,500		2,500
Project Lifetime Surplus			40,000

1.4

	Inflows (£)	Outflows (£)	Net Cashflows (£)
Investment		38,000	(38,000)
Year 1	15,000	7,000	8,000
Year 2	15,000	6,000	9,000
Year 3	18,000	8,000	10,000
Year 4	18,000	8,000	10,000
Year 5	18,000	8,000	10,000
Residual Value	3,000		3,000
Project Lifetime Surplus			12,000

Tutorial 2

2.1

	Inflows (£)	Outflows (£)	Net Cashflows (£)	Cumulative Netflow
Investment		80,000	(80,000)	(80,000)
Year 1	25,000	15,000	10,000	(70,000)
Year 2	30,000	12,000	18,000	(52,000)
Year 3	35,000	14,000	21,000	(31,000)
Year 4	40,000	18,000	22,000	(9,000)
Year 5	50,000	25,000	25,000	16,000
Residual Value	0		0	16,000
Project Lifetime Surplus			16,000	
Pays back by end of Year			5	

2.2

	Inflows (£)	Outflows (£)	Net Cashflows (£)	Cumulative Netflow
Investment		60,000	(60,000)	(60,000)
Year 1	35,000	15,000	20,000	(40,000)
Year 2	40,000	18,000	22,000	(18,000)
Year 3	37,000	12,000	25,000	7,000
Year 4	40,000	45,000	(5,000)	2,000
Year 5	50,000	25,000	25,000	27,000
Residual Value	7,500		7,500	34,500
Project Lifetime Surplus			34,500	
Pays back by end of Year			3	

2.3

	Inflows (£)	Outflows (£)	Net Cashflows (£)	Cumulative Netflow (£)
Investment		70,000	(70,000)	(70,000)
Year 1	45,000	12,000	33,000	(37,000)
Year 2	50,000	28,000	22,000	(15,000)
Year 3	57,000	27,000	30,000	15,000
Year 4	48,000	33,000	15,000	30,000
Year 5	80,000	72,500	7,500	37,500
Residual Value	2,500		2,500	40,000
Project Lifetime Surplus			40,000	
Pays back by end of Year			3	

2.4

	Inflows (£)	Outflows (£)	Net Cashflows (£)	Cumulative Netflow (£)
Investment		38,000	(38,000)	(38,000)
Year 1	15,000	7,000	8,000	(30,000)
Year 2	15,000	6,000	9,000	(21,000)
Year 3	18,000	8,000	10,000	(11,000)
Year 4	18,000	8,000	10,000	(1,000)
Year 5	18,000	8,000	10,000	9,000
Residual Value	3,000		3,000	12,000
Project Lifetime Surplus			12,000	
Pays back by end of Year			5	

NOTE

Although the project generates an overall lifetime surplus of £12,000, the initial investment is not paid back until Year 5. The project may, therefore, fail to meet Challenge Ltd's "speed" criterion and be rejected.

Tutorial 3

3.1

	Inflows (£)	Outflows (£)	Net Cashflows (£)	5% Discount Factors	Present Value (£)
Investment		80,000	(80,000)	1.0000	(80,000)
Year 1	25,000	15,000	10,000	0.9524	9,524
Year 2	30,000	12,000	18,000	0.9070	16,326
Year 3	35,000	14,000	21,000	0.8638	18,140
Year 4	40,000	18,000	22,000	0.8227	18,099
Year 5	50,000	25,000	25,000	0.7835	19,588
Residual Value	0		0	0.7835	0
Project Lifetime Surplus			16,000	NPV	1,677

3.2

	Inflows (£)	Outflows (£)	Net Cashflows (£)	7% Discount Factors	Present Value (£)
Investment		60,000	(60,000)	1.0000	(60,000)
Year 1	35,000	15,000	20,000	0.9346	18,692
Year 2	40,000	18,000	22,000	0.8734	19,215
Year 3	37,000	12,000	25,000	0.8163	20,407
Year 4	40,000	45,000	(5,000)	0.7629	(3,814)
Year 5	50,000	25,000	25,000	0.7130	17,825
Residual Value	7,500		7,500	0.7130	5,347
Project Lifetime Surplus			34,500	NPV	17,672

3.3

	Inflows (£)	Outflows (£)	Net Cashflows (£)	15% Discount Factors	Present Value (£)
Investment		70,000	(70,000)	1.0000	(70,000)
Year 1	45,000	12,000	33,000	0.8696	28,697
Year 2	50,000	28,000	22,000	0.7561	16,634
Year 3	57,000	27,000	30,000	0.6575	19,725
Year 4	48,000	33,000	15,000	0.5718	8,577
Year 5	80,000	72,500	7,500	0.4972	3,729
Residual Value	2,500		2,500	0.4972	1,243
Project Lifetime Surplus			40,000	**NPV**	8,605

3.4

	Inflows (£)	Outflows (£)	Net Cashflows (£)	10% Discount Factors	Present Value (£)
Investment		38,000	(38,000)	1.0000	(38,000)
Year 1	15,000	7,000	8,000	0.9091	7,273
Year 2	15,000	6,000	9,000	0.8264	7,438
Year 3	18,000	8,000	10,000	0.7513	7,513
Year 4	18,000	8,000	10,000	0.6830	6,830
Year 5	18,000	8,000	10,000	0.6209	6,209
Residual Value	3,000		3,000	0.6209	1,862
Project Lifetime Surplus			12,000	**NPV**	(875)

NOTES

- The project would appear not to be financially viable at a cost of capital of 10% per annum, as it has a negative NPV.
- Using the payback method of capital investment appraisal, the project may be viewed as viable, as the initial investment is paid back before the end of the project (in Year 5).

Tutorial 4

4.1

	Net Cashflows (£)	5% Discount Factors	Present Value (£)	5.7% Discount Factors	Present Value (£)
			Iterative Rate (%)		
Investment	(80,000)	1.0000	(80,000)	1.0000	(80,000)
Year 1	10,000	0.9524	9,524	0.9460	9,460
Year 2	18,000	0.9070	16,326	0.8950	16,110
Year 3	21,000	0.8638	18,140	0.8467	17,781
Year 4	22,000	0.8227	18,099	0.8011	17,624
Year 5	25,000	0.7835	19,588	0.7579	18,948
Residual Value	0	0.7835	0	0.7579	0
NPV			1,677		(77)

NOTES

At 5.7% the NPV is approximately zero.

4.2

	Net Cashflows (£)	7% Discount Factors	Present Value (£)	17.7% Discount Factors	Present Value (£)
			Iterative Rate (%)		
Investment	(60,000)	1.0000	(60,000)	1.0000	(60,000)
Year 1	20,000	0.9346	18,692	0.8496	16,992
Year 2	22,000	0.8734	19,215	0.7218	15,880
Year 3	25,000	0.8163	20,407	0.6132	15,330
Year 4	(5,000)	0.7629	(3,814)	0.5210	(2,605)
Year 5	25,000	0.7130	17,825	0.4427	11,067
Residual Value	7,500	0.7130	5,347	0.4427	3,320
NPV			17,672		(16)

NOTE

At 17.7% the NPV is approximately zero.

4.3

				Iterative Rate (%)	
	Net Cashflows (£)	15% Discount Factors	Present Value (£)	21.1% Discount Factors	Present Value (£)
Investment	(70,000)	1.0000	(70,000)	1.0000	(70,000)
Year 1	33,000	0.8696	28,697	0.8257	27,248
Year 2	22,000	0.7561	16,634	0.6818	15,000
Year 3	30,000	0.6575	19,725	0.5630	16,890
Year 4	15,000	0.5718	8,577	0.4649	6,974
Year 5	7,500	0.4972	3,729	0.3839	2,879
Residual Value	2,500	0.4972	1,243	0.3839	960
NPV			8,605		(49)

NOTE

At 21.1% the NPV is approximately zero.

4.4

				Iterative Rate (%)	
	Net Cashflows (£)	10% Discount Factors	Present Value (£)	9.2% Discount Factors	Present Value (£)
Investment	(38,000)	1.0000	(38,000)	1.0000	(38,000)
Year 1	8,000	0.9091	7,273	0.9157	7,326
Year 2	9,000	0.8264	7,438	0.8386	7,547
Year 3	10,000	0.7513	7,513	0.7679	7,679
Year 4	10,000	0.6830	6,830	0.7032	7,032
Year 5	10,000	0.6209	6,209	0.6440	6,440
Residual Value	3,000	0.6209	1,862	0.6440	1,932
NPV			(875)		(44)

NOTE

At 9.2% the NPV is approximately zero.

Tutorial 5

5.1

	Inflows (£)	Outflows (£)	Net Cashflows (£)		
Investment		80,000	(80,000)		
Year 1	25,000	15,000	10,000		
Year 2	30,000	12,000	18,000		
Year 3	35,000	14,000	21,000		
Year 4	40,000	18,000	22,000		
Year 5	50,000	25,000	25,000		
Residual Value	0		0	Net Investment	Average Investment
Project Lifetime Surplus			16,000	80,000	40,000
Average Yearly Surplus			3,200	ARR (%)	8.0%

5.2

	Inflows (£)	Outflows (£)	Net Cashflows (£)		
Investment		60,000	(60,000)		
Year 1	35,000	15,000	20,000		
Year 2	40,000	18,000	22,000		
Year 3	37,000	12,000	25,000		
Year 4	40,000	45,000	(5,000)		
Year 5	50,000	25,000	25,000		
Residual Value	7,500		7,500	Net Investment	Average Investment
Project Lifetime Surplus			34,500	52,500	33,750
Average Yearly Surplus			6,900	ARR (%)	20.4%

5.3

	Inflows (£)	Outflows (£)	Net Cashflows (£)		
Investment		70,000	(70,000)		
Year 1	45,000	12,000	33,000		
Year 2	50,000	28,000	22,000		
Year 3	57,000	27,000	30,000		
Year 4	48,000	33,000	15,000		
Year 5	80,000	72,500	7,500		
Residual Value	2,500		2,500	Net Investment	Average Investment
Project Lifetime Surplus			40,000	67,500	36,250
Average Yearly Surplus			8,000	ARR (%)	22%

5.4

	Inflows (£)	Outflows (£)	Net Cashflows (£)		
Investment		38,000	(38,000)		
Year 1	15,000	7,000	8,000		
Year 2	15,000	6,000	9,000		
Year 3	18,000	8,000	10,000		
Year 4	18,000	8,000	10,000		
Year 5	18,000	8,000	10,000		
Residual Value	3,000		3,000	Net Investment	Average Investment
Project Lifetime Surplus			12,000	35,000	20,500
Average Yearly Surplus			2,400	ARR (%)	11,7%

INDEX